BEDS

*This book is dedicated
to those who have helped me to write it,
and especially to*

THE STAFF OF CHELSEA REFERENCE LIBRARY
and
EMILE   MARMORSTEIN
MICHAEL J. LENNON
ERIC   J. DINGWALL
MARY HENDERSON
IRENE   BEESON
BEN VINCENT
FELIX GROSS
JACK YORK
and
DUFFY

A bed, a bed, Clark Sanders said. . . .

ANON.

I certainly do thank God
that I am not like Reynolds.

WILLIAM BLAKE

BEDS

WITH MANY NOTEWORTHY INSTANCES

OF LYING ON, UNDER,

OR ABOUT THEM

BY

Reginald Reynolds

1952

DOUBLEDAY & COMPANY, INC.

GARDEN CITY, NEW YORK

Contents

BEDS

Chapter 1

ON BEING BORN

A bed, a bed, Clark Sanders said. . . .
Anon.

*The whole world is bursting into blossom. I am
being born. . . . The Great Adventure begins.*
The Chrysalis (*And so ad infinitum,*
by the Brothers Ĉapec)

Sigh no more, Leda, sigh no more,
Men were deceivers ever.

THE URGENCY of Clark Sanders, in his memorable dictum, suggests that of Richard Crookback at Bosworth.
Chacun à son goût, his chosen quadruped; and I—like
Clark Sanders—have preferred the Bed. As for horses,
if my wishes would turn to steeds I tell you plainly that
they would be unicorns, one and all; and you know what
the schoolmen were wont to say concerning those
beasts.

You shall hear more of these same unicorns as occasion shall afford the excuse to whistle for them. Here be
creatures of dream and fancy, to keep us in touch with
unreality (the phrase is borrowed) whilst the bed shall
provide the solid and material centre of our Ptolemaic
firmament. For this alone shall the sun go down and the
moon show her many shapes. The multitudinous host of

heaven shall revolve around The Bed, obsequious to its purposes.

How often have the four Evangelists been called upon to bless this place. How often has the Queen of Heaven been depicted on the ceiling of ancient canopies and the crucifix been hung at the head, even though it should be the couch of the courtesan—and who but Magdalene has best occasion? In our earliest years it figured in the folk-lore of the nursery: *Diddle-diddle dumpling, my son John*—like Asher, he abode in his breeches. The cradle of civilisation is the cradle itself—what else?—and here we ought rightly to make a beginning.

For the coffin and the cradle and the purse are all against man.

For the coffin is for the dead and death came by dis-obedience,

For the cradle is for weakness and the child of man was originally strong from ye womb,

For the purse is for money and money is dead matter with the stamp of human vanity.

The beds of Bedlam are symbolic. All beds are sym-bolic, from the iron bedstead of Og to the cradle of Christopher Smart. This mystery shall be opened, begin-ning with some thoughts of infancy, when our universe is a crib, two breasts its sun and moon, with a tub to stand for all the terrors of the sea. (*And there shall be no more tub,* we said.) Every child in its cunicular days is Hercules and a serpent-killer, in spite of that loathly worm which Cowper saw in the bud of youth and in the root of age—poets and priests are forever obsessed with mortality—and those Black Gowns *who rock the cradle till they bruise the child.* Some few, like Percy B. Shelley, *cradled into poetry by wrong,* have made the best of it. But the true symbolic type of the Child is Pantagruel,

tied to his cradle by iron chains, Pantagruel breaking
loose, smashing with his feet the vast framework of his
gigantic and ponderous crib, and carrying the remnant
still bound to his back like the shell of a mighty tortoise
or an upturned ship of five hundred tons; for of such is
the kingdom of heaven. But before this pocket giant of
will and valour can hurl himself against the world he
must first be born, and here our clinical history begins.

This business of getting one's self born is so much
connected with beds—in most case histories—that it can
hardly be ignored. On the other hand, one could write
a whole book about it, which would not be such a bad
idea if so many others had not already thought of it. By
far the most entertaining, of course, is Dr. Witkowski.
His *Histoire des Accouchements chez tous les peuples* is
a vast compendium of information. He can even supply
the following information apropos of prenatal sermons
by infant prodigies:

> *Saint Furcy prêchait avant d'être né: on l'entendit
> du fond des entrailles de sa mère reprendre forte-
> ment les païens.*[1] *Le cas du dominicain Vincent
> Ferrier est aussi extraordinaire: il aboyait dans le
> sein de sa mère, annonçant à celle-ci qu'elle ac-
> coucherait d'un grand prédicateur. Saint Bonnet
> se contenta d'être sacré évêque avant sa naissance.*

Avoiding, as far as possible, the temptations offered
by such byways, we have still a few matters to consider.

[1]St. Furcy was an Irishman of the seventh century, better
known as Fursa. In a footnote Witkowski reminds the reader
of a similar miracle attributed to Mahomet. Escaping from
the arms of the midwife, the founder of Islam threw himself
on his knees, announcing his own birth (*d'une voix male et
distincte,* says Dr. W.) with the words *God is great; there
is only one God and I am his prophet.* Similar precocity was
attributed to Gautama.

Pharaoh's daughter, as we know, found a baby in a float-ing cradle, but Pharaoh's queen appears to have dis-dained a bed for the purposes of parturition—that is a modernistic notion. A bas-relief at Luxor shows her sit-ting bolt upright on the obstetrical chair, having non-chalantly given birth and handed the child to a chain of waiting slaves. The chain gang suggests that more chil-dren are about to follow but (the child having reached the third woman in the line) it appears that the queen is now handing out packages of peculiar shape. Below this scene various spirits are at work performing some form of mumbo-jumbo in aid of Mrs. Pharaoh. Some-thing of this sort has at all times been considered highly desirable when children are born; and as the bed is now generally preferred for this purpose among civilised women the matter of rites and invocations in childbirth is relevant to our subject.

Thus Propertius (*Elegies*, Lib. IV, I) tells us of the prompt relief given to a woman who had long been in labour:

> *Junonis facite votum impetrabile dixi,*
> *Illa parit. . . .*

It reads not unlike an advertisement for Juno, as though Juno were a patent medicine: in fact it shows the close similarity between the ancient divinities and their modern equivalents. In a strip cartoon the last caption would read: *Thinks: If it hadn't been for Juno . . .* But Juno was not always to be trusted. Witness the case of Alcmena, that unfortunate woman who mothered Her-cules. Jove being the father, Juno expressed her resent-ment in malice and treachery. Alcmena was not so tact-less as to invoke the aid of Juno herself, but called up Lucina (she was really the same person, when she was not being Diana—classical mythology is apt to be somewhat involved at times). The ninth book of the *Metamorphoses* tells what happened. One must bear in mind that Alcmena was having twins—one normal and legitimate, the other an outsize god-begotten by-blow—and the poor woman was going through a very bad time indeed. Lucina arrived and took a seat in the doorway, with the worst possible intentions:

> *O'er her left knee her crossing leg she cast,*
> *Then knits her fingers close and wrings them fast.*[2]

In addition to these unfavourable omens, the wicked woman (for oh, how human are these goddesses whenever we get their measure) muttered spells to delay the birth. In fact she was only defeated by a trick devised by the parlourmaid, who came to a bad end as a result. The sole relieving feature about mythological births was the much greater part played by men in this business, Zeus himself setting an excellent example. After producing Athene (out of his head, you will remember) he gave birth to Bacchus, in the most peculiar circumstances. Part of the story was reconstructed by Lucian, and reads something like this:

POSEIDON: Can I drop in on Zeus, now, Hermes?
HERMES: Quite impossible, Poseidon.
POSEIDON: Well, let him know I'm around.

[2] This form of sympathetic magic is still very common. Leemius noted that among the Laplanders a woman when lying in must avoid anything twisted or knotted in her garments. As late as 1924 it was noted that, in the Nicobar Islands, any delay in delivery was ascribed to things in the house being shut or boxed up, or containing knots. Here it is even unsafe to make a fishing net, and all lashings of canoes, spears, waterpots—even of the hut itself—are cut to ensure that there shall be no impediment (see W. R. Dawson, *The Custom of Couvade* [Manchester, 1929] pp. 29, 32, 33 and 94).

HERMES: Don't be difficult, I tell you—you've chosen an awkward moment. You can't see him *now*.

POSEIDON: Is he . . . with Hera?

HERMES: No, it's a horse of another colour.

POSEIDON: I see. . . . Ganymede is there?

HERMES: Wrong again. Zeus is—unwell.

POSEIDON: Unwell? And how? What a fishy story!

HERMES: I'm ashamed to tell you, but that's how it is.

POSEIDON: Don't be coy with me; after all, I'm your uncle.

HERMES: All right then, Poseidon; he's just given birth.

POSEIDON: Given birth? Him? Tut, tut! Who by? So has he kept it dark that he's androgynous? But his waistline hasn't altered at all.

HERMES: That's true; but he didn't carry the child there.

POSEIDON: Ah, I see: he's had another from his head, like he did with Athene. He has a fertile head!

HERMES: Not at all—it's in his thigh that he carried the child he had by Semele.

POSEIDON: O excellent God, who bears children all over him and gives birth in all directions.

Such gods took a proper interest in parturition. Their aid was regularly invoked for the bed of labour; and of all rites and ceremonies practised in this connection without doubt the most important were those concerned with sex determination. The ancients recognised that the birth of a male child is something very fortunate and proportionately did they deplore the begetting of daughters.[3]

[3]A sex distinction worthy of remembrance is the belief (in the Middle Ages) that male children received souls forty days after conception, while females had to wait four

Hence we find the concentrated knowledge, experience and energy of all the priests, wizards, scientists and sorcerers always bent upon this single purpose—in spite of which Nature continues to yield its annual surplus of women. To this subject we propose to give some attention presently.

Dr. Witkowski, who very properly includes the creation of Adam in his study of obstetrics, queries whether Genesis I:27 does not imply that Adam was an hermaphrodite.[4] Like the Hindu Manu, Adam was, it is explicitly stated, created male and female—Eve, at that time, not having made her appearance. This theory can be supported from the evidence of Plato, who maintained—— But you are right. The customer always is. I must return to my muttons. (Groucho Marx, by the way, says that one can stay awake by subtracting sheep.) It is at least certain that the birth of Eve was the result of another of those male *accouchements* for which men have received far too little credit. According to the *Malleus Maleficarum,* Eve was made from a bent rib (which is the reason for her inability to keep straight) but this work is notoriously prejudiced. The story is at least a warning of the strange things that can happen to a man in his sleep. But women too have claimed curious experiences; and while we are discussing birth it is worth recalling that tribesmen at Goumbi, in Nigeria (so Paul Du Chaillu related the matter), dared not allow ex-

---

months. Dr. Cabanès recalls the case of a midwife in Rome who made use of this fact when in a tight spot, charged with infanticide.

[4] *Histoire des Accouchements* (Paris, 1887), p. 55. *Se fondant,* wrote Witkowski, *sur ce passage obscur de la Génèse, certains auteurs croient qu'Adam était hermaphrodite. C'est ainsi qu'il apparut à la sainte veuve Antoinette Bourignon* . . .

pectant mothers (or fathers) to look at a gorilla for fear
that a gorilla should be brought to birth. Such fears have
been common enough and a variety of animals have at
different times and places been claimed as human products.

As late as 1726 the chief obstetricians in England
were very seriously concerned with one of the oddest
things that was ever alleged to have happened in a bed.
Here was Mary Toft, down at Godalming in Surrey, giving birth—so it was firmly believed—to rabbits, and all
because she had been frightened by a rabbit the previous
November. Among her converts was not merely the
local apothecary, Mr. John Howard, but the King's Surgeon and Anatomist, Nathaniel St. André, who firmly
believed that he had delivered Mrs. Toft of the better
part of two conies and reported on the matter officially in
*A Short Narrative of an Extraordinary Delivery of Rab-
bets* (etc.), published shortly afterwards. According to
Pope, all London was divided into factions by this
miracle at Guildford, and the whole matter, raised to
national importance, was taken up at top level by the desire of His Majesty, for whose pleasure Sir Richard
Manningham, Kt., Fellow of the Royal Society and of
the College of Physicians, set out at 4 A.M. on Monday,
November 28, to look into a matter far more diverting
than any mere quads or quins.

The account of what followed will be found in *An
Exact Diary of what was observed during a Close Attendance upon Mary Toft, the Rabbet-Breeder of
Godalming in Surray* (etc.) by Manningham himself—
a best seller in its day. Sir Richard's story begins briskly
enough with an Express from Mr. John Howard (described as surgeon and man-midwife of Guildford), informing Mr. St. André *that another Rabbet was then
leaping in Mary Toft.* A message is at once despatched

to Sir Richard Manningham, desiring him to stand by, fully armed with his bag of tools, no doubt, in readiness for any emergency. In vain Sir Richard tries to go to bed—messengers scurry from house to house and the hunt is up. A German surgeon, Herr Limborch, is brought into the party, and the December dawn finds the two surgeons, with the King's Anatomist, on the road to Guildford. Here they pick up the local expert, Mr. Howard, and march in force to the lodging of Mary Toft, who is now seventeen rabbits to the good and still batting.

The discussion after this point becomes somewhat technical. Mr. John Howard, who appears to be an honest fellow, seems quite convinced about the rabbits, though —as a professional man—he is distinctly perplexed. The King's Anatomist, however, is still quite prepared to believe anything after his previous adventures with Mrs. Toft. (She *was* Mrs. Toft, by the way, not Miss—in the circumstances the absence of any reference to the presumed father of such curious progeny is very neglectful on the part of the chronicler.) But Sir Richard was not a man to be so easily put upon. He had attended more confinements than he could count, and had never yet known rabbits to be born of woman. *Tuesday the 29th,* he wrote, *we brought Mary Toft to London with us and lodg'd her at Mr. Lacy's Bagnio, in Leicester Fields.* Sir Richard then confided his suspicions to the Dukes of Richmond and Montagu, Lord Baltimore and Samuel Molyneux, secretary to the Prince of Wales.

At this point the celebrated obstetrician, James Douglas, was also brought in for consultation. But it was not thought wise to breathe any word of doubt about these rabbits until the porter at Mr. Lacy's Bagnio confessed to a justice of the peace that Mary Toft had secretly procured a rabbit by his assistance. Questioned

upon the matter, Mary produced a brilliant alibi—she
had bought this rabbit to *eat* it. Why not, indeed? She
was, in fact, inordinately partial to rabbits, in every way,
and she could not wait for the next one to be born (for
she *most obstinately persisted that she was still big with
a Rabbet*). Poor Mary Toft. Nobody believed her any
more. Urged to confess by a distinguished gathering of
visitors (His Grace the Duke of Montagu, Lord Baltimore, Mr. Douglas and myself, writes Sir Richard), she
at last came clean; and the rest of the proceedings was
about as dramatic as a Russian trial for sabotage,
espionage and so forth.

Indeed, ever since the peculiar cases of Zeus, Adam
and others, where very little clinical evidence is obtain-
able, there have been numerous stories of irregular
births, all of them designed to terrify us in our beds[5]—
though I will grant that men have had less occasion than
women to be alarmed. It is a very long time since any
man had such a splitting headache as that which preceded the birth of Athene, and some time since the
incident of Adam's rib. But strange things went on hap-
pening to women right through the Middle Ages and
down into the eighteenth century. Sir Thomas Browne
gave some attention to the matter in his *Pseudodoxia
Epidemica* where (Book vii, Chap. xvi) he threw some
doubt on the activities attributed to *incubi*. The story
that Merlin had been begotten by the Devil he called a
groundless conception; but then Sir Thomas was altogether too fond of questioning things, as for example
whether Adam and Eve had navels, which he considered
an improper suggestion, because the navel, *being a part*

[5]See Harvey Graham's *Eternal Eve* (London, 1950), p. 334.
He mentions a woman who gave birth to a large rat and
another who produced two small fishes. I was sad to find
that he had dealt at some length with Mary Toft, too.

*precedent and not subservient to generation, nativity, or
parturition, it cannot be well imagined at the creation or
extraordinary formation of Adam, who immediately
issued from the Artifice of God; nor also that of Eve,
who was not solemnly begotten, but suddenly formed,
and anomalously proceeded from Adam.* I concede the
point, with Browne's rider that Adam was nevertheless
in a state of *umbilicality even with God himselfe.*

But to return to the bed, and the art of being born in
it. The more one studies the question, the clearer it becomes that the functions of the husband have, in our
time, been neglected and underestimated. And here I am
observant of some remarks in Bayle's *Dictionary* (I
quote from the English translation, 1734–41) which by
some inscrutable form of reasoning attached themselves
to the article on Francis of Assisi.

The matter under discussion was the affirmative reply
given by Peter Damianus to the question, *Utrum liceret
homini inter ipsum debiti naturalis egregium aliquid
ruminare psalmorum*—whether at such-and-such a time
a man could repeat any part of the psalms. Peter Damian
said he could, on the authority of I Timothy II:8[6]; and
Pierre Bayle, in refuting this ruling, tabled a *caveat* of
his own, remarking that one of the most celebrated com-
mentators on Aristotle would have made a very different
answer: he would have asserted that the welfare of the
state requires in this action more than any other that the
people should mind the *hoc age* (what they are about)
*and keep their minds as much as possible from wander-
ing.*

According to him the reason why the children
of men of genius and study are generally such
fools and blockheads is because their fathers don't

[6]He might have added Psalms CXLIX:5.

mind enough the business they are upon and suffer their thoughts to be exercised on other matters. On the contrary, says he, you meet with some heavy fellows who get children of admirable parts; the reason of which is, they apply themselves wholly to the affair of procreation and not merely for fashion sake. They mind what they are about and nothing else.

For this view, which affords a Shandian point of departure (and what a cinch Tristram's case would have been for a Dianetic Auditor), Bayle had medical evidence to offer, and even cited one authority who said that, *for a contrary reason, bastards are generally witty and vigorous*—an opinion which was expressed, though not entirely without prejudice, by Gloucester's by-blow in Shakespeare's *King Lear* (I, ii, 11–15). Without entering further into so delicate a matter, I come next to the vital question, how to be born a male. On this the ancients have detailed instructions; and (though I shall not attempt to exhaust this subject) some wisdom from the East surely is worthy of our consideration.

The rule is (I quote from the *Shayast lā-Shāyast,* that is to say, the Proper and the Improper) *that they keep a fire in the house, because, from not keeping the fire properly there arise less pregnancy of women and a weeping for the loss of strength of men.* Such, as might be expected, was the belief of the Fire-Worshippers, whose opinions are even more clearly expressed in the book of *Sad Dar:*

And this is also declared in revelation, that, every time they do not maintain a fire properly, pregnancy becomes scarcer for the women, fewer male children are born. . . .

The Hindu sages attached equal importance to this matter, and there is a reference in the *Vishnu-Sûtra* to the appropriate ceremony for sex determination. This is the *Pumsavana,* which must be performed before the embryo begins to move. But precautions are also taken (as the *Sânkhâyana-Grihya-Sûtra* shows) at an earlier stage. These precautions include placing a boy of good birth in the woman's lap. Into the boy's hands the bridegroom gives fruits: *Thus she becomes the mother of male children.* It all seems very simple. But it is also wise to say at the appropriate moment: *May a male embryo enter thy womb, as an arrow the quiver; may a man be born here, a son after ten months.* The incantation (in the 19th *Khanda*) continues with a request for an option on more and more male children, with a subclause somewhat selfishly wishing female children onto other women.

Should all this be overlooked (on account of other preoccupations) *au moment critique,* methods of sex determination are still possible, as already hinted. In the third month of pregnancy the husband can still bring his wife curds from a cow the same colour as herself, with two beans, and one grain of barley for each handful of curds. *What dost thou drink?* asks the expectant father; and his wife, well rehearsed, replies three times: *Generation of a male child.*

Such is the *Pumsavana* in the *Asvalâyana-Grihya-Sûtra* (*Kandika* XIII, 2 and 3). Gobhila even insists upon the fact that sex is determined in the third month of pregnancy. The ceremony begins with the wife having a good wash, seated upon *darbha* grass, which must point to the north. She sits to the west of the fire, facing the east, and her husband (who stands behind her) touches her navel and recites a verse. At this point there is evidently an interval, as the text continues abruptly: *then they may do what they like* (verse 4). Actually

there is much more to be done, but the instructions end
with the same reassuring statement or invitation. Hir-
anyakesin gives a slightly different (and somewhat
crude) version of the ceremony, but also insists upon
the third month as the correct time for it. Apastamba
says that the *Pumsavana* should be performed when the
pregnancy has become visible. The chief common factor
in all these prescriptions is the insertion of powdered
nyagrodha shoot into the wife's nostrils, an action performed by the husband whilst reciting an appropriate
verse from the Scriptures.[7]

Returning to the Fire-Worshippers, the Zoroastrian
view, as far as it can be ascertained from the *Dīnkart,*
appears to have been that sex was determined in the fifth
month; but a different view is expressed in the Zoroastrian *Bundahis,* for here sex is said to be determined
by the relative strength of the male and female seed. If
the advantage lies with the male (which is hot and dry)
the child will be a boy; if the cold, moist female pre-
dominates a girl will be born. In the event of an even
balance the result is not, as one might suppose, an
hermaphrodite, but twins. One would assume (though
it is not so stated) that this at least meant one boy and
one girl, a dead heat; but the Pahlavi text adds: *and
triplets.* The logic of this is hard to follow, as there is
no way of dividing triplets fairly except by the sword of
Solomon, severing whichever has the casting vote. But
in the Hindu Scriptures we shall find that the *Manu-
smriti* suggests a similar explanation of sex determination, with the more rational solution that in the event of
equality the balance will produce either an hermaphro-

---

[7]Suitable charms are provided in the *Atharva-Veda.* Another
(somewhat obscure) ceremony is described in the *Pâraskara-
Grihya Sûtra* (*Kandika* I, 14). See also the *Khadira-Grihya-
Sûtra* (II, 2, 17).

dite or one boy and one girl. The laws of Manu advise
men not to marry into a family, no matter how powerful
or prosperous, if male children are lacking in it[8]—indeed, Manu classes such families with those of which
the members suffer from haemorrhoids, phthisis, bad
digestion, epilepsy, leprosy or thick body hair.

European theories in the seventeenth century resemble
in some respects the ancient teachings of the East.
Charles de l'Orme, who once enjoyed considerable
prestige in France as a doctor of medicine, had useful
ideas on every subject relating to beds, including the art
of being born. He himself slept in a bed made of bricks
and recommended such beds to others because they
were designed to shut out draught and damp. Snug as a
chrysalis, one could preserve one's natural heat, to which
Dr. de l'Orme attached the greatest importance—to such
an extent that he applied his ingenuity to a device for
satisfying the demands of nature without leaving his retreat. With six pairs of stockings on and a covering of
hare skin he felt tolerably secure. But the hare skin
brings us back to the point of comparison with the
oriental sages. Why hare? Without doubt because hares
had the reputation of being *hot and dry,* like the male
seed which produces heirs male. We shall find in the
theories of Dr. de l'Orme himself an insistence on the
same differentiation by *humours* already met in the
Zoroastrian Scriptures. In order to produce intelligent
children, said Dr. de l'Orme, it was necessary to eat
goat's flesh. Goats, above all other beasts, were believed
to be *hot and dry,*[9] and the same dietetics were to be

[8]An interesting forecast of modern genetics.

[9]De l'Orme's instructions to the prospective parents that
they should *manger de la chair de chèvre avant que de
coucher ensemble* may be compared with Galen's recipe for
begetting wise children—that the parents should *eat much*

applied to the offspring, the babies being prescribed
goat's milk and later kid's flesh.

Certain things were particularly to be avoided.
Though the flesh of the hare was generally counted
among the hot and dry foods, it had been known in
France since the Middle Ages that no pregnant woman
should eat the head, or the child would be born with a
harelip (*bec-de-lièvre*)—a fact elucidated by Gascard
(*La Naissance au Moyen-âge*). So far we are concerned
only with the production of children *qui aient bien de
l'esprit* and with avoiding deformities. But an English
writer makes it clear that *esprit* is inseparable from the
male sex and both from the dietetic principles already
laid down:

> If the seed be cold and moist, a woman is be-
> gotten, not a man: and if the same be hot and dry,
> a man is begotten. . . . This therefore is to be
> noted as a thing without all controversie. . . .

> Those who seek the comfort of having wise
> children, must endeavour that they be born male:
> for the Female, through the cold and moist of
> their Sex, cannot be indowed with so profound a
> judgment.

To achieve this double object we have the following
recipe:

> The first is, the eating those sorts of meats which
> are hot and dry, provided they have not those
> qualities in too high an excess, lest thereof be in-
> gendered a man extreamly wily and malicious . . .

---

goat's milk boiled (according to T. Chamberlaine, in a work
quoted later). It may have been with some dim recollection
of these facts of life, as understood in his time, that a seventeenth-century Quaker (Thomas Aldam) spoke of the Lord
knowing the goats by their fruits.

but rather those viands be hot and dry in a moderate degree, such as Hens, Partridges, Turtles, Thrushes, Goats &c and those roasted.

Secondly, much exercise, to heat and dry the seed, whereas ease and overmuch delicacy breedeth coldnesse and moisture in the seed; and hence it comes to passe, that rich and great persons that live at ease and feed high, have for the most part daughters.[10]

In addition to such purely material precautions, a word on hagiotherapy may be appropriate at this point —a practice learnedly discussed by Dr. Cabanès, in the seventh volume of his *Moeurs Intimes,* with special reference to royal births. This practice, inherited from the Middle Ages, still played an important part even as late as the seventeenth century.

It seems that Our Lady used two shifts during her pregnancy, according to the Byzantine historian Nicephorus Calistus. These chemises, or one of them, passed into the hands of Charlemagne—a gift from the Empress Irene,[11] who was doubtless in a position to guar-

[10]These extracts are from a supplement by a certain T. Chamberlaine to the second and three subsequent editions of *The Compleat Midwife's Practice* (first published in 1656, in London. Second edition with supplement, 1659). The original work was evidently a joint effort, signed with initials only, which vary in the different editions. The identity of T. Chamberlaine is unknown to me and research has only revealed lacunae and chaos in most of the catalogue references to this work. The Index-Catalogue to the Library of the Surgeon-General's Office, U. S. Army, confuses the author of the supplement with Peter Chamberlen, well-known member of a hereditary line of obstetricians who maintained for generations the monopoly of a secret weapon.

[11]This may have been at the time when the Byzantine empress was planning to marry the Emperor of the West; and

antee authenticity. Both chemises came later into the possession of Henri III and were evidently regarded as guarantors of fertility. There were also several girdles of Our Lady—eleven were in existence in England alone when the monasteries were dissolved, and a monk was paid about a dollar for bringing one to Elizabeth of York in 1502. They were much in demand; and one of them being fortunately available at the church of Notre Dame du Puy, in Anjou, it could be obtained on loan by persons of sufficient pomp and circumstance. Indeed, it is possibly to this girdle that history owes the birth of that conceited and troublesome monarch, Louis XIV; for his mother (Anne of Austria) bore him after twenty years of sterility by having recourse to the girdle of the Mother of God and to her rosary. Anne made doubly certain by collecting the relics of St. Isidore from Spain. I am not clear as to what precisely was the therapeutic value of St. Isidore, but Anne of Austria believed in giving everybody a chance. Indeed, she had for fourteen years hoarded some fragments of St. Mary Magdalene, thinking that they might come in useful; but in this she had been disappointed.

A rival claimant to the honour of having induced the birth of the Roi Soleil was a certain Frère Fiacre. As far as I can discover he did not invent the vehicle which bears his name. Indeed, he would have scorned it: his speciality was to make pilgrimages on foot, in midwinter. In point of fact the hackney carriage of France was invented about that time but apparently took its name from the Hôtel de St. Fiacre in the Rue St. Martin, which was in turn named after an Irish saint who died in

---

no doubt the chemise was both a symbol and a gage. An unpleasant woman (she put out the eyes of her son Constantine VI), Irene is nevertheless revered as a saint by the Greek Church.

the seventh century. This original Fiacre, in addition to
being immortalised by a cab, was a patron saint of gar-
deners and useful in curing various diseases.[12] (It is all
the more confusing to find that, according to the *Catholic
Encyclopedia,* Anne of Austria was *among his most
famous clients.*) This Frère Fiacre, then, whom I have
so carefully distinguished from his more celebrated
namesake and from the even more illustrious vehicle, was
a long-distance walker; and one of his pilgrimages, *fait
exprès* and for no other purpose, coincided with the
conception of the Grand Monarque.

I am not sure whether Anne retained his services in
case of some hitch with the girdle, or whether this great
fertility hike was entirely Brother Fiacre's own idea. He
certainly assisted in this way to bring into the world a
number of distinguished persons, specialising—the
theme, it will be observed, is recurrent—in heirs male.
To the indefatigable footwork of Frère Fiacre France
was perhaps indebted for the birth of two dauphins and
two dukes.

The fertility cult of the Virgin is continued to this day
in India in connection with a Catholic church at Bandra
(Bombay). There are no chemises in evidence, but the
church was built on the site of an old Hindu temple and
inherited a reputation from its predecessor. Hindu and
Moslem women, as well as Christians, make offerings at
this place in the sure hope of receiving children as a reward. Their offerings consist of dolls, sold for this purpose outside the church—a flourishing trade of which I
saw something myself in 1950.

The honours in this matter have in times past been

---

[12]I have a dim memory that Cardinal Richelieu had recourse
to his relics as a cure for haemorrhoids, but I cannot verify
this without leaving my bed.

shared by St. Margaret or Marina,[13] whose relics—a
powerful agent not only of fertility but of happy birth—
were used by Marie de' Medici, among others. There
are references to the potency of St. Margaret (or rather
of her relics) in Rabelais and some other French writers.
She too prolonged her term of office in India, though
Dr. Cabanès could not cite an instance of her being
called into consultation after the year 1815. The association with fertility is obscure in Margaret's case. According to the *Acta Sanctorum,* she died in defence of
her virginity; and it is as a virgin, martyr and saint that
the Romans honour her as St. Margaret, the Greeks as
St. Marina. According to the *Catholic Encyclopedia,* the
chief uncertainty regarding her is chronological: nobody
knows in what century she lived.

Returning once more to sex determination, I find that
on September 28, 1776, the *Morning Post* published a
long advertisement on behalf of a certain Mr. Lattese,
described as a Piedmontese gentleman, who begged
leave to acquaint the Nobility and Gentry that by a long
course of experiments he had discovered the wonderful
secret of procreating either sex, at the joint option of the
parents. Or rather—the scrupulous honesty of the ad-
vertiser is much to be admired—he could not warrant
them the birth of a daughter (if such should be their
extraordinary whim) but only that *the chance will be
highly in favour of such an event.* Should, however, they
follow the more normal and natural course of opting for
a son they could be positively sure of satisfaction. Payment was to be on results; and Mr. Lattese was con-
fident that in families of high rank (where heirs male
were a desirable object of great importance and conse-

[13]Not to be confused with another saint, of the same name
(Marina) who lived as a man, in a monastery, and was
falsely accused of having seduced an innkeeper's daughter.

quence) a suitable reward would, without doubt, be cheerfully granted.

One public benefactor of the same period, however, was concerned not so much with sex determination as with the procreation of a generation to replace *the present puny, feeble, and nonsensical race of probationary immortals, which crawl, and fret, and politely play at cutting one another's throats for nothing at all, on most parts of this terraqueous globe.* For this purpose a special bed was designed, which was on view in the Temple of Health at the Adelphi for five shillings per head at night and a mere half crown during the day. Its owner, the celebrated Dr. Graham, appealed in particular to their Excellencies the Foreign Ambassadors, to the Nobility, Gentry and to persons of Learning and Taste. The doctor lectured three times a week at exactly 8 P.M., demonstrating the true nature and effects of electricity, air, music and magnetism when applied to the human body, as announced in a series of advertisements where he promised also that he would *delicately touch upon the Celestial Bed.*[14]

The Bed and the Temple moved later from the Adelphi to Pall Mall (near the King's Palace, the advertisements announced). Dr. Graham soon informed the public that his lectures were being attended by vast numbers—from eight to sixteen hundred ladies and gentlemen. For three evenings past there had been *an overflow of at least nine hundred ladies and gentlemen.* But in spite of having to turn them away at the door, the greathearted Graham still implored more to come and reduced his admittance charge to one shilling. Let them now, said he, come forth, or forever afterwards blame themselves and bewail their irremediable misfortune. His works, which

[14]His idea was not entirely original. Cagliostro had previously sold magical beds for painless childbirth.

were selling faster than the printer could produce them,
he reduced in price by drastic stages. For a mere two
shillings and sixpence one could also buy the *warm lecture of Vestina, the Rosy Goddess*. The original Vestina
was Emily Hart—none other than the Lady Hamilton
of later years, with whom Nelson was one day to dally
when he was not attending battles, bullying the Danes or
murdering the Republicans of Naples.

Of all Graham's many devices, offered to the public
—at appropriate charges—to enhance beauty and to increase health and fertility, the *hymeneal couch* was the
most celebrated. For a mere fifty pounds sterling the
childless couple could be sure of an heir by using this
Celestial Magnetico-Electric Bed, which rested on six
massive and transparent columns, as described by Dr.
Graham, who further assured his clients that *the bedclothes are perfumed with the most costly essences of
Arabia*. Indeed, the doctor compared his hymeneal
couch with those of proved fertility which adorned the
palaces of Persia and even to that of *the favourite sultana
in the seraglio of the Grand Turc*. It was *the fruit of the
most laborious industry and of the most indefatigable
zeal*.

I will not mention, wrote Dr. Graham, *the sums it has
cost me; they are immense. I shall only add that I have
omitted none of those precautions which decency and
delicacy have a right to exact*. The amenities thrown in
with the bed included an orchestra—consisting apparently of a harmonica, a flute and an organ—plus vocal
solos (*the charms of an agreeable voice*). But in addition to all these attractions, modelled no doubt upon
the tastes of the Shah and the Grand Turk, there was
*the truly divine energy of this celestial and electric fire,
which fills every part of the bed, as well as the magnetic
fluid, both of them calculated to give the necessary de-*

gree of strength and exertion to the nerves. Stopes herself was never more lyrical.

Few of us, indeed, have enjoyed the privilege of being conceived or born under the controlled conditions so carefully prescribed by Indian sage or Scottish physician. So far from being concerned with the mass production of male children and with increase and multiplication generally, the married couples of Europe and America have shown an increasing tendency to avoid all such responsibilities as far as possible, and the wonder is that most of us were born at all. Yet even in the matter of birth control the ancients may have known more than a thing or two. Their alleged methods were, it is true, somewhat drastic, by report, and do not appear to have been widely in use. Indeed, their efficacy and even their existence—as we shall see—have been queried by sceptics. I mention them merely because no chapter on the art of being born would be complete without some instructions as to how this misfortune may be avoided altogether. We shall also find here specifics to ensure legitimacy.

There was known to the ancients a certain herb called *leucophyllus,* native to the river Phasis—that stream up which Jason and his All Star Cast sailed in quest of the Golden Fleece. Of this *leucophyllus* we are told that it had remarkable properties—Bayle quotes Pontus de Tyard, a bishop in his time:

> *Car quiconque au Printemps en son lit cachera*
> *Cette plante trempée en Phasis trouvera*
> *Que jamais sa Vénus ne sera dérobée.*

An admirable plant, indeed. A man had but to hide it in his bed, and the fidelity of his mistress was assured. Of even greater potency was the *agnus castus,* used by Grecian women (according to Pliny) in order to preserve their chastity during the celebrations known as the *Thesmophoria,* held in honour of Ceres. Bayle has a good deal to say about this other herb, too, pointing out that women who participated in these festivals were only required to live separately from their husbands for a matter of three or four days, though Ovid implies that nine days was the total duration. No matter, said Bayle, it was *pretended that, the better to enable them to submit to this abstinence, they used to lye on certain leaves, which had a refrigerating faculty.* This pretence was sufficient to justify a Remark (or footnote) long even for Monsieur Bayle, defending the reputation of Grecian womanhood. I quote some relevant passages:

> It is common, in solemn festivals, to strew the streets with flowers and leaves. Festoons are fixed upon the doors, and rooms are sometimes adorned in the same manner. The Greeks might perhaps extend this custom to the beds, for those who celebrated the festival of the Goddess. In process of time people might think there was something mysterious in that custom; and the inquisitive might have carried their researches so far as at last to fancy that the wise ancients had there found a salutary remedy with regard to incontinence. . . .

So much for Bayle's conjectured explanation. The story itself he demolished with some severity. *Must we not,* says he, *entertain a very bad idea of their virtue to suppose that . . . married women could not live five or six nights (suppose nine) in a separate bed. . . .* Bayle felt strongly that the use of the *agnus castus* implied a confession *which might fill their husbands with the most dreadful alarms.*

> Some of these were engaged in a trade or way of life which obliged them to pass some weeks at a

distance from their families. . . . Those who
never stirred from their houses were not always
in health. . . . The same cause which would have
prompted the enjoining this remedy, during the
solemnity, to married women, would have obliged
them to prescribe it during the absence or sickness
of their husbands. . . . If both had been done
we should find in some book that no plant was
more common in all Greece than the *agnus castus*.
Every man would have had a dozen of them in his
garden; they would have been obliged to have
whole forests of it and skilful planters to look
after them. . . .[15]

It is indeed a formidable conception, once one follows Monsieur Bayle in his elaborate train of reasoning.
He imagines the elderly husbands of young brides laying
out large plantations of this necessary herb and dedi-
cating them to appropriate Ἀποτρόπαιοι, *lares* or tutelar
deities of the Bed. (Bartholomew de Glanville, by the
way, prescribed this plant for men, though the Greeks
do not appear to have considered that point of view.)
But it seems there were no footsteps among the ancient
monuments to indicate such practices, and we may find
ourselves in agreement with Bayle that *the Athenians
had too much sense to believe that certain leaves laid
between a pair of sheets had the power to bridle lust.* He
fittingly concludes the matter:

[15]Bayle's *General Dictionary*, English edition of 1734–41,
Vol. IX, article on Thesmophoria. Monsieur Bayle was at
some trouble to correct the error of Brantôme, who (when
speaking sceptically of thirty-two remedies of this kind,
offered by an Italian) specifically mentioned the *agnus castus*
as a prophylactic used by the Roman Vestals—a libel which
he fathered upon Pliny (a safe wager, for Pliny's progeny
of tall stories was beyond any man's power to count).

> I will take it for granted that there are certain
> herbs which, at the long run, may refrigerate those
> who eat of them. . . . Common justice will not
> suffer us to sacrifice the reputation of a number-
> less multitude of Grecian women, in case they did
> not deserve such an insult, to the testimony of
> Pliny and some other authors.

Such a statement was proof that the Age of Chivalry
still lived; which makes it all the more extraordinary
that anyone should have been so hardy as to call old
Pliny a liar, so firmly had the centuries confirmed his
authority. I must resist the temptation to pursue the
matter any further, in spite of a perplexing observation
by Fosbroke that Greek goddesses were *either virgins or
capable of becoming so*. They had, perchance, found
the secret with which a certain Monsieur Diderot was
later to startle the world when he announced that he had
discovered how to *faire fleurir une nouvelle Virginité,
où elle a été par hazard perdu* [sic], a matter which he
thought fit to advertise to the *Dames Angloises* in a
handbill, of which he sent a copy to the British Museum.
It must surely be this original handbill which has been
inserted into the B.M. copy of *A Guide to Health,
Beauty, Riches and Honour*,[16] being a collection of late

[16]London, 1783. Copies of Advertisements by Mr. Lattese
and Dr. Graham will also be found in this highly instructive
anthology. But little has changed in advertising except literary style. This Monsieur Diderot is not to be confused
with the celebrated Encyclopaedist, who nevertheless
meddled somewhat in medicine. In his *Eléments de physi-
ologie* he quoted Soranus of Ephesus that *un signe très
certain et point trompeur que la femme est enceinte d'un
garçon, c'est lorsque le pouls du bras droit est plus fréquent,
plus fort, plus grand que celui du bras gauche*. Denis Diderot
thus qualifies as a sex-detector but not as a determiner. As
to the restoration of virginity, it was quite outside his range.

eighteenth-century advertisements, edited by Francis Grose. Le Sieur Diderot, as he styled himself (Accoucheur, Chirurgien & Dentiste à sa Majesté très-Chrétienne), announced that he had *déjà obtenu les Lettres Patentes pour son heureuse découverte*. It is a pity that so little information is available on this subject, as Monsieur Diderot claimed to be able to supply any kind of virginity that might be required, French, Italian, Spanish, English *und so weiter*. Dutch virginities were at a premium on account, he said, of an embargo placed on the trade by the government of the States General.

The late Edward Crowley (Aleister, to his public) had, I believe, some such specific; and the idea suggests almost endless digressions into the realm of pure fantasy. But this is no way to get one's self born; and having devoted so much space to maternity, it is time that we considered the no less essential functions of fatherhood. We shall find the matter, unless I am mistaken, fortuitously relevant to our subject.

Chapter 2

ON THE PAINS OF PATERNITY

COUVADE . . . A term applied by some writers to the "man childbed" attributed to some uncivilised or primitive races, and extended to comprehend a series of customs according to which, on the birth of the child, the father performs acts or simulates states natural or proper to the mother or abstains for a time from certain foods or actions, as if he were physically affected by the birth. . . .

The recent application of the word in anthropology is due to Dr. E. B. Taylor, following M. Francisque Michel Le Pays Basque *(1857) 201, where the "man childbed" attributed to the Basques and Béarnese, is said to be so called by the latter. But this is a mistake. . . . It is not true that* couvade *was ever a name for the practice in Béarn; the Béarnese* coade *is simply = F.* couvée, *a covey of chickens. Further the pretended existence of the practice in Béarn and among the Basques appears to be merely the echo of a statement by Strabo as to the ancient Celtiberians, loosely repeated by one compiler after another as a commonplace of history. . . .*

Murray's English Dictionary, *1893*

IN SPITE OF ALL this it seems that Aitor, legendary progenitor of these same Basques, took refuge on a mountain from the Flood—that flood of almost universal race memory—accompanied (*Credite, posteri,* for this was essential if you were ever to read of it) by Mrs. Aitor. In their cave of refuge the promise of posterity appeared in the form of a son; but with the future of the race depending upon this single hope the mother dared not allow her husband to go in search of food. Like the Ark of Noah this mountaintop was a well-stocked (though no doubt carefully selected) zoo, in which, you will understand, the carnivora were well represented.

What were they to do? The decision was soon made. Mrs. Aitor was to search for food while her husband minded the baby—a responsibility of the greatest importance which may have tested his courage more than all the dinosaurs, unicorns, basilisks, bears and sabre-toothed tigers around and about. And this, said the Basques, was the origin of the strange custom among them, that when the mother was able to leave her bed after giving birth her husband took her place. And like the spirit whose breath animated the first clay that was Adam, so the Basque father, breathing courage and fortitude upon the newborn child, by sympathetic magic endowed it with his proper attributes.

It was of such a custom in Spain that Strabo told the ancient world. Among later observers who recorded the continuation of the custom among the Cantabrians and the people of Navarre, one spoke of it in terms of *humours*—doubtless having in mind the necessity of balancing these cold, moist humours of the mother with the dry and fiery humours of the father. There are sufficient independent witnesses, in fact, to prove that the practice—whatever one may say of the name saddled upon it—was continued well into the nineteenth century. Diodorus Siculus noticed this custom in Corsica, at the beginning of the Christian Era, and an echo of the same practice is to be found in an episode of *Aucassin and Nicolette*. I quote from the English version of my friend Mr. Laurence Housman.

It was at Torelore that Aucassin encountered the *couvade*. He learnt with surprise that the king had some considerable wars on hand but was unable to give them his full attention, as he was lying in childbed. Where, then, asked Aucassin, was the queen?

> And they told him that she was in the field, and had led thither the whole force of the country. And Aucassin heard it, and it seemed to him a great marvel. And he came to the palace and lighted down, both he and his friend and she held his horse, and he went into the palace with his sword girt, and fared on till he came to the chamber where the king lay in child-bed.

Asked what he was doing, the King of Torelore replied:

> *I bear a son.*
> *When my month is at an end,*
> *And I'm well upon the mend,*
> *Then to hear mass I shall go,*
> *As my ancestors did so,*
> *And my great wars to maintain,*
> *March against my foes again. . . .*

But Aucassin, it seems, was no anthropologist. Instead of taking out his notebook and asking the king how long this had been going on, what importance he attached to it and such-like questions (to which the replies might have been of incalculable value) he whips off the bed-clothes, seizes a cudgel and *taking it, he turns him about, and beat and battered him till he was like to have killed him*. Having reasoned thus with this *roi fainéant*, Aucassin made him swear to put an end to the *couvade* in the country of Torelore, and not much more was heard about it until Marco Polo recorded its existence in Chinese Turkestan.[1] From this record, relating only to the aborigines in one locality, a belief grew up—popularised in *Hudibras*—that the custom was common in China, although in fact the Chinese appear to be among the few great nations which have probably never practised it.[2]

André Thevet, who had a vast store of unlikely information on every subject, mentioned the custom in his *Cosmographie Universelle,* published in 1575 (p. 196[b]), and in the seventeenth century the Belgian geographer Jean Laet in his *Histoire du Nouveau Monde*[3] said that, among the Petivares of Brazil, when the women give birth the men retire to bed *et sont salués courtoisement de tous leurs voisins et sont traités de femmes soigneusement et largement*. As such stories began to circulate, Pierre Bayle (who missed nothing)

[1]According to a note in the third edition of Yule's translation (London, 1903), Vol. II, p. 596, Mr. H. Ling Roth tried to discredit this story on the grounds that Marco Polo *wrote at a time when the Old World was full of tales of the New*. As the editor remarked, this fact was singular so long before the birth of Columbus and nearly two centuries before the discovery of America.

[2]W. R. Dawson refers to accounts of an alleged Chinese *couvade* in Neale's *Narrative of a Residence at the Capital of the Kingdom of Siam* and in Navarra's *China und die Chinesen*. He considers that there has been a confusion between the Chinese proper and the Maiotzu, the aborigines of the country who practise this custom.

[3]Leyden, 1640. It had originally appeared in Latin, seven years previously.

took note of them in his *Réponse aux Questions d'un Provincial*. There were, he said, some things so absurd and so contrary to those customs which travellers found everywhere established that one could easily imagine they had never existed. *Telle est la coûtume de ne prendre aucun soin des accouchées, mais de faire mettre leurs maris au lit, & les y traiter comme des malades.*

Even in 1784 the good Jesuit father, Martin Dobrizhoffer, recording his own observation of the custom in his *Historia de Abiponibus* (a people of Paraguay), remarked that he had heard before of such customs but never taken the stories seriously until he saw for himself how the bellicose males of the Abipones would forsake their horses to lie huddled in skins, dieting carefully, living in privacy and generally behaving as though they had themselves given birth. Evidence was soon to accumulate of widespread usage; and those who favour the diffusionist theory have seen the *couvade* as part of a vast culture complex (including sun-worship, mummification, ear piercing, tattooing and cranial deformation) branching out from some true and original Cradle of Civilisation.

The evidence for this view has been adroitly summarised by W. R. Dawson in *The Custom of Couvade*, published in 1929 by Manchester University Press. Having unashamedly made use of this summary, and especially of its excellent bibliography, I shall presently express my gratitude in the form of some impudent and fribblish criticisms. For the moment we will follow Mr. Dawson's conjectures as to the course of the *couvade* in the heliolithic stream. Being neither a Bellamyite nor an Atlantide, Mr. Dawson begins in the eastern Mediterranean, which is the orthodox starting point. He can find no positive evidence to pin *couvade* onto the Egyptians, which is always a misfortune if one is plotting the course of diffusion, but he finds in Plutarch a story which might suggest the existence of such a custom at one time in Cyprus.

In the month sacred to Ariadne, so we are told, her death was commemorated by a curious ceremony. A Cypriot youth would simulate by voice and gesture the pains of a woman in labour—an annual custom, said to have been instituted by Theseus, who deeply regretted having marooned the wench on the island, as you will remember (though some say that he was himself shanghaied; and again it is generally agreed that all this happened elsewhere—probably at Naxos—but no matter). The lass was already in the family way—that, at least, is alleged; though again it has been suggested that Theseus was not a party to this, the father of Ariadne's children (quite a family by some accounts) being in each and every case none other than her lawful husband, Bacchus. With him, at least, she sought and found consolation for her sufferings, making a good exchange and creating a precedent; for many a broken heart has found the same comfort.

But Theseus nursed a bad conscience; and this was the form in which it found expression—a strange piece of mummery of which some say Theseus my foot. They say it is a relic of the *couvade,* and it would greatly suit the convenience of the diffusionist theory that it should be so. But the plain fact is that this play acting is not true *couvade,* which is concerned with an actual husband, a living wife, a real child and a true birth. Nor is there any positive evidence that true *couvade* ever existed in Cyprus.[4] So we pass on.

[4]There is a record that in Captain Cook's voyages a play was acted by inhabitants of the Society Islands which *concluded with the representation of a woman in labour, acted by a set of great brawny fellows, one of whom at last*

Westward the nearest possible trace of *couvade* is in Sardinia—a mere conjecture, based upon a possibly related custom. (Greece, Italy and Sicily show no evidence of it.) Reference has been made to Corsica, *couvade* has been recorded in the Balearic Islands, and Spain yields quite a wealth of evidence, including two records of its survival among the Basques in the nineteenth century. For what it is worth I may mention at this point that in a Catalonian clinic maternity even today is regarded (very suitably) as a family affair. The husband attends with the wife for the periodical examinations. There is a bed for the husband in the wife's room and he accompanies her into the delivery theatre, where he remains throughout. I have heard similar stories of Belgium. What connection this may have with *couvade* I would not like to say—probably as much as that custom in Cyprus and a good deal more than an Irish story to which we shall come presently.

From northern Spain the *couvade* can be traced into Béarn. For the rest of France the case appears unconvincing. Dawson quotes an old French saying—*Il se met*

---

brought forth a strapping boy, about six feet high. This is quoted by Dawson as a possible survival of *a reminiscence of the couvade,* with—I suggest—no more evidence than we have in the case of the Ariadne commemoration. Why should not the Cypriot ceremony be just what it claims to be and the play witnessed by Captain Cook a piece of coarse buffoonery such as we can find in any country at any time? One wonders what peculiar religious customs might be inferred from the Elizabethan practice of employing boys for women's rôles on the stage, or what might be deduced from the fact that a young woman plays the Principal Boy in a modern pantomime. And—above all—what mystic rite is concealed in popular music-hall features of female impersonation? It is apparently too simple to suggest that what amuses us might also amuse the people of Ulieta.

au lit quand sa femme est en couche—as proof that the tradition has survived. To my mind it indicates something very different; for a people who really practised such a custom would not refer to it in order to express ridicule. One might as well argue from the saying *to shut the stable door when the horse is stolen* (or its French equivalent, which is worthy of the Curé of Meudon) that such was at one time the practice in England (and, *mutatis mutandis,* in France). The people who invented such a saying as this one about going to bed when one's wife is with child may have heard tell of *couvade,* but only as something foreign, strange and quite certainly absurd.

Dawson has only two more fragments of evidence relating to France, and I find neither satisfactory. One is from J. B. Thiers, whose *Traité des Superstitions* was published in 1679. Thiers said that when a woman was in labour it was customary to cover her with her husband's breeches in order that she might give birth painlessly. A similar custom is noted in Germany, where other German customs, mentioned in Hartland's *Legend of Perseus,* are given reference as *akin to, or possibly derived from couvade.*

Sir James Frazer,[5] who cites Thiers on the therapeutic value of the father's breeches, also quotes J. W. Wolf (*Beiträge zur deutschen Mythologie,* 1852) to show how helpful the husband's trousers can be in Germany. He compares such beliefs, and some similar ones found in other parts of Europe, with certain customs known in Ireland. Thus James Mooney, in the *Proceedings of the American Philosophical Society* (Vol. XXIV, p. 146), is quoted on an old West of Ireland belief that the man's

[5]Frazer's *Totemism and Exogamy* (London, 1910), Vol. IV, pp. 250–51.

garments, laid upon the woman, relieved her sufferings, whilst causing her husband to cry out with agony.

Another authority was Dr. A. C. Haddon, who practised medicine in Connemara and reported in 1892 that a woman there would, on occasion, wear the coat of the expectant father *with the idea that he should share in the pains of childbirth.* This story, and a similar one, given on the authority of a doctor who had practised in the counties of Tipperary and Limerick, will be found in *Folk-Lore,* IV (1893), 357–59. In the Tipperary and Limerick version it is again the trousers which are used—worn round the mother's neck. Such a custom is mentioned by John Dunton, the English bookseller and author who went to Ireland in 1698. Among previously unpublished letters of Dunton's at the Bodleian (Rawl. D.71) some were made public by Edward MacLysacht in 1939. I quote from MacLysacht's *Irish Life in the Seventeenth Century,* pages 350–61:

> And surely if the curse laid upon Eve to bring forth her children in sorrow has missed any of her posterity, it must be here, many of the poorer and laborious sort of women bearing their children without any long labour or extreme pains . . . often proving their own midwives. . . . They have also a custom to wrap the labouring woman in their [sic] husband's coat, and as the delivery proves either easy or difficult, they form fancies of the man's being a good or bad husband.

But why should this be evidence of *couvade?* Can't a man put his coat or breeks upon his wife or her bed without them being taken to be a substitute for himself? I hold strongly to this point, the more so because, since we find them doing this in Ireland, I shall be lying in

ambush for Mr. Dawson and anybody else who tries to
father a *couvade* upon the Book of Leinster.

The third supposed instance of *couvade* survival in
France is given on the authority of Solomon Reinach. It
amounts to nothing more than this: that after the death
of a child in a coastal village near Coutances, it happened in that one family and on that one occasion (in
the year 1880 to wit) that both the mother *and the
father* (the italics are borrowed from Mr. Dawson) retired to bed. There they received condolences. With the
most genuine respect for the scholarship of Mr. Dawson
and the vast amount of useful work he has done in col-
lating material on this subject, I find here a perfect example of the greatest peril in all research—the tendency
to find whatever we are looking for. The poor man may
have had a cold or a bilious attack, or he may have been
literally prostrate with grief. I could offer, in fact, any
number of perfectly simple explanations (and for each
one there must be a dozen that have not occurred to me)
whilst on the other hand I suppose there is no theory so
foolish that it could not be backed by one such isolated
and dubious incident. In fact, if the poor father's reception of his visitors in bed is to be connected with any
human convention I would rather be inclined to consider
it as a survival of the *lit de parade,* which we shall discuss later.

We are now, you will observe, on the coast of the
English Channel. Our lines of communication with the
nearest stronghold of *couvade* (in the Pyrenees) are
extremely doubtful. But in spite of this a glimpse at
Great Britain may prove worth the trouble. While waiting in the customs shed it may be worth remarking that
evidences of the man-childbed have been claimed to exist
elsewhere in Europe. Warren Dawson mentions the
island of Marken, in the Zuyderzee, and the statement

by Charles Letourneau that a Russian had informed him of its survival in the Baltic provinces. . . .[6]

A note in *The Academy* (February 16, 1884) recorded from what was termed *a source beyond suspicion* a Yorkshire practice whereby the mother of an illegitimate child was said to be bound by a local code of honour not to reveal the name of the father. But the girl's mother would go in search of him and the first man she found in bed would be the culprit. As evidence this anonymous note, with its absence of names, dates, places, instances or authority, seems of dubious value, though I find it solemnly quoted by sound anthropologists. There are, however, sources of information which appear more reliable and point to the existence of something not unlike the *couvade* in England, within more modern times. It is true that the male-childbed, so called, is missing—the *pièce de résistance* of the whole system. But the sufferings of the father are on record; and the most important thing—missing in most of the accounts of *couvade*—is that (for what the records are worth) the sufferings were evidently real enough. It is in England, in fact, that we find (in place of simulation and play acting) the true, the authentic pains of paternity—a matter surely worthy of our consideration even if it takes us out of bed for a few minutes. Patriotism demands nothing less of me.

Paternal pain, generally in the form of toothache, has been recorded among expectant fathers in East Anglia,[7] but evidence from other parts of England is

[6]This is apparently the only authority for a categorical statement regarding *couvade* in the Baltic provinces to be found in the *Encyclopaedia Britannica* (11th ed.). The writer nevertheless rejected the abundant evidence of *couvade* survival in Spain.

[7]*Encyclopaedia Britannica* (11th ed.). The contributor of

also available. The well-known Egyptologist, Winifred S. Blackman, contributed a short article to *Folk-Lore* in 1918 (Vol. XXIX, pp. 319–21) on traces of the *couvade* which had received her attention in Britain. The instances she mentioned, from observations of her own and of other presumably reliable people were noticed in Oxfordshire and Cheshire. They consisted, for the most part, of cases in which sympathetic pains were experienced by husbands when women were childbearing. In one instance a sailor, though himself in the Mediterranean, bore the pain of his wife in England. Where this was the case, or at least so long as the husband's pain endured, the wife was (it seemed) immune. Thus in one recorded case a woman had replied to sympathetic enquiries with the words: *Oh, I am all right; J—— is bearing the little one this time, and he is awfully bad.* Such, indeed, was the case, for J—— was stricken so severely with morning sickness that he was obliged for a time to abandon work. It would be of some value to know how the doctor filled in the necessary certificates; but no doubt (like everything the profession does not understand) his condition was described as idiopathic. In point of fact it is noteworthy that one of the symptoms was neuralgia, a pain directly linked with anxiety, worry and a bad state of nerves.

When the practitioners of sympathetic magic first began, in England, to treat the weapon instead of the wound, and to practise on almost everything but the patient, the method had noticeably beneficial results. A little reflection on the methods commonly in use, the unhygienic applications so often prescribed and the merciless bleeding, will make it clear that sympathetic

---

the article on *Couvade* remarked that the prevalence of this belief in early times was proved by references to it in Elizabethan drama.

magic had much to recommend its use: it did at least
relieve the patient from much unnecessary suffering,
save him from much perilous therapy and inefficient
nursing, and give Nature a reasonable chance to resist
and overcome whatever toxins had invaded the system.
As the benefits of the system were proved empirically,
without doubt it gained power in proportion to the increase in faith on the part of those to whom it was applied. I make no doubt that sympathetic magic has been
equally successful in the case of the *couvade*.

In the first place, a belief in the general principles
underlying this practice must everywhere have relieved
women in childbirth from much unnecessary suffering,
artificially added to that (and the best authorities agree
that it need not be very great in a healthy woman) which
Nature imposes.[8] The infliction of a debilitating régime
and of a hundred remedies upon the husband, combined
with the belief that he really is invalescent, would easily
produce most of the symptoms described in a husband
of the English *couvade* type, and more easily if he were
sensitive and sympathetic—if, in fact, he desired in truth
to bear or share the sufferings of his wife. This would
be sympathetic magic in reality, the magic of a true
sympathy; and the visible symptoms of pain in the husband would prove the final link in this chain of causation,

[8]In one of John Dunton's letters, with regard to Ireland
(see p. 36) the bookseller makes the apposite remark that
where Irishwomen in his time fell into any great distress
(i.e., in bearing children) the barbarities with which they
were treated were *such as would make a reasonable man
believe they were used to frustrate the very intentions of
nature.* Instances follow. Fortunately, as Dunton had already made clear, most Irishwomen required little or no
assistance in those days. But where they did so the barbarities which shocked Dunton were only an exaggeration of the
ignorance and stupidity he could have found in England or
on any part of the Continent.

as such symptoms would assist the woman by confirming her belief that her husband was bearing the pain.

Modern experiments have proved beyond any doubt that the difficulties experienced by civilised women in performing a function which wild animals and primitive peoples perform with ease (almost with nonchalance) is due to wrong diet, to lack of exercise (or rather of the right kind of exercise) and to fear. There is obviously no more certain path to pain than a conviction that one is going to be hurt. The removal of this fear, by the *couvade* convention, must therefore eliminate at least one potent contributory to the experience of actual pain on the part of the woman. A final instance provided by Winifred Blackman indicates that the power of suggestion invoked by this belief may even be of fundamental importance:

> In this case the wife suffered very badly with haemorrhoids, and her husband had frequently begged her to see a doctor, but in vain. He happened on one occasion to express great sympathy with her, just before she became pregnant. The haemorrhoids were, according to my informant, immediately transferred to the husband, who has suffered from them off and on ever since. The wife, however, is completely cured.

This story is all the more valuable because the cure of this particular ailment by sympathetic magic has a very old history. In I Samuel VI (4 and 5) there will be found that curious story of the Philistines. Having been smitten (in the previous chapter) with *emerods*[9] *in their secret parts,* the Philistines consulted with priests and

[9]*Emoroides ben fuyue veynes whyche stretche out atte the eeres.* (My definition is taken from Trevisa's translation of *De Proprietatibus Rerum,* by Bartholomew de Glanville.)

diviners, who advised them to send back the Ark of the
Covenant to the Chosen People. But they were not to
send it empty. Either the Lord or the Israelites wanted
reparations, and the Ark was to be stuffed *with five
golden emerods and five golden mice. . . . Wherefore
ye shall make images of your emerods, and images of
your mice that mar the land*. There is, unfortunately, no
record as to whether the cure was efficacious on this occasion, but the representatives of the Almighty appear to
have been quite pleased with this singular tribute.

During the same year (1918) in which Winifred
Blackman published her observations on traces of the
couvade in England, Mr. Laurence Housman's novel,
The Sheepfold, appeared. Having occasion to look at
this book again recently, I was struck by an episode in
which a young husband is described as sharing the pains
of his wife when she is confined. As Laurence Housman
referred to the matter quite casually, almost as though
it had been a common and well-known phenomenon, I
wrote to ask him upon what evidence this episode was
based. Was it, perhaps, a recollection of his own version
of *Aucassin and Nicolette?* The correspondence which
followed elicited a number of interesting facts. The
father's pain, said my friend, usually comes in the form
of toothache (a fact confirmed from other sources, as
we have seen)—indeed, he knew one man personally,
who had lost a tooth for each of his three children.[10]
My friend's stepmother had firmly believed in this transference of pain and was shocked when Clemence Hous-

[10]This was the composer Moorat, who wrote the music for
Prunella (by Housman and Granville-Barker). Moorat was
of Armenian extraction, and so were the three teeth. L.H.
was unable to locate with precision information acquired
up to sixty or seventy years ago, but thought Worcestershire
and Gloucestershire the most likely counties to have been
the sources of his general information.

man,[11] quoting Uncle Remus, said it was a case of *You do the pulling while I do the grunting*. Sickness, said Laurence, was another shared affliction, and (in one case of which he had heard) the husband—during his wife's pregnancy—was *sick as a horse* every morning, his good woman escaping this inconvenience altogether.

Some such habits must surely have been carried to America by the Pilgrim Fathers. (The Pilgrim Mothers, perhaps significantly, are seldom mentioned.) My Middle West correspondent, Mr. Jack C. York, of Ironton, Ohio, states as follows:

> I have a vague recollection of hearing older members of my family speaking of something similar to *La Couvade,* but not in the sense of a custom. . . . Rather, my folks, as I remember, talked of certain men they knew who were forced to go to bed because of personal illness—violent nausea—while their wives were undergoing childbirth.

Once more, you will observe, it is no pretence of pain but the real thing, in the best Anglo-Saxon tradition. Modern Americans (male) would probably be ashamed to admit such weakness. However, as we shall see, a more complete and orthodox form of *couvade* had been known in the Americas before the *Mayflower* arrived, before the Spaniards landed, or Prince Thingamy from Welsh Wales or even the hardy Norsemen. But there is yet a word to be said about the British Isles. Thomas Pennant, in 1772, found a poor husband in Dumfriesshire *roaring with agony in uncouth and unnatural pains,*

[11]Sister of Alfred and Laurence. Though little known, she is, in my own opinion and that of her surviving brother, the best writer in that brilliant family—as posterity may yet discover.

while his wife suffered nothing at all—a fact attributed, in this locality, to a cunning art known to the *accoucheuse*. Warren Dawson, in this connection, quotes an old Highland saying about putting the pains on the man. Indeed, the plot thickens. But now we are crossing to Ireland and I am calling a halt.

There is a story in the Book of Leinster (twelfth century) and in a fifteenth-century MS at the British Museum (Harleian 5280) which has given rise to a great deal of discussion. The story, in brief, is as here follows. To the residence of a widower called Crunniuc, in the ancient kingdom of Ulster, there came a strange woman who took charge of the place without asking anyone's permission, managing both the household and the children and taking her place at night beside the householder. As might be expected, the lady in due course conceived; and on account of her condition she was unable to accompany Crunniuc to a big festival that he was after attending. Before he left home she gave him, as is the custom, some words of advice (there is, I understand, some difference of opinion as to her words, but broadly speaking, we may say that it was a counsel of prudence). And this, of course, was just Chekhov's gun on the wall which is bound to go off—the first law of drama, and of dramatic narrative—for it is no less customary for such advice to be neglected by gentlemen, once their elbows have been lifted a few times.

At this festival, organised by people of the Six Counties—or rather, by a narrow strip of them from Lough Neagh and the river Ban to the sea—there, was, of course, horse racing; no big occasion in Ireland would ever have been complete without that. The King of Ulster naturally carried off all the trophies: it is said he had some magnificent horses, though for all I know the whole thing was a boat race, for we have sufficient evidence about the character of this particular king to doubt whether any but the royal jockeys would seriously have considered riding to win. It may have been with some such thoughts in his mind that Crunniuc, being asked rhetorically whether anything could be more fleet than the king's horses, replied (perhaps with the bitterness of a man who has just been defrauded by jiggery-pokery, after putting all he had on what should have been a sure thing) that *his wife could run faster*.

The story having supplied no previous evidence of Mrs. Crunniuc's M.P.H., we can safely assume this remark to have been intended in a derogatory sense, implying that the royal horses of Ulster were so many caterpillars. This, which would be the normal sense in which a man would use such words, is particularly clear in view of Mrs. Crunniuc's condition—of which the good man cannot have been ignorant. To his dismay he soon found himself under arrest on a charge of *lèse-majesté,* while messengers were sent to fetch his wife forthwith, and enter her against the insulted beasts.

The second Mrs. Crunniuc was a reasonable woman. She said that Mr. C. was quite wrong, and no doubt went on to explain that people said that sort of thing but it meant nothing at all. As this did not help she pleaded her present condition and made an application for delaying the race. It was all in vain; and she was hauled off to the racecourse, where her fervent appeals to the cruel tyrant proved utterly unavailing. Promising that the king should suffer a greater wrong than that which he had done to her, she declared at last who she was— Macha, the daughter of Sainred, the son of Imbath (Ocean). She was, in fact, on one side at least, a goddess.

The poor woman must have seemed a very unlikely runner; we do not know what odds were quoted, but only that there was no pity in the hard hearts of Ulster.

To the amazement of everybody, however, she won the race. Then, at the winning post, she gave birth to twins and died. Emain Macha they called the place, and the capital of the Ulates it long remained. But the curse which Macha put upon the king remained with him and all the men of his country, from generation to generation. And this was the *Cess Noiden,* the pains of childbirth which each grown Ulsterman must suffer once in his lifetime.[12] What was more, it was prophesied that the *Cess Noiden* would incapacitate the Ulates in the time of their utmost danger, and this fell about when Ulster was invaded by Queen Medb, in the days of King Concobar. The hero Cuchulain, being (by a special dispensation) the only Ulsterman exempt from this curse— perhaps because he was no true Orangeman—seems to have taken on almost the entire armed forces of Eire singlehanded.

I first came across this story myself in an unpublished MS by an Irish friend who had made his own English version of the *Táin.* When I first considered including some discussion of the *couvade* in this book I must confess that there seemed to me to be some connection between this tale and the widespread custom of the man-childbed. I consulted my Dublin friend, Mr. Michael J. Lennon, and he had in due course completely convinced me that the story was irrelevant when I found that it had already acquired an accepted position in literature relating to the *couvade.* Irrelevance alone would not, of course, have prevented me from using the story if I had

[12]This does not appear to apply to the present occupants, mostly descended from a gang of brigands posted in Ulster by Cromwell. Whether those whom the godly man drove *to Hell or Connaught* carried the curse with them has not, so far as I can ascertain, been the subject of any investigation. Probably most of those whom Cromwell did not massacre soon died of starvation, anyway.

felt a mind to do so. But the fact that Dawson mentions the story and compares it with the old yarn of Herodotus about the Scythians who plundered the temple of Aphrodite—to which I shall allude presently—makes the *Cess Noiden* relevant, if only in the sense that its relevance needs to be refuted.

H. d'Arbois de Jubainville in the *Revue Celtique,* t. VII (1886), 225–30, had an informative article on a translation of the Macha story which had been made by Windisch, two years previously. He did not mention *couvade.* Michael Lennon thinks the first to place the Ulates *dans cette galère* was Heinrich Zimmer, but I cannot find evidence for this. The fact remains that the *Cess Noiden* was not an instance of *couvade* in any accepted sense of the term, and that the only possible peg on which a genuine Irish *couvade* could possibly be hung is a note five lines long among the Miscellanea of *Folk-Lore,* in 1899 (Vol. X, p. 119). There a writer (without giving any details) speaks of a saying reported to him. He said it was used in Ireland when speaking to an expectant father: *You'll soon have to go to bed with the old woman and be nursed, like they did years ago.* That —we must admit—would be suspicious if there were anything else besides a few old coats and pairs of breeches to back the assumption. But further evidence is entirely lacking.

The *Cess Noiden* has been much discussed, though without making the main facts very clear. Sir John Rhys in his *Lectures on the Origin and Growth of Religion* (London, 1888), pages 362–63, explained that it was called the Nine Nights' Sickness because it lasted either four days and five nights or five days and four nights. I have no comment to make on this extraordinary arithmetic—there are several pages of it, in which one can easily sink up to the neck—but it is surely important to

decide whether the *Cess* of the Ulates was a *couvade* or
not. To Sir John it appeared so; it was *the Ultonian
couvade*. This strange custom, he said, was known in
Ireland, at least in Ulster (p. 627). On page 628 he finds
that *the persistence of the myth of which the Ultonian
inactivity formed an integral part would naturally come
to be interpreted sooner or later in the light of the only
custom that seemed to make it intelligible, namely that of
the couvade*. Intelligible, one asks, to whom? Judging by
the context, Rhys appears to have been referring to
those Irish poets and storytellers who handed on a tale
already ancient *before any Aryan wanderer had landed
in these islands*. But this begs the question; for what has
to be proved is that the custom of the *couvade* was, in
fact, known at all in Ireland, except on the evidence provided by this same *Cess Noiden* of Ulster. An alternative
reading would make Sir John Rhys's ambiguous statement refer to the anthropologists of his own time (and
since) who would certainly interpret any and every
phenomenon *in the light of the only custom that seemed
to make it intelligible*—or, better still, in the light of
some fashionable fad of whoever happened to be around
and about, making most noise at the time—e.g., Dr.
Freud, in the 1920s.

But on the very next page (629) Rhys was asking *who
ever heard of a couvade that included all the adult males
of a whole province at one and the same time?* Well,
whoever did? Certainly not the Irish, for they had never,
in all probability, heard of any manner of *couvade*. Nor
is it possible to explain the story of Macha as an attempt
of the Gaelic conquerors to account for an existing custom. The story of Macha is itself much older than the
Táin Bó Cúalnge, probably much older than the Great
Gaels of Ireland. It is worked into the *Táin* as a *remsceal*
or introductory story, justifying the singlehanded de-

fence of Ulster by Cuchulain; but it was not invented to
account for that feat of arms or for the indisposition and
absence from the field of the other Ultonians. It stands
by itself, a tale ancient even in the days when the story
of Cuchulain was first told in Ireland. Whatever its
origin, there is absolutely no reason to connect this
legend with *couvade*,[13] especially in the absence of any
positive evidence that such a custom was ever prevalent
in the country. The same general objections apply to
such pure guesswork which has already been noticed in
the case of Ariadne and Cyprus.

In tracing the course of *couvade* southwards from
the eastern Mediterranean, Warren Dawson finds some
difficulties, especially the lack of Egyptian evidence. It
is not until we come to the Congo that we find evidence
of the full *couvade*, though customs have been recorded
further east which are believed to be related to it. On any
diffusionist theory, once the poverty of the eastern Mediterranean is compared with the wealth of material in
Spain and East Africa, the claims of *Atlantis* appear to
outweigh, as a hypothesis, the more orthodox claims of
the Levant; while this absence of evidence in the case
of Egypt must be particularly distressing to those who
would father everything upon the Pharaohs.

To the east of the Mediterranean and south of the
Black Sea there lived in ancient times the Tibareni, who
were said to practice this custom, the husband retiring to
bed and groaning when his wife gave birth. Thus Apol-
lonius Rhodius tells us of these same Tibarenes that
when they bring forth children to their husbands the
men lie in bed and groan, with their heads close bound,
but the women bring them food and prepare for them
childbirth baths. Valerius Flaccus said much the same,

[13]I have since found this view categorically stated by Eleanor
Hull in *The Cuchullin Saga* (London, 1898), pp. 292–93.

speaking of the green lakes of the Tibarenes, *where she that has given birth binds her husband's head with indolent turban, and herself tends him after her babe is born.*[14]

Dawson (as already mentioned) is inclined to link with the *couvade* a story of Herodotus (I.105) to the effect that the Scythians who sacked the temple of Aphrodite at Ascalon were afflicted with some disease. Herodotus did not himself state the nature of this disease, but only that it was female and that you could see for yourself by visiting Scythia. I have myself suggested elsewhere (in *Beards*) that the disease was nothing more nor less than shaving, which was enough to make any man resemble a woman to Greek eyes—and ill, at that. This hypothesis also meets the point made by the historian, that you could see for yourself what was wrong with these Scythians.

At least my version has the advantage of ruthless simplicity, as it disposes by one stroke of the Scythian disease and of the Amazons—who have also crept into the *couvade* legend, on the grounds that their children were reared by men, these attending to domestic tasks while the women wore the trousers. My simple suggestion (that these Amazons—those of Pontus, at least—were merely shaven Scythians) relieves me of any necessity to discuss them further. What, after all, more closely resembles a female archer without breasts than a shaven man with a bow and quiver? This version has the enormous advantage of evading the difficult question: *Who breast-fed the Amazon children, and how?*

Couvade is found next on the west coast of India, in Malabar. Further examples are found inland, and its existence has been noted round the Bay of Bengal from

[14]In each case I have used the translations given in the Loeb classics.

Assam to Malaya. Examples are quoted from the Nicobar Islands, from Indonesia, Borneo, the Celebes, the Philippines and Melanesia. The Hairy Ainus of Japan once practised the *couvade*—the men being as anxious to simulate women in childbirth as their wives were to imitate men by tattooing moustaches on their faces. Traces of the custom in Kamchatka[15] may provide the link with the Americas. In North America there is no positive evidence of its widespread use, though its survival has been claimed in Ontario and it certainly reached Greenland by one route or another. In South America and the West Indies the evidence is abundant.

Various are the explanations of this fascinating custom. The legendary Basque explanation, whereby manly virtues are sympathetically instilled into the child by its father, appears to have been endorsed by Solomon Reinach. On the other hand, the practice is known among the Koramas of Mysore; and one man, when questioned, explained that the father deserved more attention than his wife, because his function in the birth of the child was more important than hers. Very different again was the explanation given in another part of India, in an account similar to that recorded by Marco Polo concerning the people of Zardandau. He was told that, the woman having had a hard time, it was only fair that the man should take his share. In one part of Scotland it was believed that whoever rose first from the bridal bed would bear the pains of childbirth; but I do not know whether the competition to which this must have given rise was motivated by selfishness or the spirit of

[15]Recent ethnographical researches by Maria Stepanova indicate considerable early migrations *from* Alaska *to* Siberia. This raises once more the question of the direction taken by the culture stream and its place of origin. It will be observed that the link between the Far East and Asia Minor is very weak.

honourable self-sacrifice. The article on *couvade* in Funk and Wagnalls' *Standard Dictionary of Folklore* suggests yet another popular explanation—source unstated: *that the child has been separated from the father and that both are weak and in need of care and nursing.*

The anthropologists have expressed a great divergence of opinion. A French Catholic missionary of the eighteenth century (J. F. Lafitau, in his *Moeurs des Sauvages Amériquains comparées aux moeurs des premiers temps*) decided that the custom derived from some obscure knowledge of Original Sin. Later in the century the *couvade* was attributed in another French work to male vanity. By the end of the nineteenth century a French authority had come to the conclusion that its object was *de faire oublier ses douleurs à la femme, de lui donner une innocente révanche de la réproduction.* A German writer of the early nineteenth century had already explained that the real object was simply to have the husband handy at a time when he might be useful—what better way was there to pass the time than to lie daydreaming? Another German—none other than Max Müller—said that (quite on the contrary) the father took to his bed from self-defence, as an escape from female tyranny. Some even saw in the male-childbed the survival of a habit from a distant past when mammals (as surmised by Darwin) might have been androgynous, both sexes giving milk to nourish the young. This theory was discussed at some length by contributors to *Notes and Queries* in 1889 and 1890.[16] Numerous instances were offered of men suckling children, until the editor took the course (unusual in *Notes and Queries*) of announcing that *Further discussion is not invited.*

[16] Seventh Series, Vol. VIII, p. 442, and Vol. IX, pp. 9–10; 54–55.

Another theory links the *couvade* with a hypothetical revolution of individualism against primitive communism. Yet another finds in it the symbol of a changing order, when matriarchy gave way to patriarchy and men asserted their paternity by a formal ceremony of adoption. Or again it was an ingenious scheme to cheat the Devil. The chief difficulty has always been the fact that the *couvade* takes so many forms. Strict dieting of the husband is a very common feature. Among the Tagals of Luzon (according to Dawson, quoting Blumentritt) the father *must forbear from the enjoyment of double fruits . . . otherwise his wife will have twins, which Tagals by no means wish to happen.* In some other cases the father must avoid sneezing—a subject with regard to which whole volumes could be written (St. Augustine tells us that in his time a man who sneezed while putting on his shoes, and on certain other specified occasions, would instantly retire to his bed).

Usually we find the father lying abed *wailing and acting the part of the accouché,* as Karsten said of the Caribs, or receiving congratulations, as George Murdock[17] remarks in the case of the Witotos of the northwest Amazon. His wife is up and about—indeed, it is not easy to see just what the husband is imitating in a primitive society where women do their part with such ease and grace.

Thus Daryll Forde,[18] writing of the Boro women in another part of South America, notes that on the birth of a child the mother will go out the same day to dig her manioc patch. It is the father who must remain for a month in his hammock—a rectangle of fibre netting, stretched by two sticks and slung from convenient house posts. But among the Arawak we find another variation

[17]*Our Primitive Contemporaries* (New York, 1938).
[18]*Habitat, Economy and Society* (London, 1934), p. 145.

of the South American *couvade,* both father and mother remaining in bed for a week together.[19] A similar variation is apparently found in the Nicobar Islands, where E. H. Man speaks of both husband and wife being fed by relatives. In view of the derivation of the word *couvade,* as shown in our quotation from Murray's *Dictionary,* it is curious that Man should remark upon the same custom among the Nicobarese being *likened to the sitting of a hatching hen.* (This suggests yet another possible origin of the custom—no more fanciful than some which have already engaged our attention— that it might be an imitation of the habits observed in the domestic life of certain birds, the cock sharing the duty of sitting on the eggs.)

There are, again, the Nayādis of Cochin, among whom the father does not retire to bed but sits shampooing his abdomen, as Edgar Thurston remarked in a passage quoted by Dawson. It is usual for the man to refrain from all heavy work—a precaution taken by the Nicobarese fathers months before the birth. In this case the extension of the privilege may possibly be connected with the reputation of the Nicobarese for laziness, but the prejudice against heavy work appears to be widespread among fathers throughout the world. On the other hand, the ordeals through which some must pass are such as to suggest anything but a man's preference for an easy life, and they are even calculated, one would imagine, to afford a drastic remedy for careless procreation. Thus Tylor described the Carib fathers in the West

[19] A. L. Kroeber in *Anthropology* (New York, 1948). Kroeber also mentions another case of primitive women taking the business seriously—that of the Utes of North America, where the mother, after giving birth, spends thirty days on a bed of hot ashes. The usual *couvade* procedure is, however, to leave all this sort of thing to the father while the woman applies herself to domestic and other chores.

Indies as fasting and dieting to such an extent that it was a marvel they could survive. After a long period of abstinence, sufficient to weaken the poor wretch to the limit of human resistance, the father was scratched all over his body[20] with the teeth of the agouti, a native rodent. Pimento was then rubbed into the wounds. . . . We have already noticed that in England there is evidence that some fathers really suffer when their wives have children[21]; but in the West Indies they took no chances in this matter. As a universal practice in a world threatened with overpopulation this quaint old Carib custom has much to commend its adoption.

It is with such tortures in mind, plus the practice of fasting or unpleasant dieting (sometimes also bleeding) with which the *couvade* may be accompanied, that I have considered an unorthodox dichotomy. Sir James Frazer and others long since attempted to divide the *couvade* into two separate customs, one connected with the welfare of the child and the other with that of the mother. So far as I can discover no anthropologist has so far made a similar distinction between those aspects of the customs which are conducive to the father's welfare and comfort and those which are unpleasant and probably detrimental. A careful survey of the more pleasant, engaging, attractive and enviable aspects of the *couvade* throughout the world and an equally intensive survey

[20]Scratching appears to have some obscure significance in the *couvade*. Among the Indians of Guiana the father was not allowed to use his fingernails, even for his own relief, while in childbed, but could use a splinter.

[21]A phrase employed by one observer, quoted by Dawson (p. 52), seems to imply some real disturbance in the case of the Jivaro Indians of Ecuador. The father in this case is said to coddle and diet himself *until he has recovered from the shock produced upon his system by the increased weight of his responsibilities as a father.*

of its disadvantages, as found in so many local variations, would surely be very helpful. In considering its general adoption we could then decide whether it is more important to give the father a good time or to discourage him from functioning. No less an authority than Malinowski[22] has testified to the social value of this custom and (however obscure may be its origin) utility should surely be the test.

Of all the mysteries which surround the *couvade,* none is greater than the fact that it is most common, and is generally found in its most highly developed forms, among those primitive peoples whose womenfolk make least commotion about the business of parturition. The alternative suggestion that the man is imitating, not the wife, but the child, does not fit the facts, except possibly in certain instances. It is the woman in labour who appears to be simulated as a rule; and even the exceptions which Frazer made, in his attempt to differentiate between two types of *couvade,* do not appear convincing.[23] Funk and Wagnalls' *Standard Dictionary of Folklore,* however, takes a similar line in discussing the *couvade* in South America, insisting that it is *not* a mock confinement. The use of his hammock by the father is, it is suggested, *the normal behaviour of any Indian who has nothing to do.* Of course, if we accept this idea it spoils all the fun. And Brett, in his *Indian Tribes of Guiana,* definitely says that the father, on taking to his hammock, *remains some days as if he were sick.*

If such a custom should have developed where birth was attended by much pain, much preparation and aftercare in the case of the mother, it would have presented us with an understandable form of imitation. That it

---

[22]*Sex and Repression in Primitive Society* (London, 1927), pp. 215–16.
[23]See *Totemism and Exogamy,* Vol. IV, pp. 244–47.

should be, as often it is, an apparent imitation of a maternal experience which is unknown to the imitators is something as yet unexplained. Not only is this the most outstanding fact in any general survey of the custom, but it disposes automatically of many attempted explanations which ignore the impossibility of imitating an unknown phenomenon.

Warren Dawson's book, in spite of my own amateur criticisms upon certain points, remains (in my view) the best general survey of the *couvade;* and his final verdict as to its significance is IGNORAMUS. If the diffusionist theory is correct we need not be too much troubled by divergence of practice and of the local explanations offered: a local form which no longer fulfils its original function and an accepted reason which bears no relationship to that function would both be completely compatible with the existence of some such common origin, long lost among the centuries and the milestones of ancient migrations. Dawson himself seems momentarily to forget this fact in discussing the difference in local practice and local theory, though he returns to it eventually in summing up the evidence.

Difficult as it is to find a local origin or to trace a clear track from point to point, the diffusionist theory seems to be the only one which really accounts for the *couvade;* and the divergence of practice argues strongly in favour of this theory. Had practice been reasonably uniform, had the reasons offered by those who practised it been closely analogous, the spontaneous origin of the *couvade* in many parts of the world might reasonably have been suspected as a natural human reaction to a common human experience. But it is too much to assume that, for a variety of reasons, a variety of customs arose having (quite fortuitously) certain peculiarities in common. If this reasoning be cogent, we are left with the certainty of a common origin but complete uncertainty as to what that origin was or even where we should look for it. We only know that it must have followed the discovery of paternity; which should not lead us into the argument (*post hoc, propter hoc*) that the *couvade* must necessarily have been instituted to mark this revolution, as some have suggested.

At least the pains of paternity have been fairly established and another use suggested for the bed, for which there are some hoary precedents. But I recall that I promised to say something about the cradle, and fortunately we have not far to go.

Chapter 3

HERCULES IN HIS CRADLE

> *The most shameless and indecently irrespon-*
> *sible persons among us are not drinkers of wine*
> *but drinkers of milk; and all these infants have*
> *something in them of the qualities displayed by*
> *Rabelais' Titanic babes.*
>
> > John Cowper Powys

> *I must immediately mobilise soldiers*
> *To kill, dismantle and massacre the children.*
>
> > King Herod (*in a Breton Mystery Play*)

THIS VERY MORNING, as I was musing in bed (like sweet Miss Oliver), I fell to thinking of my earliest sensations, which were really very similar, for they consisted of very little but warmth, comfort, the sense of security and a disinclination to leave my cot.

Very different was the fate of our forefathers, whose first memories must have provided nightmares for their later years. Not content with Job's swaddling band of thick darkness, the parents swathed their children in solid material bands, till they resembled embalmed corpses. Thus Jeremiah speaks of those he had swaddled and brought up, while Ezekiel, likening Jerusalem to a neglected child, says *thou wast not salted at all, nor swaddled at all.*

Dr. Cabanès, in his *Moeurs Intimes du Passé* (Vol.

VI), discussed this ancient form of torture. He considered that it was not originally practised among the Ethiopians and the Egyptians. Sparta was also at one time
innocent of the practice; and the Greeks generally appear to have allowed some small freedom of movement
to the child, though one of their doctors in the second
century gave some strict instructions, which included an
injunction to tie the child's arms to its body. It was, however, in the Middle Ages that swaddling probably became most stringent and was most widely in use. The
work of the primitives shows us children like mummies
or chrysalids enduring with stoic resignation the blind
tyranny of custom. Even movement of the head was
restricted. For the rich these bonds were often objects
of extravagance. Jewelled ribbons might be used in place
of the usual bandages of cloth.

With some modification swaddling continued well into
the eighteenth century. It even had the formidable support of Dr. Mauriceau, the famous French obstetrician,
who declared that swaddling was necessary in order to
give the child *l'attitude droite* and to prevent it going
on all fours. In spite of a general decline of this practice
from the end of the eighteenth century, Cabanès noted
its survival as late as 1920, in Turkey and Italy, also in
certain rural districts of France and other European
countries. It evidently survived among the Greeks, too,
in the late nineteenth century, as Viollet-le-Duc observed
that they still made their cradles of hollowed trunks,
with holes through which the bandages were passed.

Such were, indeed, the first cradles, rocked upon Nature's own rollers; and I suppose that there have been
worse. Among many of which I have seen descriptions,
the baskets used by the Arapesh and the Mundagumor
of New Guinea strike me as peculiarly uncomfortable.

Margaret Mead[1] has described these portable cradles—the net bag of the Arapesh, flexible and so designed as to curl the child's body into its prenatal position; the Mundagumor basket, stiff, dark within and designed to hold the child's body prone, arms pinioned by the rigid lines of its plaited cocoon. But we need not ransack the records of antiquity or of modern anthropological research among primitive peoples to discover the miseries of the cradle. In seventeenth-century Europe the midwives of Paris even deformed the shape of children's heads in order that baby girls might grow up to wear the fashionable *fontange*—an astonishing headgear which, of course, was long *démodée* by the time the misshapen heads were old enough to wear it.[2]

Other practices of the eighteenth century are described by William Hone in his *Every-Day Book* (July 9, 1831). It had been usual, he said, to roll the child's body tightly in a strong cotton swathe, about six inches wide and from ten to twenty feet in length. With its first breath the infant received oil of sweet almonds and syrup of blue violets by the spoonful. These were *unctuosities,* presumably to oil the works, but they did not protect the child from the inevitable convulsions caused by constriction. The convulsions were treated with *Dalby's Carminative,* and the victim was next subjected to overfeeding, until a surplus of sugared milk and pap produced further symptoms of distress and *Daffy's Elixir* was poured into the regurgitating stomach, so that the overfeeding could be continued. As this meant that the child was soon far

[1]*Sex and Temperament in Three Primitive Societies* (London, 1948).

[2]With more logic one of the Incas (Lloque Yupanqui) ordered cranial deformation simply to keep the people stupid. He considered that this would make them law-abiding, hundred per cent Peruvians.

too ill to sleep, it was drenched with a dose of *Godfrey's Cordial,* unswathed, reswathed and tortured in every known way until (wrote Hone) *in a few weeks or months it died.* . . . Such customs continued, according to Hone, until about 1790, when the survivors evidently decided to adopt some other expedient for maintaining the percentage of infantile mortality.

The cradle itself was in those days an elaborate affair in wealthy homes. It had grown from the simple wooden structure of the seventeenth century (the cradle of Dean Swift is an example—still to be seen, I believe, in the church at Brede, in Sussex). As though to mock the captive child within, many eighteenth-century cradles were cunningly carved and richly upholstered. Simplicity was as foreign to that age as it is to our own, though our taste runs to elaborate gadgets rather than to ornament. The latest thing in cradles that I have seen is the picture of a Travel Crib, invented by a New York manufacturer —a combination of cradle and play pen that folds into a suitcase.[3] But the old ways tell us more about young Hercules: was it not for fear of his strength that they bound him and in honour of his divinity that they spent a fortune in decking his crib?

A royal birth—be it at Bethlehem or Versailles—is always an event that stirs the mind. It is a paradox, this combination of power and helplessness, where His Royal Highness has to submit like any other to the awful indignities of napkins, tubs and talcum powder. And, as every babe is a prince or princess in its own household, the royal tableau is worth consideration: it is but common life seen through the microscope. Many a child must have echoed—as soon as he was old enough to lisp the words—the complaint of the future Louis XIII: *J'aimerais mieux qu'on ne me fist point tant de révér-*

[3]*Newsweek,* May 10, 1948.

*ences et tant d'honneur, et qu'on ne me fist point fouet-
ter.*

The ceremonies appertaining to a royal birth in France
have been discussed with some detail by Dr. Witkowski
(*Les Accouchements à la Cour*), who describes the bed
upon which Anne of Austria, Maria Theresa and Anne
of Bavaria gave birth. The fittings included two pegs, a
foot in length, fixed one on each side of the bed so that
they could be seized at the critical moment. Witkowski
also published an interesting manuscript by Dr. Deneux
on *La Naissance des Enfants de France.* Here, once
more, is a description of a bed (evidently of later and
more elaborate design) *avec ses poignées en fer, ses
pantoufles fixées à des courroies, susceptibles d'être ral-
longées ou raccourcies*—a bed, as Deneux truly remarked, so frightening that it reminded one of the mediaeval torture chamber.

To this same Dr. Deneux we owe an account of the
procedure prescribed by court etiquette. Having been at
pains to consult the oldest and most reliable authorities,
he set them down for his guidance and that of posterity.
At the moment when a royal child was about to be born
it was the duty of the *accoucheur* to announce *à haute
et intelligible voix:*

S. A. R. VA ACCOUCHER

When the royal lady gave birth he was not to forget
(in the excitement of the moment and of his purely
functional duties) to proclaim *à haute voix:*

S. A. R. ACCOUCHE

And finally, when the child was born, the *fait accom-
pli* was to be announced with equal pomp and circumstance, after which *l'accoucheur prend l'enfant et le*

présente à Sa Majesté, de manière à ce qu'elle puisse en reconnaître le sexe.

In spite of all these precautions Deneux himself may be said to have failed in his first efforts as a royal obstetrician. When he helped the Duchesse de Berry, in the year 1817, to produce her first child, the infant was placed in a room so overheated, so evil-smelling, that it was hardly possible to breathe within its walls. For some reason six beds had been brought into the child's bedchamber and supplied with mattresses from the lumber room. The wool with which these regal mattresses were stuffed was so full of worms that they could be picked up by the handful from the floor. In heat and stench the first hope of the Bourbons died of asphyxia. It was not the good doctor's fault—he had given unheeded warning. The royal infant died, a victim of ignorance, stupidity and dirt—all three as common in an early nineteenth-century court as they were in a contemporary cottage.

The careful court procedure described by Dr. Deneux had, of course, the justification of reason and experience. It was part of an elaborate arrangement to ensure and record the fact of a royal birth. Ever since the origin of James Francis Stuart had been disputed and made the pretext for the Great Rebellion in Britain, every royal family had good cause to take precautions. There must be no more stories circulated of children smuggled in warming pans into royal bedchambers. It is odd, in one with such avidity for historical mysteries as Dr. Cabanès, that the story of the warming pan and England's Old Pretender receives only the barest mention in his account of royal births, with the unusual remark that *la solution ne tente pas au surplus notre curiosité.*[4] The solution, however, was simple enough: the warming-pan legend was an invention to satisfy Tory consciences and part of

[4]*Moeurs Intimes du Passé,* Vol. VII, pp. 35–36.

a plan to rationalise rebellion by a series of pretences: firstly, that James II had abdicated, and secondly, that his son was a cuckoo in the Stuart nest. But the story, such as it was, determined the future course of procedure at royal births in England and no doubt had its effects on the Continent. If legitimacy could not be guaranteed it was at least determined that every prince should be indubitably his mother's son.

Infantile bed-life is at best a monotonous routine. Even without swaddling it remains a long and ineffective revolt of the individual against the oppression of government and society. Of course, there are exceptions. Some precocious infants have already been mentioned in the first chapter of this book; and to these I must now add St. Nicholas, who began fasting on Wednesdays and Fridays before he was weaned. From such beginnings the path to canonisation must surely have been an easy one. He became, in due course, an archbishop and was credited with one of the most remarkable miracles on record. It seems that two schoolboys arrived at Myra, in Lycia, where Nicholas was archiepiscopating in the time of Constantine the Great.[5] The boys, who were on their way to Athens in search of education, put up at an inn where they nearly came to grief, for mine host was one of those—we shall come to them shortly—such as Thomas Deloney and Wilkie Collins described in their time.

He thought nothing of murdering the boys in bed, chopping them up and salting them, with every intention of selling the product as pickled pork. But a bishop who had fasted even at the breast might be supposed to be

[5]It will be observed that this makes Nicholas a contemporary of Arius, whose ears he is said to have boxed at the Council of Nicaea. In short, he was a sound Catholic, though Athanasius does not appear to have known about him.

an exceptional person with unusual powers. St. Nicholas not only knew of these goings-on at the inn, but he called there the following morning to reproach the innkeeper for his churlish conduct. The story ended happily enough, for the inhospitable innkeeper apologised and the chunks of pickled boy were suddenly reassembled; and no worse (except perhaps for the salt) the young travellers were able to continue their journey to Athens with the saint's own blessing.

Patron saint of virgins, sailors, children, Russians, bakers, travellers and parish clerks, St. Nicholas still fills stockings with good things for good children, but has for some reason bequeathed the three golden balls which were once his emblem to the pawnbrokers for all time. His relics, seized in a piratical raid made *exprès,* for this purpose alone, by the citizens of Bari, have been credited with many miracles. His nocturnal acts of charity, originally a feature of his own reputed birthday (December 6), have been transferred in most countries to Christmas Eve; and as Santa Claus or Father Christmas, his title may be taken to include the patronage of children's bedrooms. Under his care the young need no longer fear the night that ends in the pickle jar, but can sleep in certain and happy anticipation of unearned increment through the saint's munificence.

Bed, it is true, is still very often (for children) a place of punishment. It seems strange to remember, as one lies between the sheets, that once it was both a penalty and a disgrace to be sent to this desirable place. It has also had its fears, as Lamb recalled when he claimed that from his fourth year to the age of seven or eight he never laid his head upon his pillow without an assurance of seeing some frightful spectre. These appeared as characters from an illustrated history of the Bible. Restif de la Bretonne also recorded the terrors of the night which were among the memories of his childhood and Forrest Reid had similar recollections. For fear of ghosts that poor worm Boswell could not sleep alone till he was eighteen. But the worst terrors must surely be things of the past. Did you ever read *The Fairchild Family*? My father claimed that it played an important part in his education. I remember one incident in that book which —if it in any way reflected contemporary life—explains a good deal. It concerns a child who told a lie, and how his loving parent took him from his bed that he might carry him to a desolate place where a hanged felon swung from a gibbet. This was just to learn him to tell the truth—morality was not administered in homoeopathic doses in those days.

One old custom designed to put the fear of God into the young was derived from the Malthusiasm of King Herod, who took drastic measures to reduce the population of Palestine. This long served as a pretext for beating children on Innocents Day (December 28), the ostensible reason being a reminder of the worse fate escaped by more fortunate generations. The day itself was considered unlucky—no wise person, for example, would marry at Childermas, and many other taboos applied to it: *we dread*, wrote Aubrey (in his *Remaines of Gentilisme*), *to doe any businesse on Childermasse day*. But the day, for all that, afforded great sporting opportunities for those so inclined, mediaeval tradition having established the right of any person who caught a child or young person in bed that morning to treat the matter as an offence and administer summary correction. In France, particularly, the custom appears to have been popular: *bailler les innocens, donner les innocens* or simply *innocenter* were the expressions used by those who rose early and set out, whip in hand.

Such a popular pastime could not, however, be long

restricted by any age limit. Good-looking wenches—
especially servants, who had little or no opportunity for
seeking redress—were especially liable to be victims, and
sportsmen thought nothing of pursuing them into the
road. In some parts of France the game even began on
Childermas Eve (which must have made it very unsafe
for potential victims ever to seek their beds) and it continued until the following evening; so that for twenty-
four hours there was little safety from those enthusiasts
who were not too particular as to the rules of play.
Other variations are suggested by some lines of Clement
Marot:

> *Très chère soeur, si je sçavois où couche*
> *Vostre personne au jour des Innocens,*
> *De bon matin j'irois à vostre couche*
> *Voir ce gent corps que j'aime entre cinq cens. . . .*
> *Et si quequ'un survenoit d'avanture,*
> *Semblant ferois de vous innocenter*
> *Seroit-ce pas honneste couverture?*[6]

For the child there were no such gentler variations.
Once a year, at least, his bed was a place of terror, to
be avoided before the grey dawn roused his tormenters,
eager to impress upon him his good fortune in that he
was not born in the days of King Herod. When one considers all that children have survived, and especially in
their cradling and bedding, it is enough to make one's
elderly blood creep. But, as I have remarked, every child
is Hercules. It is a solemn thought that if the organising
capacity of children were equal to their vital energy they
would easily rule the earth, because in any struggle for
power they would be the last to be worn out. And the
more I think of it, I doubt if many of them came to grief

[6]Quoted by Cabanès in *Les Indiscrétions de l'Histoire,* Vol.
I.

on Innocents Day; for I never yet knew a household where they were not the first to rise, shattering sleep for all others as effectively as Macbeth himself. Even as I write I hear them out in the road—Christopher and Pauline, bless them and blast them—making me feel nothing but a lazy, wicked, sick, cowardly, slovenly, pampered, doddering old man. And my hot-water bottle is cold.

Chapter 4

LIT DE JUSTICE, LIT DE PARADE AND LYING-IN

This expression (lit de justice) *literally denoted the seat or throne upon which the king of France was accustomed to sit when personally present in parliaments; and from this original meaning the expression came in course of time to signify the parliament itself.*

John Timbs

An excellent thought, indeed: the place, as it was said, where Justice sleeps. According to Timbs, in his *Curiosities of History,* the last Bed of Justice *was assembled by Louis XVI at Versailles . . . at the commencement of the French Revolution.* From that time the long insomnia of Justice is supposed to have begun, though I suppose that the Woolsack is still a comfortable place to recline.

Cecil and Margery Gray,[1] in discussing the *Lit de Justice,* find that its origins *remain shrouded in mystery.* They trace it back to the beginning of the fourteenth century, when the King of France first attended his *Parlement* reclining upon a bed; and personally if I ever attended Parliament that is exactly how I would prefer

[1] *The Bed* (London, 1946), p. 72.

to be. In fact the only time I was ever in the House of Lords they would all have been better tucked up between the sheets, for an Appeal was being heard before a number of sleeping Peers of the Realm, lulled by the interminable drone of a gentleman in a wig, who mumbled inaudibly the words of a vast document. But as to the origin of the *Lit de Justice,* it is always a pleasure to catch a *savant* napping, and I have already discovered the solution of this mystery—in fact I have dealt with it at greater length in my book on *Beards.* Briefly, it is as follows.

Robert, Duke of Normandy—my authority is none other than Serlo, Bishop of Séez, as recorded by Orderic Vitalis—frequently lay in bed until 3 P.M. for lack of bread to eat or clothes to wear. Bishop Serlo categorically states that he was lacking in trousers, stockings and shoes. In fact he was nothing but a bum, and never went to church for the same reason. Now I conjecture from this that Robert conducted his ducal functions from his couch—what else could he do? I well remember in 1938 crossing a bridge which then marked the boundary between Yugoslavia and Italy. It was very early in the morning. For some reason (and here I must ask for your credulity) the Yugoslavian boat that had brought us to Susak was ahead of schedule. A sleepy sentry knocked at the door of a hut several times. Receiving no answer, he opened the door and switched on a light, waking an official who lay on a small bed with a rug over him. Here, it seemed, passports were examined and we were sent round the room fetching such things as pen, ink and rubber stamp while the official, on his *Lit de Justice,* reclined at his ease.

Not until I saw his neatly folded trousers hanging on the back of a chair did I realise that this was no matter of mere laziness or a peculiarity of Yugoslavian etiquette, but sheer necessity. Such must have been the case with Robert Curthose; and why not with the kings of France, who must have spent most of their time from 1346 onwards in dodging their own vassals and the English Goddams? Even Henry of Navarre, some two and a half centuries later, had hardly a shirt to his back and probably thought his breeches dear at half a crown, like King Stephen in the ballad. What better reason for holding court in bed?

Custom, whatever the origin, made the practice honourable. The fashion spread, as fashions do, from the court downwards. Women, debarred from the Bench, found compensation in the *lit de parade,* where a successful courtesan might hope for posthumous publicity, her painted features being exhibited to the admiring populace. According to the Sieur des Réaux, the notorious Marion Delorme was thus exhibited on a *lit de parade,* wearing a virgin's crown after her death at the age of thirty-seven; but there appears to be some doubt about her death (not to mention her title to the crown) as another report of it places its date nearly a century later in her hundred and thirty-fifth year. Whatever the truth of this particular story, a study of French customs of the eighteenth century shows that there is nothing original in certain practices which have come into being in modern America.

However, no woman who desires admiration will be content to wait for such an opportunity as this. The practice of women holding court after a child had been born was, from this point of view, more gratifying. For queens and courtesans this meant the *lit de parade;* for lesser persons it at least involved a ceremonial lying-in, with vast numbers of visitors and a great deal of entertainment. The visits rapidly acquired a certain formality, an etiquette of their own which included the bringing of presents to the recumbent hostess. While these presents became increasingly extravagant, the hospitality offered became a matter of prestige and rivalry, leading to lavish expenditure in any household blessed with a child. One can imagine the internal domestic disputes which arose —the wife insisting on entertainment at least as ostentatious as that provided recently by some relative or neighbour, with every intention of even exceeding it in cost and display.

The good man may well have had a different point of view; and in the sphere of municipal government (a male preserve) he soon found courage to assert himself. Municipal decrees eventually limited or totally prohibited these orgies of feminine pride. At Milan—for the custom was no less common in Italy than it was in France and England—sumptuary laws were passed restraining expenditure on bedclothes for ladies lying in. They were not to use counterpanes of embroidered silk or stitched with gold or silver thread, the women themselves being forbidden to wear silk camisoles when entertaining visitors in their bedrooms.

Dr. Cabanès, who gives several examples of such legislation in his *Moeurs Intimes du Passé* (Vol. VI), shows that, as early as 1537, the Senate at Venice attempted to limit the list of those who were permitted to pay these formal visits to relatives of the family. Baptisms evidently provided a similar occasion for overspending, and during the sixteenth century efforts were made in Alsace to limit expenditure at both baptisms and *accouchements*. The indication is clear that citizens in council could fortify one another's courage so that here they dared what they could not have attempted unaided as fathers and husbands. But it took a woman to protest against another abuse in the rite of baptism—the use of spittle. None other than that staunch papist, Mary Stuart, was (according to her son, James I of England) *so far from being superstitious or jesuited* in her Catholicism that she sent word, when young James was baptised, to say *she would not have a pockie priest to spet in her child's mouth*. A jollier baptismal custom was one which Edmund Campion dug out of Giraldus Cambrensis and set in circulation to discredit his fellow Catholics of sixteenth-century Ireland: his story was that the Irish priests, when baptising male children, did not baptise the right arm, so that it might remain pagan and strike more deadly blows. But the folklore of the font must lure us no further, for I have still some notes on the *lit de parade*.

In the seventeenth century the entertainments which accompanied a royal birth and the lying-in of court ladies included dancing; and one has to imagine a scene in which a very primitive maternity hospital is attached to a magnificent ballroom. One precaution, however, appears to have been common—certain odours (unspecified) were considered harmful to the heroine of the occasion; and in order to be certain that no guest should bring any of these undesirable smells into the house a guard was posted at the door to sniff at all who entered. . . . As to the expense, it is best realised by considering the sum of £52,000 odd which was spent on the confinement, in 1605, of Anne of Denmark—the gay consort of James I, who had a reputation for *making the night more glorious than the day*. It is hardly to be imagined that this fortune was spent on professional attention— indeed, we know what was paid out; and it would not have absorbed one pound in five hundred. The rest was disbursed in celebrating the event.

Even in the lives of our ancestors, however, the number of children born of any one mother had a limit. Yet other occasions had to be sought and one was found in

bereavement. C. and M. Gray give interesting examples
of the extension of this practice, showing that women
often received their visitors in bed when they required
consolation for the death of a husband. (Six weeks was
at one time considered a suitable period for a Queen of
France to spend in bed after the death of her consort.)
Madame de Montespan, on the other hand, thought the
bed a suitable place to receive the compliments of friends
after the marriage of her niece; and Mademoiselle de
Fontanges was so overcome by her good fortune in becoming a duchess that she, too, received the congratulations of the court—and of her royal benefactor—lying
cosily beneath her quilt. Mary Wortley Montagu frequently received visitors in bed without any excuse whatsoever.

Apart from the Cardinal de Richelieu, who eventually
took to his bed and travelled in it (his retainers breaking
open the walls of any house that he proposed to occupy), customs such as these do not appear to have
reached such extravagant proportions among the male
population—perhaps because men tend to regard a bed
primarily as a place in which to sleep. Male exhibition-
ism, as I have pointed out elsewhere,[2] took on even more
peculiar form, in that many important persons, from
Louis XIV to Marshal Suvarov, held receptions whilst
seated on the *chaise percée*. But beds of great person-
ages have often acquired a sanctity of their own, and
the habit of making reverence not merely to royalty but

[2]In *Cleanliness and Godliness*. C. and M. Gray, however,
quote a satire by Jean Loret (1650), mentioning a man
who:

> Durant trois jours au lit s'est mis
> Pour recevoir de ses amis,
> Avec grandeur et bienséance,
> Les compliments de doléance.

to royal beds is to be noted in seventeenth-century France. *This cult of the bed,* write Cecil and Margery Gray, *extended even to the Kingdom of Heaven.* Our Lady, too, had her *lit de parade;* and as early as 1548 the birth of Christ was represented in the Chapel of the Virgin at Rheims Cathedral in a bed worthy of the occasion—a bed fit for a Farnese or a Medici.[3]

As for the Infant in the manger—let Witkowski tell his own story: *A Sainte-Marie-Majeure, on venère le berceau de Jésus-Christ, mais les magnifiques plaques d'argent dont il est orné ne ressemblent en rien à l'auge traditionelle de la sainte étable.* Dr. Witkowski noted also that the swaddling clothes in which the Child was originally swathed were to be seen at Rome in the Church of St. Paul, whilst in Lorraine they could boast of the original sainfoin used in the manger.[4] Many artists, in spite of such reminders, followed the tastes of their own age. (The cradle ordered by Napoleon for his son, the King of Rome, was designed by Prud'hon and took one of the most skilled artisans in Paris six months to complete. It was eventually purchased by a collector for £5200; but by that time an historical sense had developed and the world was spared—for that reason alone—pictures of an Infant Christ modelled upon a baby Buonaparte, in a combination cradle-cum-musical-box.)

From the *lit de parade,* as used in the Courts of Earth and attributed to that of Heaven, my mind turns naturally to other excuses devised for remaining in bed and

[3] See *The Bed* by C. and M. Gray, p. 78. Representation of the Virgin in bed is rare, as Witkowski notes. The reason for this reluctance is obscure.

[4] *Histoire des Accouchements chez tous les Peuples,* pp. 89–90. Dr. Witkowski adds other peculiar relics, less relevant to my own theme. But his long footnote on this subject is well worth reading.

the many historical precedents for doing so. Let us consider first the Ancients, but not, I promise you, too thoroughly. I have no intention of rivalling the indefatigable zeal shown by the Grays, who even dug up Paulus Silentiarius and his friend Agathias to prove that mosquito nets were in use by the sixth century A.D. Not that mosquitoes are uninteresting—for in due course we will consider the story of St. Macarius. (He at least disdained anything made with interstitial vacuities.[5]) But let us for the moment consider the uses of the bed as a throne, the bed public and convivial.

Among the early pioneers of the *lit de parade* was Alexander the Great. As to the Romans, a dreary, brutal, unimaginative people (who built an empire because they were too stupid to care what it cost them or anybody else), they had this one redeeming weakness: that they liked their beds and even banqueted in a sort of dormitory-dining-room. Some have found reason to believe that the ancient Hebrews had a similar use for the bed. Sir Thomas Browne quotes Ezekiel XXIII: *Thou didst wash thyself, paintedst thy eyes, and deckedst thyself with ornaments, and sattest upon a stately bed, and a table spread before it*. Besides, says Sir Thomas, there was *the custom of Discalceation, or putting off their shoes at meales*. Some thought this was in order to keep the beds clean, but it is a flimsy conjecture: discalceation at mealtimes is practised all over India for quite a different reason. More apposite are Sir Thomas Browne's quotations from the Vulgate, which imply a reclining posture at a Jewish feast. Thus, in Matthew XXIII:6, our A.V. translation (*love the uppermost rooms at feasts*)

---

[5]The definition is, of course, Dr. Johnson's, and should be compared with his no less celebrated effort on network: *anything reticulated or decussated at equal distances, with interstices between the intersections.*

appears in the Vulgate as *Amant autem primos recubitus in coenis*—the word *recubitus* being sharply distinguished from *cathedra,* which describes, in the same passage, the coveted seat in the synagogue (*et primas cathedras in synagogis*). By contrast to this Pharasaical behaviour the disciples (in Luke XIV:8) are told: *Cum invitatus fueris ad nuptias non discumbas in primo loco.* Our English *sit not down* gives a very different impression.

There is further evidence to be found on the subject of beds at Jewish banquets in the Gospel according to St. John (XIII: 23): *Erat recumbens unus ex Discipulis ejus in sinu Jesu quem diligebat,* which gesture (I quote once more from the *Pseudodoxia Epidemica*)[6] *will not so well agree unto the position of sitting, but is naturall, and cannot be avoyded in the Laws of accubation.* However, our Special Correspondent on all matters affecting biblical criticism—Jack Hoyland, of Woodbrooke, Birmingham—assures us that Sir Thomas was on a wrong scent. The Greek, as he reads it, gives Luke XIV:8 as *don't slump yourself down into the chief chair,* and Matthew XXIII:6 my friend construes *they love the chief chairs at dinner-parties.* Leonardo, says Jack, may have been right; for he finds much doubt as to whether the Jews—other than Hellenised Sadducees—reclined at feasts in the Graeco-Roman fashion. For the rest, beds in many biblical references appear to have been no more than rolls of bedding such as every traveller in the East

[6]Book V, Chapter vi. There appears to me to be some impropriety in the parallel which immediately follows in Sir Thomas' text when he points out that *the very same expression is to be found in Pliny, concerning the Emperor Nerva and Veiento whom he favoured.* Sir T. Browne deduces that the expression *bosom friend* was derived from this alleged gesture of accubation.

includes among his luggage[7]—beds, in fact, that one can take up, and walk.

But even if we must rule out the Jews, the *lit de parade,* in its broadest sense, has a venerable history; and I am only concerned at the moment with the essential respectability of lying in bed, for one reason or another, in broad daylight. This is a matter of *amour propre* and self-respect. The *lit de parade* was revived by Florence Nightingale, in her old age, and by Dr. Mossadegh, the Persian premier, during the oil negotiations of recent memory (August 1951).

It is a comforting thought that so many great men have been sluggards. Dr. Johnson, it is true, said (according to the obsequious Boswell), *I tell all young men, and tell them with great sincerity, that nobody who does not rise early will ever do any good.* Yet in the same breath the doctor admitted that he himself lay abed till noon; and elsewhere he confessed that he often continued there till two in the afternoon. But then Johnson considered that anyone who thought of going to bed before midnight was a scoundrel—which suggests an interesting syllogism, as the doctor also considered that a scoundrel's last refuge was patriotism. I am not sure where this takes us, but it appears to justify my own habits, so we will proceed—in spite of Isaak Watts and his nasty little doggerel.

On the other hand, it must be admitted that Jeremy Taylor considered three hours' sleep sufficient, while Richard Baxter was a close runner-up with four. And the Ancients were early risers—some have even included Homer, though upon what evidence I cannot imagine. But Virgil, Horace, Seneca, Marcus Aurelius and that intolerable prig, Cicero, appear to have been in this

[7]Except where the *scympodium* (mentioned in next chapter) is indicated.

category. Buffon even ordered his valet to eject him forcibly, if necessary, at the stroke of six. Walter de la Mare, who mentions most of these examples of early risers, and some others[8] remarks that Sir Thomas More was another of them and that the citizens of his *Utopia* no doubt continue to *attend lectures before sunrise.* Groucho Marx makes the ingenious point that if Thomas Edison slept only four hours a day, as claimed, it would amount to eight if he doubled up in bed.

I return with relief to persons of more human habits. Chesterton, who resembled Johnson in so many other ways (though a far greater man and as truly jovial as the doctor was essentially pompous), appears to have favoured lying in bed—at least in theory. His well-known essay on the subject, in *Tremendous Trifles,* suggests the meditations of an experienced practitioner. Characteristically, G.K.C. explained that misers were early risers —a thought which, of itself, suggests Chestertonian verse—and *burglars,* he said, *I am informed, get up the night before.* To Chesterton *the alarming growth of good habits* was a positive menace to good morals, and above all he distrusted any rationalisation of one's own laziness: *If a healthy man lies in bed let him do it without a rag of excuse; then he will get up a healthy man.*

I cannot at the moment remember what bishop it was who said of early rising that it was conducive to all the worst possible results, conceit all the morning, fatigue all the afternoon and bad temper all the evening. No one would have said that of Oblomov. It might very reasonably be argued that we should not today have *Paradise Lost* (unread, on our shelves) if Milton had not composed most of it in bed—where else would he have found time even to read the proofs?

To the bed (the only perfect climate, as it has so

[8]*Behold This Dreamer* (London, 1939), p. 35.

justly been called) we owe much of Mark Twain's work.[9]
With Robert Louis Stevenson it was often a matter, not
of choice, but of necessity, so we will not subpoena his
ghost with pen and flageolet. But Rousseau and Voltaire
were known to work in bed by preference. To the same
class belong Macaulay, Napoleon, Alexander Woollcott,
the poets Gray and Pope and—naturally—Trollope.
Proust was of their number; and surely we should add
Max Beerbohm, credited with the remark that his ideal
of happiness was a four-poster in a field of poppies. I
am half inclined to claim Shakespeare, on the strength
of four lines in the sonnets, as a bed-worker:

> *Weary with toil, I haste me to my bed,*
> *The dear repose for limbs with travel tired,*
> *But then begins a journey in my head*
> *To work my mind, when body's work expired. . . .*

However, it appears that Shakespeare (or Bacon)
only lay awake thinking about the Dark Lady (or Mr.
W.H.), and there is no evidence that this was continued
on the following forenoon. We will include him out, to
borrow a famous phrase. Campbell began *Lochiel's
Warning* in his sleep and woke up to finish it—like that
celebrated British peer who dreamed he was speaking
in the House of Lords and woke to find it was true. In
Campbell's case coming events had indeed cast shadows
before them, for those were approximately the very
words of his dream. Longfellow had not the same excuse: he was wide awake, suffering from acute insomnia,
when he dashed off that rhyme about the schooner
Hesperus and the skipper's tiresome daughter. A couple
of aspirin might have saved the ship.

[9]Mark Twain was nevertheless the first to point out the risk,
based upon the high proportion of deaths which occur in
bed.

Of the composers, Rossini, Paisiello, Michal Glinka
and—I believe—Puccini worked in bed a good deal. In
Rossini's case one can well imagine that the end of the
William Tell Overture was suggested by an alarm clock.
Gaetano Donizetti is said to have been so lazy that he
rewrote a sheet of music rather than pick up his first
draft, which had slipped off the bed. This was probably
a saving of time, as Donizetti was a fast worker. Among
British politicians—all Conservatives—Lord Balfour
stayed in bed till noon when he could, and Lord (Chuck-
it-Smith) Birkenhead worked among the pillows with a
cigar in his mouth, like Churchill (whose day begins
with this oppressive odour—a horrible thought). Mary
Somerville, the greatest bluestocking of her age—and a
very fine woman at that—was another ornament of the
bed, where she did much of her scientific writing. But I
weary of this catalogue: it would probably be easier,
where writers are concerned, to make a list of those who
(if they can avoid it) ever work anywhere else.

Paul Morand once wrote in *Le Figaro* that in bed he
felt like a rajah on his elephant, superior to the times
and their problems. I would have understood this better
if he had not at the same time confessed to the presence
of radio and telephone. For myself I will have neither of
these nuisances, nor, above all, will I allow the newspapers near me. There is no value in the elevation of
one's elephant if the political pygmies and other pests
are to be suffered proximity. Like the Clerk of Oxenford,
who would rather have

> *at his beddes heed*
> *Twenty bokes, clad in blak or reed,*
> *of Aristotle . . .*

I favour books, and old books, at that, though I can
manage without Aristotle for the moment. But the art

of lying in bed, as Lin Yutang has observed, has been neglected by the Western world. It is worth considering some of its possibilities and advantages.

Let us admit for the start that there is a time and place for everything. In December 1947 a case was heard at Knoxville, Tennessee, where the jury awarded to a worker in the textile mills the cost of boarding and lodging the defendant—a woman who had come to his home for dinner and remained in one of his beds from July to November on account of her arthritis. She was, it appears, uninvited; and her claim that she was a fourth cousin of the plaintiff does not appear to have impressed the Court. Such another uninvited guest was Charles XII of Sweden, who arrived in Turkey after his defeat at Poltava and took to his bed for sixteen months. This was some sort of stay-in strike, designed to induce the sultan to visit him.

We will, therefore, confine ourselves to those who lie in their own beds, without causing too much inconvenience. Only a few years ago an article appeared in the *Lancet* which caused much interest because it advocated lying in bed as an end in itself.[10] The doctor who wrote this admirable article pointed out that our ancestors slept with closed windows and that we need not fear to do the same. Comfort was the all-important thing—including the bedside carpet (preferably Shiraz), gratifying to bare feet, choice literature at hand, the essential table, lamp, ash tray and even (for those who desired one) a spittoon. Above all, the place should be one of relaxation and enjoyment—no mere utilitarian convenience for the sordid purpose of sleep. That should

[10] *Time* (May 6, 1946), for some reason, commented upon the matter as a *clinical report on an unclinical subject*. I do not know what was intended by this curious observation, for nothing more purely clinical could have been imagined.

be no more than an incident in the use of the bed.

According to *Time* (December 12, 1949), Joseph P. Fanning, a bedding manufacturer of Chicago, attributed a boom in the sale of beds to the fact that in 1949 people were *going to bed to escape domestic and international complications*. This I find very understandable and it has my wholehearted sympathy. If only the politicians would all go to bed and stay there long enough there would be no crises and the rest of us could eventually emerge with a little optimism. Bed as refuge from crisis is probably the best place. There was an old lady living in South Wales during the war who survived a number of air raids which were fatal to many of her neighbours. She was interviewed by a press correspondent as one of the survivors of a blitzed street and she gave him her own recipe for security. From this it appeared that each night, before going to bed, she read a chapter of the Bible; a second chapter was read in her bedroom and a third in her bed before she blew out the candle. *And then,* she concluded, *I pull the clothes over my head*. This clearly completed the ceremony and enabled her with confidence to mutter unrepeatable words about Hitler beneath the blankets. In this particular use of the bed it is the ideal substitute for returning to the womb, a very natural inclination for any sane person precipitated into a mad world. On a very similar principle E. V. Lucas claimed that he once slept off the terrors of an earthquake after the first upheaval.

The idea of holidays in bed was already being discussed in the nineteenth century. The medical pros and cons need not be considered at the moment—I am concerned this morning merely with pleasurable ways of passing time. Leaving out of account for the moment those extremists who have spent many years in their beds, merely from a strong disinclination to get up, I have always been impressed by the good sense of hibernating animals. Consider for once as your model, in place of that totalitarian drudge, the miserable Stakhanovist ant, our individualist friend the bear. Having built for himself a cunning hibernacle, he fills his body with almost anything he can find and—if the hunters can be believed—plugs himself *a tergo* with a *tappin* or *dottle* of pine needles, so that his winter feed shall not escape during his long sleep. Who would not be a bear on those dark, cruel winter mornings when we crawl from warmth and blessed peace to face all the horrors of human destiny? This, at least, was the opinion of President John Adams.

I can even feel sympathy with that Spanish physician—said to have lived in Galicia during the latter half of the nineteenth century—who became so weary of visiting the bedsides of his patients that (out of envy or malice) he retired between the sheets himself and there remained. In 1891 *El Imparcial* reported that he had kept snug for sixteen years and that his patients, no longer able to summon him to their beds, had perforce to reverse the normal procedure. His practice and his reputation had, in fact, profited equally from his behaviour, which conserved his energy and absolved him from any necessity of affecting a bedside manner by placing the onus on the other party.

The case of Mrs. Hallock, of Elmira (New York), was, in my view, less laudable. Her retirement to bed was in response to a spirit message directing her to remain there for ten years, which she did. The interference of the spirits in a matter so essentially personal appears to me unwarrantable. Indeed, it nearly caused Mrs. Hallock grave inconvenience, as she had to manage a large farm; and farm management is not generally conducted from a *lit de parade*. Nevertheless, Mrs. Hallock, being determined on no account to disregard her psychic instructions, remained resolutely beneath her eiderdown and successfully conducted all her business until the term expired. She had been up and about for no more than a month when a second message directed her to return to bed at once for the rest of her life; which order she unhesitatingly obeyed.

Other reasons have been offered for prolonged voluntary incarceration which may appear more reasonable. I read once of a man so violent that, after doing some damage to his sweetheart and twice attempting suicide in his remorse, he retired to bed as the place where he was least likely to be a menace and a nuisance—a fine example of public spirit. Then there is the case of Raoul Duval, the Frenchman, who caused quite a sensation when it was discovered in 1946 that he had been in bed for eighteen years at Abbeville because (as reported by the *Daily Express*) he did not wish to *see the world nor talk nor think about it*. The old Athenian in his cave spoke not more bitterly of mankind than this Timon of Abbeville. Asked of what he had been thinking all those years, he replied that sometimes he thought how much he hated men and women; but remembering they were not worth thinking about, he would stop thinking. He would never read a newspaper nor allow his parents to tell him of the outside world. By mere chance he had learned that the war was over. Raoul was at that time thirty-eight years old, and has spent his time abed ever since he graduated.[11]

I do not know whether any of the citizens of Colombia have become bedridden as a result of the laws, but

[11]I understand that Abbeville was heavily dive-bombed in 1940—a test of Raoul's conscientiousness, if the story in the *Daily Express* is true.

I have read that it is prohibited by Colombian law to arrest any person while in bed in his own home. According to information received, a Colombian citizen, wanted by the police in 1947, had long eluded the police by wearing his pyjamas night and day and leaping into bed whenever an attempt was made to put the arm on him. The police, so it was said, had all the humiliation of seeing this man walking in his garden or sitting in his porch, but were never agile enough to beat him to the bedside. The principle involved seems to resemble that which was implied in those cities of refuge, known to the Jews and to the Red Indians—or it might be compared even more closely with the sanctuary of the altar which mediaeval tradition normally respected. But in a really serious case of felony I should have thought the race from the porch involved too great a risk: one could always trip up somewhere. The really prudent criminals of Colombia must surely remain permanently in *lits de parade,* surrounded by their admiring friends; and doubtless it was to keep them there without expense to the Prison Commissioners that this cunning law was devised.

In contrast to such peaceful scenes, we read continually of people who never go to bed at all,[12] but sleep in chairs, or standing up or (for all I know—I expect daily to hear tell of such a thing) balanced on a perch, like a hen. Or again there are those who go to bed but claim they have not slept for years. How *sympathique* do our clinophiles appear when compared with such monsters, how natural by contrast. . . . Even those who have put their beds to the baser use of perennial sleep seem to be nearer to humanity than these sleepless devils; for perpetual insomnia is Satan's punishment, and no privi-

[12]Willard, one of the proprietors of the City Hotel, Broadway, in the early nineteenth century, had this reputation.

lege. There is nothing horrible in the thought of Washington Irving's hero, nor in the memory of those white-bearded kings (there are many of them) who

In dim glades sleeping, murmur in their sleep. . . .

Barbarossa (or was it his son?), Good King Wenceslas (so fond of the bottle), Genghis Khan, Arthur at Avalon, Charlemagne, Ogier and all the Peers of France are of that pleasant and friendly company. Dr. Marek Wàjsblum has just informed me that I may add the names of Boleslaw the Bold (of Poland) and Tamerlane—the latter according to stories which my informant heard himself from the Uzbeks.

Instances of protracted sleep are common enough. Stowe relates that on April 27, 1546, William Foxley, potmaker for the Mint in the Tower of London, fell asleep and so remained for fifteen nights, in spite of efforts to attract his attention by pinching, burning and other drastic methods. Not even the king could awaken him by a personal visit. It appears to have been an isolated attack, from which William eventually awoke in perfect health and lived another forty years. Chambers, who recalled this account in his *Book of Days* (April 27), remarked that such cases were not uncommon, but that of those on record an overproportion referred to females.

Though it is an error—symptomatic of the gross materialism of our age—to regard a bed merely as a place in which to sleep, it is also a mistake to regard sleep as dull, devoid of entertainment or even unprofitable. The art of inducing delectable dreams at will is already known to some and may one day become common knowledge, whilst the new game of dianetics suggests infinite possibilities of exploiting the unconscious mind. In March 1950 shoppers in Connecticut Avenue,

Washington, were mildly surprised to see a beautiful young woman in a strapless nightgown going to bed in broad daylight. She was none other than Washington's Beauty Queen, Mary Jane Hayes; and her purpose was to demonstrate a method of learning languages in one's sleep—a scheme sponsored by the Educational Services Organization. I must confess that I shudder at the thought—a loudspeaker was under her pillow. . . . They say that every child falls out of bed at some time—or rather, that if he does not do so he will grow up a fool— but that we learn the art of staying put through the development of an unconscious mechanical control. It is impressive to think of all that goes on in our minds without our knowing anything about it.

As for occupations while awake, they appear to be almost infinite in their variety. There was, for example, Sir John Suckling, whose conduct in 1639, during the English campaign against the Scottish covenanters, was the subject of a famous ballad.[13] His efforts at the card table were more successful than his soldiering, a fact which was attributed to his habit of practising in bed. Swift, according to one spiteful story, spent supine morning hours snugly thinking up wit for the day's work; but sometimes—by his own account—he used the time in writing letters to his girl friends. Pepys, who sometimes lay long, used to drink in bed on occasion and liked his wife to read to him. In this he may have resembled, at least in certain respects, Queen Elizabeth's chosen champion, Sir Henry Lee. According to John Aubrey,

[13]See *Sir John Suckling's Campaign* in Percy's *Reliques,* Series II, Book III. This is really a footnote to my *Cleanliness and Godliness,* where I omitted to mention that Sir John was the only Captain Courageous of song and story who was ever recorded to have withdrawn from a battle on account of the necessities of nature. How, in those prolonged conflicts, did other warriors make do?

he was never maried, but kept women to reade to him when he was abed. (Unfortunately there is some doubt about this story, as the first statement was definitely false—Sir Henry married and even produced a legitimate daughter.)

But for the most part it will be observed that solitude is a prerequisite of bedcentricity. Fantin-Latour sitting up in bed in top hat, overcoat, scarf and gloves, drawing by candlelight, is essentially a solitary picture; though fortunately Whistler called and recorded it. And those who are given to sudden inspirations must needs sleep alone if they wish to commit their thoughts to paper. (How much easier this is in the days of fountain pens and bedside lights. William Oughtred, who was half mathematician and half charlatan, had a tinder box always by him *and on the top of his Bed-Staffe, he had his Inke horne fix't.* John Aubrey, who is responsible for the story, claimed Oughtred as one of his lie-abeds, who studied late and rose at eleven or twelve o'clock. If Aubrey is also right in his assertion that Mrs. Oughtred *was a penurious woman, and would not allow him to burne candle after supper,* William must have practised his vices in secret, which argues that he slept alone.)

I will pass over Frank Scully's handbook on hospital recreations, *Fun in Bed,* in which I found little leaven. Of the great James Brindley (an almost illiterate prodigy of mechanical intuition who designed the Grand Trunk Canal and revolutionised engineering in the eighteenth century) the *Dictionary of National Biography* informs us that *when he had a puzzling bit of work he would go to bed and think about it.* Such is the way of genius— its best work is done in bed, and even sometimes asleep, like Coleridge before the Person from Porlock tore his dreams to shreds. (The fact that Coleridge was not actually abed is immaterial to my argument. Indeed, if he had been, *Kubla Khan* would have been completed.)

Thomas Hobbes, who was something of an eccentric, was alleged to have used the sheets and even his own thighs as tablets on which to draw and work out calculations. He also sang at such times, having first made fast his bedroom door—for, as John Aubrey observes, it was not that he had a very good voice but for his health's sake. (*He did beleeve,* wrote Aubrey, *it did his lungs good, and conduced much to prolong his life.*)

In sharp contrast to such delightful vignettes I cannot forbear from mentioning those ascetics who so mistrusted their beds that they not only spent the very minimum of time in them but would rise in the middle of the night to immerse themselves in cold water. Of these Dom Louis Gougaud (*Devotional and Ascetic Practices in the Middle Ages*) mentions several examples, especially among the Celts. St. Patrick thought nothing of spending a winter night shivering in a pond; but I am happy to relate that Heaven often had more pity on the saints than they had for themselves. In the case of St. Brigid the pond in which she proposed to mortify Sister Ass was miraculously dried up; and in four other recorded instances (all Irish) the hot tap was turned on supernaturally. One of the beneficiaries was St. Kevin of Glendalough, who spent one hour of each night praying in the lake.

In two of these hot-water stories, by malice or mischance, the temperature rose to boiling point, the victims being conceited monks who, thinking themselves the equals of Saints Comgall and Fechin, had attempted to imitate their austerities. St. Fursa—that same prodigy whom we have already met reprehending the heathen prenatally *du fond des entrailles de sa mère*—is discovered in later life unable to recite his psalms with accuracy unless standing in a well with the coldness of snow. While he had breath he would yet praise the Lord. St. Colomba and St. Kentigern, Bishop of Glasgow, both achieved the marathon feat of working their way right through the psalter at each nocturnal immersion. The same is claimed with regard to Cuannatheus—a saint whom I cannot identify unless this is another variant of Cuanna, otherwise known as Cathaldus or Cataldus, alias Cartualt, of whom very little is known at all, anyway.

In fact the cold-water recipe, as Dom Louis has made very clear, was widely in use not only against the temptations of sloth and comfort but against every other weakness of the flesh. Even to read of this in your warm bed is surely to feel the creeping cold that is the end of all courage and all concupiscence. It was definitely with this latter end in view that a certain Irishman called Scothine took to the water—another of those Gaelic ascetics whose problems are described in a poem of the ninth century to which I shall refer later. St. David used the same remedy, also St. Bernard and many another, to trounce the rebellious flesh. But you must go to Gougaud for the rest. I only mentioned the matter because this overwhelming desire for cold baths seems most commonly to have taken people in the middle of the night. Mediaeval ascetics appear to have been fairly evenly divided on the question of baths: those who did not practice total immersion in cold water *pour passer le temps* during those long, loveless nights went to the other extreme and made it a point of honour never to bath or wash in any way whatsoever. For them the nights must have been even more insufferable.

With less drastic intentions Benjamin Franklin (alas, an early riser) used to parade in the nude in an unheated room, for ten minutes each morning before he dressed. He believed that the exposure of one's body to the cold air was beneficial to health; and for a similar reason (to prevent overheating at night) Franklin had four beds in his room so that he could use them in rotation, moving on as each bed became warm. One can only assume that he was kept busy and slept very little. Disraeli seems to have had some such notions in his head, for it is on record that when he arrived at Berlin (in the course of those highly dishonourable negotiations from which he was to return bringing *Peace with Honour*) he was provided with two beds in his room at the Kaiserhof. Keyhole espionage—for the second bed had aroused curiosity—established the fact that the British prime minister rotated on the Franklin principle.

I do not propose to discuss those alarming statistics, beloved by American sociologists, which profess to tell us what percentage of (a) men and (b) women talk in bed, listen to the radio, pray, smoke, eat or do all these things at once or in their various permutations and combinations. One such survey, purporting to give the nocturnal habits of 131 Manhattan families, is included by the Grays in their collection, and I found it singularly depressing. Indeed, the only joy I had of it was to discover it reproduced in a German paper under the title, *Schlafzimmerstatistik*. Phrases such as *eine Forschungsgruppe für Behausungsfragen* have a scholarly sound and completely transfigure dull ciphering, investing it with the academic pomp of dons who

> *bawl*
> *The absolute across the hall.*

The only statistics which I feel inclined to quote are some which were published in the *Science Digest* for April 1949. They originate, astonishingly enough, from the United States Department of Agriculture, which appears to have been worried about the time spent by women in *making* beds. The average housewife in America—so I learn from this source—walks four miles and spends twenty-five hours each year merely in making and remaking one bed. Unless I am mistaken the remedy will soon be discovered in such a progressive country—it will be found cheaper and quicker for the lady to buy a new bed every morning. This will easily be realised when one considers the estimate of the Department of Agriculture that in a family of four the wretched mother spends the better part of a week every year in this dreary occupation and wears out a pair of shoes per annum in the course of this single duty. Meanwhile the Department has offered advice on better methods, no doubt devised by men. But since we appear to have finished with the pleasure of lying awake it is time to switch out the light.

Chapter 5

OF BEDS AND BEDDING

For the bed is shorter than that a man can stretch himself on it: and the covering narrower than that he can wrap himself in it.
Isaiah XXVIII:20

I have made my bed in the darkness.
Job XVII:13

JOB WAS UNFORTUNATE in the matter of beds, as in most other things. Even when he said, *My bed shall comfort me, my couch shall ease my complaint,* he was scared with dreams and terrified through visions. For some reason he likened himself to a whale on this account.

Biblical beds are frequently mentioned in a sinister manner. Here is the place where (according to the psalmist) the wicked man devises mischief.[1] Solomon, whose observations were always those of a man of the world, asked reasonably enough, apropos of nothing in particular, *If thou hast nothing to pay, why should he take away thy bed from under thee?*[2] It can hardly be imagined that such a catastrophe ever occurred to the king himself, what time he lay and comforted himself with apples.

[1] Psalms XXXVI:4. Compare Micah II:1, where the bed is used for the same purpose.
[2] Proverbs XXII:27.

But he must have needed quite a number of beds and felt strongly on the matter, although he lived rent-free in Jerusalem. The words were probably spoken on the occasion of one of those celebrated judgments, and we know how these passages often stray into other contexts.

We can imagine the scene. In the crowded court at the King's Bench the sensational case of Og v. Mammon is being heard before Mr. Justice Solomon. The plaintiff (Og, giant, of no fixed abode) is bringing a suit of *habeas lectum* (you've got my bed) against Mammon, described as a company promoter, of Jerusalem. The plaintiff's case is that he is a retired monarch, formerly King of Bashan, where he ran into debt. He had a number of prize bulls, which he was obliged to sell, also some fine Bashan cows.

MR. JUSTICE SOLOMON: Like the women of Samaria? (*Laughter.*)

OG: Exactly, My Lord.

MR. JUSTICE SOLOMON: What became of them? I mean the cattle.

OG: They went into involuntary liquidation, My Lord.

The plaintiff's counsel at this point intervenes to explain that, according to Ezekiel XXXIV:18 and 19, the children of Israel drank the blood of his client's cattle and found it intoxicating.

MR. JUSTICE SOLOMON: Were the premises licensed? (*Laughter.*)

OG: No, My Lord, but the cattle were removed by my creditors. I was left with nothing but my bed.

MR. JUSTICE SOLOMON: What, that old iron one with brass knobs?

OG: The same, My Lord. May I refer Your Lordship to the Sale Catalogue in Deuteronomy III:11?

A full description of the bed is then read in court. It is described as a bedstead of iron, nine cubits long and four in breadth.

MR. JUSTICE SOLOMON: Quite a large bed. (*Laughter.*) Where is it now?
OG: In Rabbath of the children of Ammon, My Lord. The defendant pinched it.
COUNSEL FOR THE PLAINTIFF: I submit, Me Lud, that my client, being the last of the giants, as admitted in the Sale Catalogue, is the only person entitled *de jure* to occupy this bed *de facto,* and that he was deprived of its *usus fructus* by *malice prepense.* Your Lordship will observe that in consequence of this deprivation *sine die* my client has been obliged to suffer *peine forte et dure* in beds of inadequate proportions.

It was doubtless at this point that Mr. Justice Solomon, overruling a plea of *tu quoque* on behalf of the defendant, gave that heavy hint to the jury which established for all time the right of *non sequitur,* whereby a man's bed does not follow when creditors collect the rest of his chattels. By various statutes the debtor was also allowed to retain a chair (*Ex Cathedra,* Exodus XXVI:34[3]) and a table (*Mensa mensa mensam,* Psalm XXIII:5[4]) for which he was to be allowed reasonable

[3]This was known as the Mercy Seat. Even the unfortunate Job appears to have been allowed a chair, though he had no *locus standi* except the street (Job XXIX:7). Chairs were a frequent cause of dispute. The Scribes and Pharisees all sat in that of Moses (Matthew XXIII:2) and the psalmist begins with a warning about occupying the seat of The Scornful. Hence Amos (VI:3) refers to a seat of violence—evidently an object of disputed ownership.
[4]This was the table prepared in the sight of one's enemies, i.e., the creditors. The psalmist (LXIX:29) expresses the hope that this table will become a snare to its owners *and*

locus standi. Some doubt has been thrown on this account by the suggestion Og had been dead a long time before Solomon delivered his famous judgment; but, legal procedure being what it is, the case might easily have been dragging on since the time of Moses. Moreover, I have a great personal affection for Og and propose to return to his story later.

It was a lapse on Solomon's part that he should ever have given that deplorable testimonial to the ant, for Solly was obviously a very bedworthy person who knew the joys of sloth and described them from pleasurable experience. Who but an experienced bedman would ever have described the slothful turning upon his bed like a door on its hinges? It is a highly imaginative picture. There he lies, his hand on his bosom, too lazy to pick up a cup of tea (Proverbs XXVI:15) and dreaming of lions in the street. In the Song of Songs he becomes even more lyrical, but you all know about that. Did you ever notice, though, that he even mentions the colour of that bed, which was apparently green?

Some person of whom Isaiah disapproved apparently took his bed onto the top of a high mountain and for some reason enlarged it (Isaiah LVII:7 and 8). In spite of Solomon's ruling we find some people described by Amos (III:12) all living in Samaria in the corner of a bed; but (whatever caused this shortage of beds and houses) a writ of *non sequitur* would have had no force

---

that which should have been for their welfare, let it become a trap. This sentiment is echoed by Paul (Romans XI:9), who referred to the table also as a stumbling block, but I find this interpretation too literal. The real danger of having a table is indicated by Nehemiah (V:17 and 18), whose table must have been very large, as he was obliged to entertain 150 Jews and rulers, plus others, who daily consumed an ox and an unspecified quantity of poultry.

outside Judea. And even in the time of Luke (XI:7 and XVII:34) we find evidence of overcrowding in the beds of Palestine. The last legal reference is that obscure one in Revelations II:22, where Jezebel is condemned to be cast into a bed, which seems to me rather like throwing Brer Rabbit into the briar bush.

Cursing the rich in one's bedroom appears to have been a popular pastime, as Solomon advises against it on prudential grounds in Ecclesiastes (X:20). It may usefully be noted as another way of passing the time. For luxurious tastes there were beds of ivory, described by Amos, who did not approve of them; and it would not have been upon such beds as these that the saints were exhorted to sing—more melodiously, one hopes, than Master Hobbes—by the writer of Psalms CXLIX:5.

The Talmud provides further valuable information regarding the beds of Israel. There was, for example, the *dargesh,* a very low bed with leather strapping reserved for the Domestic Genius. It was not put to any other use, but brought good luck to the house. Nashim V (Nedarim) gives some facts about this bed, but does not say whether it was remade each day and the mattress shaken. Beds were lowered in time of mourning. According to Nashim VIII (Kiddushim), the Rabbi Judah is credited with the curious observation that an unmarried man must not tend cattle nor may two unmarried men sleep together under the same cover. *But the sages permit it.* That seems a dead end, but the use of the *dargesh* suggests comparison with the old ballad, *The Wife of Usher's Well,* where three ghosts occupy a bed made for them by their mother.

The beds in which Homer's heroes slept were always described as well gimleted or as turned on the lathe. For the rest I can find no bed literature relating to the ancient world which is worthy of comparison with the rich store of Jewish bed-lore; and the rest is better skipped except for a very brief reference to Fosbroke's *Encyclopaedia of Antiquities*. Fosbroke is good enough to supply some names applied to types of beds used in classical and mediaeval times. Of the *sperulati lecti*, mentioned in the *Acta Sanctorum*, he says that Du Cange supposed them to be beds on castors, for the sick. *Grabatum*, a sordid word, was used to describe the low, portable bed used *by the Roman slaves and our rusticks*. The *Architectile* was a wooden bedstead provided only with straw. The *scympodium* was something between a bed and a chair. But of special interest, surely, is the *Gyrgatus*, which was *a bed used for lunatics when bound*. The *truckle-bed* in the room of a person of note would be occupied, according to the place and the period, by a musician, by a person to read aloud (or maybe to tell stories in the manner of the Arabian Nights' Entertainment), by the Good Man's wife, by a servant or by the Chamberlain. Fosbroke gives references for each of these various uses.

Little, however, will be found in these pages regarding the design of beds in various ages. There are any number of reliable works on the history of furniture; and the changing styles, so far as they affect our subject, have been admirably explained and discussed by C. and M. Gray, to whose work the dissatisfied reader is recommended if he wishes to know—for example—the precise difference between beds Baroque and Rococo. There also he will find an excellent anthology on this subject, showing that authors in all ages have been bed-conscious; but that again is not my present concern. All this I leave in the capable hands of the Grays; and if I sometimes note one of their omissions, believe me it is because they are such a clever pair that one can be reasonably proud of occasionally stealing a march on them. My own search, however, crosses only occasionally the course of *The Clinophile's Vade Mecum*. The customs associated with the bed, the ideas and associations connected with it and above all the symbolism of the bed are my present preoccupations.

Its importance can hardly be denied. To quote Groucho Marx, another contemporary who has given some thought to the matter, we spend a third of our time in bed *or, if you are an actor, two thirds; or if you live in Peoria, three thirds.*[5] But even the Groucho Marxist interpretation of the subject hardly attempts— well, there is no need to say it. His theme has struck literary minds periodically with the thud of a blunt instrument. Even Sir Thomas Browne succumbed to it: *Half our days we pass in the shadow of the earth and the brother of death exacteth a third part of our lives.* Maupassant made the same discovery, and so did Xavier de Maistre in his celebrated *Voyage*—the passage was appropriately recalled by the occupant of Wilkie Collins' *Terribly Strange Bed.*

> *And from the perspicuity of Burns*
> *The patient reader learns*
> *That homo sapiens is homo sapiens.*[6]

You will perceive my meaning: the point requires no labouring.

[5]Groucho Marx, *Beds* (New York, 1930). This statement is further elucidated by the author in the following footnote: *If you live in Peoria, make it Gaylesburg. If you live in Gaylesburg you have no one to blame but yourself.*

[6]In justice to Burns, however, it should be pointed out that his banal statement showed him to be an accurate, though somewhat cautious, anthropologist. In this respect he is to be preferred to Percy Bysshe, whose reckless ornithological observations have caused so much confusion in the schoolroom.

The reproachful morning sun now streams through my window, reminding me that poverty comes as one that travelleth and want as an armed man. Poverty and squalor are only picturesque in novels and newspapers; and I must clothe my carcass to go in search of something about St. Macarius. While I am shaving here is a poor thing but mine own—*Eheu, Fugaces!*—which shows just what I mean: a revel for any Zola or his readers, but no place in which to live. And this room is beginning to resemble it all too closely.

> *How often I've read*
> *   sad tales in the* News
> *of the World about bed*
> *   sitting-rooms in a Mews*
>
> *in Mayfair and Blooms-*
> *   bury, flowery places*
> *where brides and their grooms*
> *   enjoyed tragic embraces.*
>
> *Gas ovens galore*
> *   and curates degraded—*
> *the crimes only bore*
> *   and the hemlock is faded.*
>
> *The torsos in trunks*
> *   look shabby and shoddy;*
> *Korea debunks*
> *   the romance of a Body,*
>
> *the beds of the 'Thirt-*
> *   ies, the thighs and the thews;*
> *and iron are the curt-*
> *   ains that hang in the Mews.*

O when will a crim-
inal ever again
or love, for a whim,
give pleasure in pain?

The furniture of the bed has varied considerably and I propose no general account of it, but I have not looked up Macarius for nothing. According to the Golden Legend, St. Macarius of Alexandria dug up a dead pagan and used him as a pillow. It is not clear whether this was done out of contempt for paganism or as a form of self-mortification, but the latter explanation appears highly probable as Macarius was something of a specialist in mortifying the flesh. This is made very clear from a notable incident in his career when the saint killed a gnat which was biting him after the manner of its kind. Macarius soon realised that by his rash and precipitate action in destroying the gnat he had deprived himself of an opportunity for unhappiness. There is a strong flavour of existentialism in the saint's remorse and in the remedy he sought; for he went straight off to some pestiferous marshes which bred an outsize in *Anopheles maculi-pennis* (or some such creature) and there remained for six months until his flesh was mortified out of all recognition.[7]

As to this peculiar pillow then, I will assume that St. Macarius used it solely for its unpleasantness, in which he found his only pleasure. (Did not his very name

[7]This story will be found in the *Acta Sanctorum* for January 2. In the *Acta Sanctorum* there is an even stranger story, to which I have elsewhere referred, showing that devils take the form of flies. It will probably be said that I have confused St. Macarius of Alexandria with another gentleman of the same name who lived at the same place and at the same time. They were, moreover, both born in January, and the Orthodox Church has amalgamated them. In spite of Palladius, I think the Greeks acted very sensibly.

signify happiness?) Devils came by night and invited the
pagan to accompany them, but the corpse told them to
get to Hell out of that place. He said he could not move,
on account of a pilgrim who lay atop of him. Unaccount-
ably Macarius at this point intervened in the dispute by
beating, not the devils, but the corpse, whereby in some
obscure way he caused the devils to throw up the sponge
and Macarius was declared winner of that contest. It
was, however, only one of many, for one way and another this good man had a great deal of devil-trouble:
they seem to have had some special grudge against him.

A worme is Man, whom flies their sport can make!
Poor worme, true Rest in no Bed can he take,
But one of earth. . . .

Macarius would certainly have endorsed the verdict of
Joseph Beaumont; but there were others who thought
very differently. The inhabitants of Sybaris—the first, as
I believe (and perhaps the last), to sleep literally upon a
bed of roses—would not suffer a cock within their walls
lest it should disturb their matutinal slumbers. (Thus
Digby in his *Mores Catholici.*)

I always thought we owed our covering to a gentleman
called Thomas Blanket who invented blankets in 1340;
but my dictionary disappoints me:

blanket, n. Large woollen sheet used for bed covering, for horse cloth, & by savages for
clothes[8]; *wet b.* person who extinguishes
conversation; *born on wrong side of b.*
illegitimate. [f. OF *blanquette* (*blanc*
BLANK+ette)]

Bang goes St. Thomas Blanket, an exploded myth.
The history of the pillow might prove more interesting.

[8] I take this as a personal affront.

Apart from Macarius, there was Jacob, who made his pillow of stones, and passed a disturbed night. St. Ciaran of Saiger, whose laurels Patrick stole (for Ciaran was clearly senior to him in the Irish business), is also said to have laid his head upon a bolster of stone. If, as some would have us believe, the stone that the English long since stole from Scotland (with recent and dramatic consequences) was that upon which Jacob once laid his head, it may as likely be true that this same stone, having passed some time in Ireland, was once used to support the head of St. Ciaran. The chief difficulty about that story is that the plural is used in Genesis—not one stone but perhaps many. The Romans, too, laid their heads on hollowed slabs of stone until their Eastern subjects civilised them a little.

The correct use of the pillow is another matter of historical doubt. Even in modern times I have read a news item (*Coronet,* September 1947) informing me that *The cartoonist, Rube Goldberg, sleeps with a pillow under his feet instead of under his head.* This might be just another of those publicity devices for which we all fall at some time or other; but it happens that peasants in some parts of Europe do really—so they say—lie that way with the very reasonable explanation that their feet work harder than their heads. It would be of interest to know where those who do not overwork at either end place their pillows.

The use of the bolster in Anglo-Saxon times is obscure. As Fosbroke remarks, it is often shown pictorially in a longitudinal position, for which I cannot accept his explanation of bad drawing. It can hardly have been used, like the *Dutch Wife* in Indonesia, as a means of keeping cool. Perhaps it kept the back warm—I have sometimes found some such arrangement useful myself. It is of interest that the Saxons used sheets—a refinement hardly to have been expected among a people who commonly covered themselves in bed with *sisurna,* i.e., skins with the fur on them. Speaking apparently of the Middle Ages generally, but supplying at the same time a valuable comment on his own period, Fosbroke remarks that *Under the pillow were put their valuables, as now breeches.*[9]

The question of night attire has been learnedly discussed by Dr. Cabanès, who showed in the first volume of his *Indiscrétions de l'Histoire* that it was unsafe to generalise, as many writers have done, on the habit of sleeping naked in the Middle Ages. There were many exceptions to this common practice. That some people even wore their boots in bed is clearly indicated by the order of Bishop Hugo Gratianopolitanus that a monk should not do so—*ut de caligis pedules abscinderet.* Equally clear was his order that monks should wear their clothes and socks at night (*nam dolebat nonnullos in religioso habitu ad sanctitatis injuriam tibiis dormire nudatis*[10]). This monastic habit seems to have become common and died hard; for as late as 1830 Dr. Robert Macnish is found warning the public against sleeping in stockings as a bad and unclean habit.

By comparison the common mediaeval habit of sleeping naked was certainly more hygienic. Cabanès cites evidence from Destigny's *Histoire de Cathérine de Médicis* that the nobility of that epoch used black woollen or satin in place of white linen *afin de faire mieux ressortir la blancheur de la peau.* Clearly, however, we cannot judge general behaviour by the customs of the court. Other evidence sometimes cited loses relevance

[9]Fosbroke, *Encyclopaedia of Antiquities* (1825), Vol. I, p. 229.

[10]See Du Cange, *Glossarium,* under *Pedules* and *Pedana,* where two authorities are cited on the Bishop's bed-laws.

on account of special circumstances. There is, for example, a thirteenth-century illustration at Dijon, mentioned by Cabanès, showing Mrs. Potiphar in bed wearing nothing but her long locks. But the occasion is a special one: *Elle s'est relevée sur le séant, laissant tomber les couvertures sur les cuisses, et saisit par sa tunique ou par sa chemise le pauvre Joseph qui se sauve.* There is no reason to suppose that Mrs. Potiphar would have been assumed to sleep in this manner when Joseph was not around the place.

Another mediaeval exception is mentioned by Cabanès. *Les statuts du grand hôpital de Paris . . . composés en 1220, défendaient expressément aux soeurs et aux frères qui le desservaient de coucher nus, leur enjoignant de ne pas quitter la chemise pendant la nuit.* By the time when Tallemant des Réaux was writing his *Historiettes* it was necessary to explain that a man was in the habit of sleeping without a shirt—this was in his story of the Chevalier de Miraumont, who was visited one morning, while he was still in bed, by a woman to whom he owed money. In order to discourage this tactless creditor from repeating the attempt to dun him in his house, the Chevalier, a perfect gentleman, insisted on accompanying her to the street door—*tout nu, car il couchoit toujours sans chemise.*

The case of Charles de l'Orme, mentioned in our first chapter, is no doubt exceptional. His six pairs of stockings may be regarded as evidence of individual eccentricity. But stockings do appear to have been worn in bed in sixteenth-century England. William Cecil, Lord Burghley, evidently slept in them normally, for in 1585 he wrote of being forced to keep his bed without any hose.[11]

[11]Letter to the Earl of Leicester, January 12, 1585–86. He said he had sore shins. (See Camden Society, 1st Series,

The sleeping habits of the early Tudors are indicated in the well-known account of Sir William Roper's brief courtship of his wife, a daughter of Sir Thomas More. More, who (as Aubrey reminds us in telling the story) had explained his views on the matter in his *Utopia*, received an early visit from his future son-in-law, who had called in that casual Tudor fashion to say that he would like to marry one of More's daughters.

He does not appear to have been particular as to which it should be, but his host was anxious for him to make a fair choice. The two girls were still asleep; and the first point worth noting is that they slept two in one truckle bed, in their father's chamber. When Sir Thomas *takes the sheet by the corner and suddenly whippes it off*, the girls are discovered in their smocks. They did not sleep naked, but the difference in this case was purely nominal, for the girls' smocks were up to their arms, and they swiftly turned over on spying a stranger. Roper, with the same nonchalance that had characterised the whole episode, remarked that he had seen both sides and staked his claim with a pat on the behind for the lass of his choice. *Here*, wrote John Aubrey, *was all the trouble of the wooeing*.

Andrew Boorde, in his *Dietary of Helth*, had some useful observations on sleeping habits. He advocated a fire in the bedroom (and let it here and now be placed upon record that no central heating has ever replaced this luxury or ever will. What can compare with the *pas seul* of an open fire, projecting its own fantasies on a low ceiling?). Like all his contemporaries, Andrew believed the night air to be dangerous. Windows were there-

---

No. XXVII, p. 56.) Leicester himself had a nightshirt of damask—ordered on his behalf by the queen, when buying velvet for her own nightdress.

fore to be closed—a practice less to be censured in the days when vast chimneys functioned as ventilators, assisted by the friendly fire. (By contrast Dr. Macnish, writing in the grim nineteenth century, described fires as exceedingly hurtful and even condemned the common custom of warming the bed—this, he said, except with delicate people, and during the very cold seasons, was pernicious.) A bedroom scene at an Elizabethan inn is worth considering at this point: it provides us with a fairly complete picture of sixteenth-century bed-life.

The author of the *Orthoepia Gallica* (1593), that unfailing guide to Elizabethan behaviour on all common occasions, does not omit the art of going to bed in an hostelry. The anonymous hero of John Eliot's dialogues finds himself a little ill after supper. *My stomacke greeveth me,* says he, *Mine Oast I will go to rest.* Mine Oast replies that his daughter will show the guest to his room, when the following instructive conversation takes place between the sick man and the young woman:

> *She:* You must mount this way, Sir. See your chamber. See your bed. There are the privies and here is your chamber pot.
> *He:* Draw these curtines. Lend me a kercheffe or a coiffe. I have a night cap in my bosome.
> *She* (*defensively, I suggest*): Your sheets are cleane.
> *He:* Look that they be verie drie, I pray you.
> *She:* I have ayred them at the fire.
> *He* (*doubtless in that querulous tone peculiar to invalids*): Pull off my hosen. Cover me with my gowne. I have too little covering. Give me another pillow, I cannot lie so low.
> *She:* Are you well now? Will you have yet more heling? Would you nothing else?

He: Not now.
She: Sleepe well.

This should be the cue for the curtain. But evidently the young man's *stomacke* has ceased to grieve him, and he changes his tone somewhat abruptly. Bearing in mind that these dialogues were written in French and English, to serve as phrase books, it may be conjectured that Eliot wished to provide for other situations likely to arise (as the old quatrain has it) *While English Inns have feather beds.* So we proceed.

He: Hark, Gaudinetta, kisse me once my sweet heart, before thou depart.
She: I had rather die, than kisse a man in his bed.
He: Kisse me, and I will give you your bracelets againe, that I took from you the other day playing with you.

This certainly comes as rather a shock, since we have but now seen the wench to all appearances showing the guest his room for the first time, and explaining (as the saying is) the geography of the house—even the geography of the bedchamber. Gaudinetta's reply, however, confirms that something has already been going on.

She: Speake no more to me, I pray you of kissing nor of love, but give me my bracelets againe, for otherwise what will my father and my mother say to me? They will be angrie with me.
He: They will not: they will not.
She: But they will, I assure you: but tis no matter, I will say that a theefe hath stolne them from me.
He: Harke, I pray thee, Gaudinetta, tell me one thing, which of us two loves one another better: whether you me or I you?

She (*piously*): As for me I do not hate you: for as God commandes I love all the world.

He: But to the purpose, are you not inamoured of me?

She: I have told you so many times that you should not use any such speeches to me, if you speake any more to me I shall shew you that it is not to me that you should address your selfe.

He: You are verie obstinate, I see well.

She: Give me my bracelets then if you will.

He: How now my love your bracelets? I will not, I swear a great oath: but I will give you others. Had you not rather have a silken girdle &c.

She: Harke some bodie cals me.

Gaudinetta is right enough. Alarmed by her daughter's long absence, the innkeeper's wife is heard belowstairs. *Gaudinetta,* calls the voice, *what do you above so long?* It is a reasonable question, but it receives a somewhat evasive reply.

She: I come by and by mother.

He (*returning to the main issue*): Will you not kisse me before you depart.

She: Another time, I am cald now. I shall be chidden. I cannot kisse men. My father will be angrie. My mother comes. What will you do? Let me go. I shall be kild by and by. God give you goodnight, Sir.

He: Goodnight faire mayden. Goodnight, Gaudinetta.

How easy it is to linger among such scenes—how much pleasanter than cataloguing the beds of our ancestors with all their historical and geographical variations. . . . Here the bed is a living thing, though still some-

thing of a novelty for the common man. In spite of the
great beds of antiquity, few in England had enjoyed such
comforts until the reign of Elizabeth. William Harrison,
noting the changes of his own age, marked among them
the amendment of lodging. Old men in his own village
recalled days when they

> yea and we ourselves also, have lain full oft upon
> straw pallets, or rough mats covered only with a
> sheet, under coverlets made of dogswain, and a
> good round log under their heads instead of a pil-
> low or bolster. If it were so that our fathers or the
> good man of the house, had within seven years
> after his marriage purchased a mattress or a flock
> bed and thereto a sack of chaff to rest his head
> upon, he thought himself to be as well lodged as
> the lord of the town. . . .

In this world pillows had been considered meet only
for women. Servants had been fortunate if they had any
sheet over them—another argument against the univer-
sality of sleeping naked, for they must needs have kept
clothed for warmth, even if they had no thoughts of
decency. Nor had such servants, in the days of which
Harrison spoke, anything beneath their bodies to protect
them from *the pricking straws that ran oft through the
canvas of the pallet and rased their hardened hides.*
There is good reason to doubt whether such conditions
had disappeared as completely as Harrison claimed,
during the reign of Queen Elizabeth, but certainly there
were new standards of comfort which were reaching a
growing number of the people. Even in Chaucer's time
it was assumed that a miller—none other than the butt
of the Reeve's Tale—could provide a decent bed for his
guests,

With schetys and with chalouns fair i-spred.

The *chalouns* (chalons) were the blankets. The fact that the miller (with disastrous consequences) was not also furnished with a guest room, and obliged to house his guest in the same room as himself, his wife and his daughter—an arrangement evidently not considered remarkable—shows that manners in those days were still somewhat primitive, though they may not have been quite so crude as Harrison imagined. But in Tudor times came such luxuries as the perfuming of sheets, at least in some royal and noble households. Thus we read that *The gromes shall gadyr for the Kinges gowns and shetes and othyr clothes the swete flowres, herbis, rotes, and thynges to make them breathe more holesomely and delectable.*

The nightcap—not in the modern meaning of the word—was taken for granted. The anxiety shown by generations of people to protect their heads when in bed is somewhat curious. But it is, after all, only within our own time that wearing a hat has become optional when walking abroad. Fashion long conspired with curious notions regarding health to compel the covering of the head at night and at any time in the street. Once more Andrew Boorde's ideas compare pleasantly with those of Dr. Macnish, nearly three hundred years later. Merry Andrew—he was surely the original one—insisted strongly on the importance of mirth as the prerequisite of sound sleep and good health. *To bedward be you merry,* he said, *or have merry company about you.* Anger, heaviness and sorrow should not disquiet a man at such a time, nor even *pensivefulness.* And again: *Go to bed, as I said, with mirth.* It was surely for this reason and no other that Andrew advocated nightcaps of scarlet —symbols of this bedward gaiety. Macnish, on the other hand, had no time for such counsels. He could think only of utilitarian things—hard beds and hard pillows, not because they are really more comfortable (as they are) but because soft ones *effeminate the individual, render his flesh soft and flabby, and incapacitate him from undergoing any privation*. As to nightcaps, here is no scarlet for mirth, only this pedagogical injunction:

> We should wear a thin cotton or silk night cap; and this is still better if made of network. Some persons wear worsted, or flannel caps, but these are exceedingly improper. In fact, the chief use of this piece of clothing is to preserve the hair, and prevent it from being disordered and matted together.

Even in Dan Chaucer's days the nightcap was in use, and it is strange that it should have lasted so long, for it is never mentioned as an article of elegance. The old rake in the *Merchant's Tale*—he interested me when writing *Beards* because of the *thikke bristles of his berd unsoft* when *he was shave all newe in his manere*—that same old rascal is represented in his most repulsive guise as he sits up in bed in nightcap and nightshirt. (Notice that nightshirt again as a comment on rash generalisations.) As to his young bride,

> *Whan she him saugh, up sittinge in his sherte,*
> *In his night-cappe, and with his nekke lene,*
> *She preyseth not his pleying worth a bene.*

It was probably a mistake to have worn the nightcap; also for the old gentleman to have insisted on singing, whereby *the slakke skin aboute his nekke* wobbled as he warbled. Whether the *nightcap wig* of the eighteenth century was less repulsive I do not know. We have unfortunately no description of it. But a man of any age in nightcap and nightshirt must at any period have been hard for a bride to take seriously, even if he did not sing.

In the Notebooks of Leonardo da Vinci there are some terrifying words: *There will be a great host who, forgetful of their existence and their name, will lie as though dead upon the spoils of other dead creatures, by sleeping upon the feathers of birds.*[12] Here indeed was the future of the bed for years to come. Such was that goose-feather bed chosen to epitomise all the luxuries which the lady in the song forsook in favour of the cold open fields and the love of a gypsy lad. The Sybarites and Acrasia's self lay not more softly upon rose petals, nor did Gargantua discover more epicurean employment for a goose; yet these were of all beds the most horrible and Leonardo spoke wisely. They were beds of mortality and devised for *smooring*—of which more anon.

Great ingenuity has been shown in the designing of beds; but lying on my simple divan, I find no envy in me for anyone. I think of the Persians with their charcoal braziers to warm them, inhaling carbon monoxide. (A friend informs me that he came across a similar arrangement in Costa Rica, and in the Gobi Desert they obtain the result by burning dung.) I think of mediaeval sleeping places, built into the thickness of the wall—a practice inherited from the ancient world, for such niches were found at Pompeii. Survivals could be found in Scotland within the last hundred years, for surely the Caledonian box-beds derived from this source.[13] I have also seen the expression *Murphy bed* for a type which folds up horizontally by the wall—Murray's *Dictionary*, which does not mention them, offers Murphy as a corruption of

[12]I quote from MacCurdy's edition of 1938 (Vol. II, p. 516).
[13]For the peculiar designs used in Gorbals, see *No Mean City* by A. MacArthur (and tell me if you find anything interesting: having once or twice been in Glasgow, I cannot even bring myself to read about this place. It is too easily remembered).

Morpheus, suggesting a possible origin (*the arms av Murphy*).

In the offices of the Hansa Merchants at Bergen (now the Hanseatic Museum) there are similar beds in cupboards, where the apprentices slept—apparently seated, as even a boy could not have stretched himself to his full length. (In the room occupied by the merchants themselves there was a shutter in the wall at the head of each bed so that it could be made by a Norwegian servant without her entering the room, which was forbidden.) I think of Esquimaux huddled in promiscuous igloos and of German beds with little square eiderdowns, designed to freeze one end of a man while the other end sweats, so long as they remain balanced upon the tossing body—Jerome's description of this *Bettproblem* in his *Diary of a Pilgrimage* is still the last word on this subject.

I think of the house somewhere in Newfoundland where my good friend the Rev. James Whittle, then a stranger to the country, found a peculiar bundle in his bed. It was a baby, kindly placed there by his hostess to serve as a hot-water bottle. I think of mediaeval illuminations in which people are seen sleeping at such an angle that they seem to lean rather than to lie. I think of curtained solemnity, of four-posters and of the Cast Iron Age, when the Industrial Revolution planted its grim standard over birth, marriage and death. I think of beds like coffins in the Salvation Army homes of the nineties,[14]

[14]There is a formidable illustration showing such beds in *Our Mothers*, edited by Alan Bott and Irene Clephane (London, 1932), p. 87. The Emperor Charles V rehearsed his own death (with full honours) but I do not think that he actually slept in his coffin. William Edson, of Wisconsin, was, on the other hand, one of those who slept there regularly. His case is much better established than that of Sarah Bernhardt, who is also said to have had a bed fifteen feet broad. Perhaps she enjoyed variety.

of Sarah Bernhardt and of the Paris hairdresser who even now, so I am told, prefers a coffin for his couch; also of Trappists who are alleged to have the same preference.

One of my relatives, so I am told, used to travel with a hearse in attendance during her latter days. But she did not go to such extremes as Mr. E. T. Sarman, a gentleman of whom I know nothing except that he drove in a hearse from Bainbridge, Indiana, to West Palm Beach, Florida, in the year 1946, having furnished the hearse with a bed so that he could use it as a sort of caravan.

Without envy I call to mind those beds of stone, used sometimes by the ancient Assyrians, beds of sheet iron in tropical Mexico, that of Heliogabalus, made of solid silver, and the 413 luxurious beds of Louis XIV, who cannot possibly have rotated with sufficient speed to keep them all aired, even if he had the combined agility of Queen Elizabeth and G. Washington. The Koreans slept —in the days when Koreans were permitted to sleep—on floors tempered by an indigenous form of central heating. But these were surely the more fortunate among them. For most of the millions of Asia the bed is where you happen to lie down, sweating or frozen; and the bedclothes are such as you may be fortunate enough to have upon your back.

Then there were the ancient Egyptians—the privileged, who lay on their narrow couches of bronze, alabaster, gold, ivory or inlaid wood, richly cushioned. Some few used bedsteads of wicker, but the poor lay on pallets of palm boughs, with wooden pillows hollowed for their heads. Such pillows of wood (suggestive of the guillotine) are used to this day by African tribesmen, also by Japanese women to keep their hair from being disarranged. Among the peasantry of Russia and Poland those for whom there is no room on the oven share the floor with whatever livestock they may possess. As there is unlikely to be space for more than one to cook himself on the stove, that space will probably be claimed by the master of the house. The thought of a Russian floor adds greatly to my present sense of comfort just where I am.

The chambers of the great have even less fascination for me. Let others discourse of baldaquins and lambrequins, pendants and tenterhooks, counterpoints of tapestry, silken celures, testers of Dornick and Arras, traverses of taffeta and Tartarin. All their pomp did not provide those uneasy heads with such peace as I enjoy in my Chelsea basement. Their guards and their greatness preserved them from the many only to make them the victims of courtiers and lackeys (the indispensable body servants from whom they knew no privacy) and the élite of the *ruelle*—those privileged to enter the alley between the bed and the wall. It would be a thin man who could so intrude in my present dwelling and a bold one who would dare to try, whether I sleep in my bed or lie writing about it. Did the princely Doria sleep better or laze with more repose because his silver bed at Genoa was studded with agates, cornelians, lapis lazuli, turquoises and pearls? Queen Eleanor's bedstead, discovered in the last century (for some reason it was in a cave between Beyrout and Damascus), is of interest to me, not on account of its gold and silver and precious stones, but because it may have been the scene of that alleged seduction of Saladin, a boy of thirteen at the time. The discovery of this bed in a cave seems to lend credence to an otherwise improbable tale.[15]

The fact that such a bed as this was considered mobile

---

[15]Eleanor was then Queen of France. After her divorce, which I have discussed in *Beards,* she married the Duke of Normandy, later Henry II of England.

is worth comment, for it is true that the grandest and most magnificent beds were often moved about in the past. Such was that of Richard III, a cumbersome structure which he took with him everywhere—*on dit*—pretending that he could sleep on no other. Upon this bed he had slept his last night at Leicester, before his untimely end at Bosworth. The owner of the house where he stayed appropriated this bed—perhaps Richard had not paid for his lodging and Solomon's Law could hardly apply to a dead man. At least we are told that the appropriator of Richard's bed became suddenly very rich, and after the manner of very rich men he became mayor of his town. In due course the good man died, leaving a wealthy widow, who was murdered for her money by a maidservant. At the trial the truth came out: Richard's bed had also been his secret safe deposit, and it was for this reason that the king had been unable to sleep comfortably on any other couch.

Then there was that vast bed of Cardinal Richelieu—he travelled not only with it, but on it, his minions battering down walls to allow its admittance. But the extravagant habits of kings, queens and cardinals were hardly suitable models for others as life became mobile beyond the Atlantic. It is true that a recent emigrant to South Africa (a musician by the name of George Martin) was reported by a South African paper[16] to have taken his favourite Elizabethan bed by air from London to Cape Town, after considerable struggles at Croydon Airport. But that, too, must have been a costly undertaking. Many of the first emigrants to the New World took their Gargantuan beds with them; and we have astonishing accounts of such gear among the travelling equipment of passengers on ships. But such objects, though majestic, were highly unsuitable for a population

[16]*The Argus,* May 27, 1947.

of pioneers; and I suppose we owe much to American experience and ingenuity in the development of the modern bed, the bed on which I lie.

The earliest American records describe beds very similar to those used in Europe, many of them doubtless brought by the first settlers. Even the press beds which were so built as to fold up and lie flat against the wall or in a cupboard—an obvious means of economising in space—were known in Britain and are still, I believe, to be found in Brittany. Murray quotes Pepys and Boswell under this head, though the Boswell reference indicates something more like a trundle bed—it was evidently on wheels. The true press bed was nevertheless in use, though probably less common in Europe than it was in America. Alice Morse Earle[17] describes in some detail the turn-up bedsteads which replaced the alcove beds in New England farm kitchens—the warmest places at night, but hardly the most convenient during the day for the type of bed still in general use on the other side of the Atlantic.

Field beds (as they were called), of lighter material, with an arched frame for the canopy, were already beginning to replace the heavier European styles about the middle of the eighteenth century. There seems to have been a reaction from this pure American style in Napoleon's time. Increased intercourse with Europe brought the dead-sea fruits of the Empire to the Atlantic seaboard, beds becoming heavier and abominably carved. But this influence was of short duration; and by 1840 the graceful sleigh beds emerged, marking a fresh assertion of cultural independence—they owed their name to their shape: bed without posts, having curved boards at each end. The trundle bed seems to have had a longer life in America than it had in Europe, and once more

[17]*Home Life in Colonial Days* (London, 1906).

the reason was probably one of space: a small bed on wheels, suitable for a child's use, could always be kept underneath the big double bed of the parents.

Early American beds were still high enough for the old or infirm to need bed steps, though this necessity was sometimes occasioned not so much by the height of the frame itself as by the habit of piling several feather beds on top of it. I am told that such mountainous beds were known in Normandy within the present century. But such luxurious ways were unknown to the great majority of those who had left the seaboard and the larger settlements. There is also an interesting account of the teamsters who drove the Conestoga wagons, in which Alice Morse Earle shows how roughly these pioneers of traffic lived and slept. Carrying with them their blankets and narrow mattresses, these wagon drivers would find a doss on the floor of some tavern, lying with their feet to the fireplace, though sometimes they were provided with boxes like coffins (complete with lids) in which to lay their bedding. At the Pease Tavern, Shrewsbury, Massachusetts, the room provided for the teamsters was on the second floor. In order that they might reach it without passing through the house they were expected to climb the outer wall, using small niches as footholds.[18]

In such taverns even the more privileged traveller found often that he must share a room (yes, and a bed) with a complete stranger, those who objected being regarded as obnoxious and unreasonably fastidious. Richardson Wright, in his *Hawkers and Walkers*,[19] quotes the rules of the Buckthorn Inn, New York City, a high-class establishment which would not give entry to razor

[18]Alice Morse Earle, *Stage Coach and Tavern Days* (New York, 1905), pp. 248 and 291–92.
[19]Philadelphia, 1927, pp. 24–25.

grinders or tinkers, and compelled organ-grinders to sleep in the washhouse. The respectable gentry admitted into the beds of the Buckthorn were charged fourpence, or sixpence with supper. Not more than five were permitted to sleep in one bed, and boots were to be removed before retiring—showing how little human nature had changed since the time of Bishop Hugo Gratianopolitanus.

Stray survivals from the Good Old Times can still be found, I am told, in spite of the pre-eminent efficiency of the modern American hotel. I enjoy the implications of a sign noted by my Middle West correspondent, Mr. Jack C. York, of Ironton, Ohio:

> *Beds, per night, 15 cents*
> *Safe beds, per night, 25 cents*

This imponderable announcement was posted, so I am told, outside a rooming house in Birmingham, Alabama. With a deplorable lack of the spirit of hilarious research (A. Huxley) Mr. York did not sample the safe and the unsafe to investigate the nature of clinical dichotomy in Birmingham. He is even reticent as to the reason for his presence in that quarter of the town.

Volumes could be written on American bedding, especially regarding coverlets and quilts, in the making of which an extraordinary amount of time and ingenuity was spent. Leonardo's opinion on feathers had been confirmed by experience—even John Locke has deigned to discuss the subject: he favoured a hard bed and *rather Quilts than Feathers,* holding that *being buried every night in Feathers melts and dissolves the body.* This terrifying warning was but slowly grasped by mankind, for (as Locke himself had remarked) new opinions are always suspected . . . without any other reason but because they are not already common. (This even applies to America.)

Sarah Lockwood[20] has described the many types of coverlets and quilts with which American women made beautiful the homes of the New World. First there was the crewelwork of the earliest settlements, whereby hangings and covers were embroidered with wool, vegetable dyes being used to produce those soft and restful colours which are now so rare. After the Revolution and the great migrations the loneliness of life in the log cabins encouraged greater effort and many innovations. The patterns had individual names, gay, topical or nostalgic; and I am once more indebted to Jack York for names of a few coverlet and quilt patterns which are still being made in the mountains of eastern Kentucky, Tennessee and the hills of Ohio:

> Rosy Walk, Baltimore Beauty, Girl's Love, Queen's Fancy, Devil's Fancy, Wheels of Fancy, Batchelor's Fancy, Boston Beauty, Perry's Victory, Wedding Ring, Pansies and Roses in the Wilderness. . . .

The list continues and Jack adds names of quilt patterns typical of his own part of the country: Rising Sun, Log Cabin, Love-Knot, Rose of Sharon and (a very odd one) Snake Shed. As is the fate of all beautiful things under the tyranny of fashion, these homemade works of love suffered a temporary eclipse. The Industrial Revolution produced its plethora of stereotyped shoddy and the old coverlet on which grandmother had spent months before her marriage became a horse blanket or a floor mat. It was the same with everything. (My father knew a man who broke up about fifty grand-

[20]*Antiques* (New York, 1926).

father clocks for fire-wood because he couldn't sell them
—the new Swiss timepieces had become the rage.) But
in happier days quilts of patchwork and piecework gave
a new life to disused garments—a wedding dress or even
the robe of a London lord mayor in one instance—and
when white bedcovers became fashionable at the beginning of the nineteenth century ingenuity went into the
corded quilt, a sort of *bas-relief* of needlework. It was
the final flourish of a doomed craft.

Meanwhile, beyond the settlements where wife,
daughter or seamstress plied a pretty needle, stern, tough
men slept upon bundles of small shoots—balsam, hem-
lock or pine, with blankets thrown over them. Such were
the beds of hunters and prospectors; and they have not
greatly changed, though civilisation with its spring mattresses is perpetually chasing such couches into the re-
ceding wilderness. And do (I wonder) the cowboys still
sleep as they did when the flicks were still young and
schoolboys used to read Zane Grey—rolled (the cowboys, I mean) in blankets with their saddles for pillows?

I am feeling too full of unslept sleep to continue this
chapter much longer. I meant to talk of the development
of the modern bed, the bed I lie on, but instead of that
I find I have been eulogising American home crafts—
what irony that the world's greatest industrial country
should have preserved these crafts longer, in all probability, than any country in western Europe! But then,
in this land of paradoxes even Henry Ford wore hand-
woven tweeds, I am told, and was a connoisseur of such
material, also of folk music. This is the riddle of America
and the reason I want to go there—for after all this fine
talk I must admit that I never set eyes on these treasures,
except those eyes of the imagination which have seen
even stranger countries.

But as for the modern bed, its genealogy is perhaps

better skipped after all. It would involve the perilous traverse of the nineteenth century, when the ugliest of all beds were deliberately designed and executed in cold blood. No; it is enough that we arrived at the divan, an ideal companion—at night an intimate friend and by day self-effacing, unpretentious. . . . Like the bed of Queen Victoria (I mean, at least, the one which she occupied when first she exerted her right as a queen not to share a bed with her unpleasant mother—the bed which was certainly hers in 1838), my couch is small and hard, and that is how I prefer it to be. *But it must be warm.*

The warming of beds needs little comment. Everybody knows that this was done at one time with the warming pan, later by smoothing irons or bricks, heated in the oven and wrapped in flannel. I have used such foot warmers myself in my youth when staying in the country. But the hot-water bottle is the best and most friendly of all inventions, though it had to fight its way, like everything else, to recognition. Dr. Macnish, of course, disapproved of bed warming, and even at the end of the nineteenth century there was quite a widespread belief in England that the hot-water bottle was injurious to health and (in some vague and unspecified way) *immoral*. This probably had something to do with Puritanism with its endemic distrust of comfort.

Or, again, it may have derived from a recollection of I Kings I:1–4, which shows us to what depravity a man may sink once he begins to worry about warmth in bed: it is only a short step (they may have argued) from the hot-water bottle to Abishag the Shunammite, that human bed warmer who was chosen for her beauty to comfort a wicked old king in his dotage. However that may be, I suggest that a study of the hot-water-bottle graph, showing increasing sales, would probably prove it to be closely related inversely to a graph showing the decline of Puritanism, double beds and the birth rate.

And another good thing was the invention of pyjamas. So long as the choice was between nightshirts and nudity a man could only be decent by becoming ludicrous, unless he slept fully clad, in contempt of the laws of hygiene. It is, by the way, one of the things I have against the Boers that they pretended to be civilised people, bringing light to the Dark Continent, when their sleeping habits (less than a hundred years ago) would have justified any *really* civilised nation in treating them exactly as they treated the native Africans—justified, I mean, by their own moral law, which is brute force and bloody ignorance. According to a recent book, privately published,[21] *The old-fashioned farmer people in South Africa, at least in those days* (circa 1870) *did not take off their clothes when they went to bed.* The writer tells of a young girl who broke off her engagement on hearing that her betrothed undressed for the night. She would not marry such a lewd person. . . . But she could not be more shocked than I am to think of Dr. Malan as the leader of a would-be *Herrenvolk* which has barely two generations of decent bed manner behind it. The old *sjambok*-and-Bible-thumpers must have smelt very unpleasant. Outside of the blankets I gather that there has been little or no advance in the Boer civilisation, as their treatment of Africans testifies.

In another part of Africa, so Dr. Cabanès claimed, it was customary for a man and wife to share the same nightshirt, each having one sleeve.[22] This was in Abys-

[21]Arnold Wilhelm Spilhaus, *Reminiscences and Family Records,* edited by M. Whiting Spilhaus (Cape Town, 1950).

[22]*Les Indiscrétions de l'Histoire,* Vol. I, pp. 31–32. I am inclined to regard this as one of the indiscretions of the otherwise reliable author, at the end of a heavy day. On

sinia; and if there is any truth in the story it would indicate that the Ethiopians were more civilised than the Boers—that much, at least, it is not hard to believe.

In vindication of the honour of Harvard I beg leave to point out that the order of 1754 which forbade Harvard students to wear nightgowns did not refer to an article worn in bed, but to a kind of dressing gown.[23] It has been claimed (see *Time,* May 6, 1946) that in our own time the bottoms of the pyjamas without the tops are usually worn in the East, and the tops without the bottoms for some reason in America. I find the information about America, which I have often heard from other sources, very distressing. The author quoted (an English doctor) remarked that in our English climate it is generally best to wear both coat and trousers, and I am happy to say this is the common practice in Britain. A paragraph in the *Sunday Express* (July 24, 1949) also announced grave news: so few Americans were wearing pyjamas that manufacturers had become seriously disturbed. The fate of the industry was in the balance and a national campaign was under consideration, to make men pyjama-conscious. Sales had gone down to sixty-five per cent of the previous year's output and half that of the year before.

This, however, does not mean that Americans have adopted South African habits. The present tendency is, apparently, to sleep in the raw, which has certain advantages.[24] But whilst in England bed-wear is considered

---

the previous page he had succeeded in confusing Frederick Barbarossa with a Saracen admiral who sported the same *sobriquet.*

[23]See Earle, *Home Life in Colonial Days,* p. 294.

[24]I cannot at the moment remember which was the asteroid who woke one night in her nightdress and cried out in alarm: *I've been draped.*

a purely personal matter, in America it can become of national importance, especially for those whose home address is at Hollywood. Skolsky's *Tintypes of the Stars* made considerable capital out of their sleeping habits. Thus Janet Blair hit the headlines with her angora sweater and shorts, while Van Johnson's bed-life also made news when it was known that he wore a sleeveless pullover with a monogram. I am glad to record that the law which forbids citizens of North Dakota (*Pioneers, O Pioneers*) to wear shoes or boots in bed is now as obsolete and superfluous as the monastic regulations of Bishop Hugo.

One could devote a whole book to the nocturnal cosmetic habits of the female, but one crowded chapter is enough for me and that has been done by the late Mr. Runyon, of indelible memory, in *My Wife Ethel*. My own wife Ethel gets along very nicely without any of that, so I could not in any case speak from experience. Time was, as the Brazen Head remarked, time was when even strong men went to bed in masks made of flour, cheese and white of egg. These were the *Mignons* of Henri III, *roi de France incertain et de Pologne imaginaire;* and they did but follow the royal example. They also wore gloves in bed—gloves soaked in cosmetics to preserve their elegant hands.

From what tortures have we escaped. The refined Miss Myrtle, in *Bessie Cotter,* even wore her pince-nez in bed—a symbol and guardian of her respectability. And her husband, Al the Dropper (the only man, you will remember, who ever went to a solitary bed in that establishment—a privilege for which Bessie must have envied him), was never allowed to see Miss Myrtle without those pince-nez. But I hope all the sweet old ladies who will be reading this book won't forget to remove their spectacles before switching out the light.

Chapter 6

CUBICULAR TERATOLOGY

Homo-soi-disant-sapiens supposes
Life's a pre-fabricated bed of roses
(Made by Procrustes for a plastic body,
When Eve stopped spinning yarn and purchased
shoddy)
Convinced that Adam's race have found their
souls
Pneumatic-drilling mass-production holes. . . .
From *The Indictment of Babylon*

WELL, in point of fact, what was that bed of Procrustes? Cecil and Margery Gray, in the introduction to their very erudite anthology, *The Bed*, gave Procrustes but three lines—which was treating him as brutally as ever he served his guests. (Indeed, they served poor Og little better, with a mere four lines from Deuteronomy, which is small compass for the Last of the Giants.) You may read in that anthology of a bed of silver—presented to Catherine of Braganza at a cost of £7000 by the States of Holland—and of another silver bed used by Nell Gwyn, the patron saint of my adopted Borough of Chelsea; but devil a word more of that Great Iron Bed of Og, and even less of the bed Procrustean.

Cubicular teratology, an expression first used by

Reynolds in his definitive work on beds,[1] has been defined as the science, philosophy, study, hobby or pursuit of large, monstrous, horrible or sinister beds.[2] Though scientific study of this subject is still in its infancy, it is hoped that a bed will soon be endowed at one of the older universities to further what may prove to be a very fruitful line of research. The subject was by no means unknown to the ancient world; and investigation may well establish the indebtedness of Adam Smith to Procrustes for his conception of Supply and Demand. The Father of Political Economy, that Jaganath to which so many generations have been sacrificed,[3] must surely have been influenced by Old Procrustes when he wrote that *the average produce of every sort of industry is always suited, more or less, to the average consumption; the average supply to the average demand.* But Crusty was more practical. He was no mere armchair theoretician, no phrasemonger of academic abstractions. The quintessence of Applied Procrusteanism lay in the bed itself, the field of action. The very name of this pioneer signified *the stretcher,* but the modern stretcher bed is probably a much debased form of the original, of which no specifications have as yet been discovered.

In the case of Og we are more fortunate. Although there is no record of the case of Og *v.* Mammon, already discussed (it was necessary to reconstruct this as they do the prehistoric animals from a single jawbone), the Bible and the Talmud are rich in information relating to

---

[1] *Beds* (New York, 1951).

[2] Ibid., p. 130.

[3] Whose was the epigram? I remember it well from the First World War:

> *Tell the professors, ye who pass us by,*
> *They taught Political Economy*
> *And here, obedient to its laws, we lie.*

Og and the Bed. We know the material and the measurements of the bedstead from Deuteronomy III:11. The owner was ruler of Bashan (*Ogque Bashan Rector,* as Nicholas de Lyra says, though *Rector* sounds vaguely incongruous); and Bashan was a land with a great hill (Psalms LXVIII:15) where there were great bulls (Psalms XXII:12), also fatlings, goats and rams (Ezekiel XXXIX:18). The king or *Bettmann* of this country was the last of the giants (Joshua XIII:12) and given to nostalgia, as we know from his wife's bitter complaint in *The Doggerel of Og.*[4] To her words of reproach, you may remember, the king—who was lying as usual in his iron bed in broad daylight—replied:

> ... *Damn*
> *I was dreaming of a ram,*
> *A fat cow of Bashan and a little baa-lamb.*
> *Why can't you leave to my dreaming, Mrs. Og?*
> *Bring another pillow and another glass of grog. ...*

A convivial old rascal, you must admit. But he and his kingdom came to a bad end. Lebanon, said Isaiah (XXXIII:9), is ashamed and hewn down: Sharon is like a wilderness; and Bashan and Carmel shake off their fruits. The prophet Nahum (I:4) recorded the languishing of Bashan, Carmel and the flower of Lebanon. The bed—as already noted—was removed to Rabbath, and there (we are told):

> *Og's bed of iron*
> *The bed he used to lie on*
> *When iron beds were new*

was exhibited in a peepshow by Mammon for a small *in capita* charge.[5] The fate of the famous bulls has

[4] *Og and Other Ogres* (London, 1946).
[5] *The Doggerel of Og,* lines 36–44. Though of late origin, this ballad appears to corroborate our reconstruction of the

already been discussed; and Solomon's wisecrack during the lawsuit about the women of Samaria being
Bashan cows may be compared with Amos IV:1—it
was probably a current form of abuse after the slump in
fat-stock prices, when Og went bankrupt.

Since Og is clearly described as the last of the giants[6]
some doubt has been thrown on the authenticity of the
Doggerel regarding his family. It is said that they were
begotten in the Great Iron Bed and furthermore that

> *They were all giants*
> *Who dabbled in science. . . .*

One of the descendants, Dr. Ogg of Rothamsted, is
certainly a distinguished man of science, though I regret to add that he is a great exponent of chemical
fertilisers, which were never used in Bashan during its
period of prosperity. But although I have a standing
invitation to see Dr. Ogg's baa-lambs any spring at
Rothamsted (which I suppose to be the Mecca of
mechanisation and Dead Sea salts) I have not yet been
able to see for myself whether the Ogs or Oggs of the
present generation are giants. Nor has good Dr. Ogg
yet had an opportunity to correct what he once called
my lamentable ignorance of agriculture. The flocks I

---

lawsuit. If it was Mammon who went off with the bed it
would naturally have been with the intention of making
something out of it.

[6]On the other hand, it has been pointed out that the statement in Deuteronomy and Joshua, that Og was the last of
the giants, is also suspect. Giants of a later vintage have
been recorded in all parts of the world. See *Fee Fi Fo Fum*
by H. J. Massingham (London, 1926), passim. (I will pass
over the obvious case of Goliath, which may have been invented by the Israeli Ministry of Information, or whatever
they called professional liars in those days—a piece of pro-
David propaganda.)

know best are admittedly those in my mattress; but the old King of Bashan was such another bolster-boy as myself and that is good enough for me.

Now it has been said of this same Og, the true and original archiprotoclinophile, that he was an antediluvian. And W. A. Clouston, in his *Flowers from a Persian Garden*, greatly misled me in my youth by saying that Og was saved from the Flood by riding on the back of a unicorn, which Noah had taken in tow because it was too big to enter the Ark. The unicorn, said Clouston, was made fast by its horn. If there is one thing that excites my imagination more than a halcyon, a chimera, a basilisk, an ant lion or even a poh,[7] it is a unicorn. It was once my intention to write a book on this creature, which I would have done had I not discovered that Odell Shepard had already said all that was worth saying on the subject. But the connection between Og and the unicorn proved to be a mirage, and the true story is as follows.

It seems that some people, other than the passengers on the Ark, did indeed escape the Flood, because it is clearly stated in Genesis XIV:13 that one of them came to Father Abraham. From the context it might appear superficially that this person was merely a refugee from Sodom or maybe Gomorrah; but the Rabbi Johanan—as you may see for yourself in the Talmud—says that the reference is to someone who had escaped the generation of the Flood, and that this person was none other than Og. This same Rabbi Johanan was

[7] The *Shan Hai King* describes an animal as existing among the plains of Mongolia, having the appearance of a horse, with a white body, black tail, teeth and claws like a tiger, which howls like the roll of a drum, devours tigers and leopards, and is capable of being used instead of soldiers; it is called Poh (Charles Gould in *Mythical Monsters* [London, 1886]).

probably in a position to know, because he may have been the hero of a strange adventure to be found in the Babylonian Talmud, *Seder Tohoroth*, in the seventh tractate of the Mishrah editions, known as *Niddah*.

Abba Saul, or (as some say) Rabbi Johanan, being at one time a gravedigger, was (surely unofficially?) pursuing a deer one day when the prey took cover in the thigh bone of a corpse. Abba Saul (or Rabbi Johanan) naturally followed; and the deer led him a chase down three *parasangs* of this remarkable femur before he gave up and returned home. Now a *parasang* is a *Persian* mile (about 4000 yards) and a man with a thigh bone over seven miles long is a very large man indeed. So Abba Saul or Rabbi Johanan figured this must sure be the thighbone of Og, King of Bashan, and none other. A good deal of further information about Og is supplied in the Talmud. It appears that he had a brother called Sihon; and the Lord (who was on intimate terms with Moses) told Moses to *fear him not*. Perhaps he was not so big as Brother Og. These two were grandsons of Shamhazai, one of those disreputable angels who— where is it? Ah, Genesis VI:2—*saw the daughters of men that they were fair; and they took them wives. . . .* The result of this, as we read later, was that *There were giants in the earth in those days.* Of such distinguished lineage was Og, one of those *mighty men which were of old, men of renown.*

That Og escaped the Flood is clear enough. But in the *Niddah* version the unicorn is not to be found. All that we discover is the *re'em*, a large animal—so large that the Rabbi ben Bar Hanah, who once saw a baby sea-re'em only a day old, estimated its size as equal to that of Mount Tabor. Indeed, a ball of its dung once blocked the river Jordan. One of this species, without the usual provision for mating, was taken in tow by the crew of the Ark, who tied it by its horns. The plural is fatal to all unicorn theories and we have to look for an animal with at least two horns in order to identify the *re'em*. The best authorities are now agreed that it was none other than the aurochs (*bos primigenius*), known to the Romans as *urus* and to the Assyrians as *rimu,* a beast now extinct, but believed from its remains to have been about twelve feet long and seven feet high. Though this hardly compares favourably with Mount Tabor,[8] it is a good size for a bull and—allowing for rabbinical hyperbole—may account for the description of the baby sea-*re'em*. Caesar described these brutes (*De Bello Gallico, VI, 28*). He said they were called *uri,* that they were *magnitudine paulo infra elephantos* and found in the Hercynian forest, where the hardy youths of Germany *these, captured in pits, studiously killed (hos studiose foveis captos interficiunt)*.

It had not been my intention to discuss the sleeping habits of animals in this book; but with the Gallic Wars staring at me it is hard to resist some mention of that extraordinary animal, the German elk, to be found in the previous chapter (VI, 27). How far Julius is really reliable I do not know. I have always felt myself that the schoolboy's essays on Caesar summed him up very well: *Nec beneficit, nec malefecit, sed interfecit.* I would prefer to be equally noncommittal regarding his accuracy as a naturalist; and there is even some doubt about his authorship of these chapters. But in spite of all such doubts the description of the elk is still remarkable, and the more so because this preposterous beast was another claimant to the status of unicorn—the confusion being evident in Shakespeare's *Julius Caesar* (II, i, 203).

[8]It has been suggested to me that the sea variety might have been larger, but this is pure hypothesis and *non ad re'em.*

These animals, who are called *alces,* we are told, have
no joints in their legs and they do not lie down, even
quietis causa. Indeed, if by any chance they fall they just
cannot get up again. To these are trees for couches
(*His sunt arbores pro cubilibus*)—they lean on the trees
to sleep. To catch these miserable creatures we are
further informed that hunters track them to their haunts;
and there the artful men dig beneath the tree roots or
saw nearly through the trunks, so that the trees will fall
with a slight push. Along comes the unwary elk, leans
trustfully on the treacherous tree, and down fall tree
and elk to the ground. The moral to this, very clearly,
is that one should sleep in a bed.

But about Og: there are various stories of his escape
from the Flood and his connection even with the *re'em*
(let alone the unicorn) is obscure.[9] One says that the
Flood only reached Og's ankles, another that he sat on
a ladder hung outside the Ark and had his food pushed
through a porthole. (But not without a *quid pro quo:*
Noah, who gave nothing away gratis, made him swear
to be his slave and the slave of his children forever.)
In longevity Og must have been Methuselah's only
rival: a contemporary of Noah, he lived until the time
of Moses. The date of the Iron Bed is uncertain; I
conjecture that it was probably constructed after the
deluge, but if not, Og and the *re'em* must have somehow kept it above water between them.

The source of Clouston's error will probably be found
in the Bible. It is unfortunate that the excellent men
who gave us the English Authorised Version raised

[9]Job may have had Og in mind, of course, in his cryptic remark (XXXIX:9): *Will the unicorn be willing to serve
thee, or abide by thy crib?* (Unicorn is, of course, the A.V.
rendering of *re'em;* but *crib* would be a curious word to
apply to the vast iron bed of Og.)

so many false hopes and caused so much confusion by rendering *re'em* as *unicorn*. The matter has been fully discussed by Carl Cohn (*Zur Literarische Geschichte des Einhorns* [Berlin, 1883]) and more recently by Odell Shepard (*The Lore of the Unicorn* [London, 1930]), with the result that the unicorn has no longer a leg to stand on. Actually a great deal of trouble would have been saved, in the case of Og, if only someone had realised the cogency of a simple syllogism:

All persons capable of catching unicorns were virgins.

Og was not a virgin.

Ergo, Og was not a person capable of catching a unicorn.

It is a perfect inference in the second figure of the second mood (*Camestres*) and there is no getting out of it.

Turning to *Berakoth* (which sounds like a variant of *Felapton* but it is really nothing of the sort—it is one of the books in the Talmud), we find an account of Og's death, which is very instructive. Og, it appears, decided to discourage the children of Israel (who were marching in on the milk and honey, etc.) by uprooting a mountain and using it as a sanction against the camp of these aggressors. Having selected his mountain (the equivalent of an atomic bomb), he returned with it on his head, full of zeal for the cause of the United Nations of his time. But the tribal divinity of Israel sent an army of ants, which bored a hole in the mountain, and down it fell like an outsize millstone round his neck. The King of Bashan tried to free himself, but in vain—his teeth, evidently of the rabbit type, stuck out and caught in the hard rock. A reference to this—so the Talmudic writer assures us (I beg you to believe that this is no invention of mine)—is to be found in Psalms III:7: *thou hast broken the teeth of the ungodly*. Such, at least, was the opinion of the Rabbi Simeon ben Lakish, who held that the text was corrupt and ought to read: *thou hast lengthened* (*shirbabta*). That is to say, Og's teeth (and he was long in the tooth already) were miraculously lengthened in order to trap his head in that mountain.

As to the size of Og's teeth we have excellent evidence, for it is known that out of one single tooth Father Abraham made his famous Ivory Bed, possibly mentioned—with disapproval—in Amos VI:4. (Little did you guess how relevant was this long Oggression.) Hampered by the mountain, the unfortunate gentleman was eventually done to death by Moses, who (being a mere ten cubits tall—about fifteen feet[10]) leapt his own height into the air and struck Og in the ankle with an axe. The king's ankles were tender as the heel of Achilles, along of lying in bed so much of his time; and he fell like an Og. He was a great man in every way. He ate 1000 oxen *per diem* and his stride was estimated at 40 miles; why, even in his cradle (*vide* my remarks on Hercules and Pantagruel) he had to be tied with iron chains—or so Nicholas de Lyra informs us. The man, his size, his exploits and his Great Iron Bed are all symbols of profound mystical significance, as is clearly shown by the frequent references to them in the Jewish Scriptures.[11]

[10]W. A. Clouston quotes a very near estimate. According to an old MS at Lambeth Palace, of the time of Edward IV, *Moses was XIII fote XIIJ ynches and a half*. As to the *longitude of men followyng*, we are given various figures: *cryste VJ fote and iij ynches, our Lady VJ fote and Viij ynches* (and so on).

[11]It is perhaps relevant, but maybe not, to recall that the Celtic Heaven, which flows with wine and honey, a land of

(At this point someone asks if I am including the beds of the martyrs. No, I am not including the beds of the martyrs. The best ascetics, *en tout cas,* scorned beds. Look at St. Simeon Stylites—why else is he on a pillar but to be looked at?—and you will see what I mean. But if you want to know how to suffer, read of St. Rose of Lima in the *Acta Sanctorum.* I had hardly written these words before I was told that in this very month of May 1951 photographs had arrived from Rome of an Indian who was doing a long fast on a bed of broken glass, surrounded by snakes of all sizes. The Indian was apparently smoking Camels: an advertisement?)

Iron beds seem to have gone out of fashion after Og's death. They are hardly mentioned until the eighteenth century, though an inventory of furniture at the castle of Nerac mentions *un lit de fer et de cuivre,* with figures of Holofernes and Judith.[12] The choice of the figures is curious. To anyone who recalled the story—the horrible murder of Nebuchadnezzar's general in his bed by Judith, and how she went off with his head in her shopping bag—these figures can hardly have been reassuring to contemplate as one crawled under the blankets. The moral, no doubt, is that one should keep Judith out of it.

The fear of being murdered in one's bed—a thought apparently more fraught with terror than that of murder in general—must be a very old one. It provides the horror *motif* in the story of Grendel and the hall of Hrothgar. What really terrifies is the idea of the assassin stealing in upon the sleeper—one dreads losing con-

---

youth, where there is neither age nor death, is called *Tir na n'Og.*

[12]See *Encyclopaedia Britannica* (14th edition), article on Beds.

sciousness, and every bed becomes a potential death-bed. Stories of trust and treachery give life to such fears, and of them all I have always found that of Jael and Sisera the most terrifying, as recorded in Judges IV:17–24. The story follows closely on another treacherous murder—the Old Testament is really a textbook on treachery—that of Eglon, who was probably done to death in a privy (as I have mentioned in another place[13]), which is almost as bitter to contemplate as murder in the bedroom.

The story of Sisera is that of a Canaanite field marshal who was defeated in battle by the Israelites. Hunted and weary, he comes to Jael's tent—for why?—*there was peace between Jabin* (Sisera's boss) *and the house of Heber* (Jael's husband). Relying upon this, the wretched man seeks sanctuary, and Jael even goes out to meet him. She addresses him in the most friendly terms, invites him inside and tells him to fear not. Once she has him safely in the tent, Jael persuades the fugitive to go to bed, tucks him in with a mantle, gives him milk to drink and for some reason (as we learn later) butter in a lordly dish. She then promises to stand guard over him while he takes forty winks.

As soon as the credulous Canaanite is asleep what does Jael do but take, of all horrible weapons, a hammer and a large nail. She steals up to Sisera (*for he was fast asleep and weary,* says the shameless chronicler) and knocks the nail so well and truly through his temples that it pins his head to the ground. The chronicler adds laconically: *So he died*—which seems not improbable. The credit for this revolting assassination was duly given to God and the whole of Judges V is devoted to a eulogy of Israelite achievements that day in the form of a duet by a horrible woman called

[13]*Cleanliness and Godliness* (New York, 1946).

Deborah and the Israelite freebooter, Barak. Specially
mentioned in dispatches is Mrs. Heber (Nail 'em Jael),
who is to be henceforward blessed above women in the
tent. The story is rehearsed once more, lyrically, treachery and all, with a special gloat on the murder itself and
on the feelings of Sisera's unfortunate mother.

But it is the bed as *itself an engine of destruction*
which probably strikes the greatest terror; for here is
true cubicular teratology. That *Terribly Strange Bed* of
Wilkie Collins, wth its sinister canopy, engine of suffo-
cation, was surely descended from the contrivance of
Dr. Procrustes. Such another was that of which Thomas
Deloney tells, in the inn at Colebrooke, where Thomas
of Reading met his end in spite of his own premonitions
and the piteous cries of the screech owl. (*And anone
after,* says Deloney, *the night raven sate croking hard
by the window.* The stage was well set for tragedy long
before Poe borrowed that fowl.[14]) Having talked a
little in a melancholy fashion and made his will, the
landlord's *fat pig* retired to that gruesome couch so
conveniently situated in a room above the kitchen—*in
such sort that by the pulling out of two yron pinnes below . . . downe would the man fall out of his bed into
the boyling cauldron . . . where being suddenly scalded
and drowned, he was never able to cry or speake one*

[14]Compare also *the twa corbies making a mane.* The raven
was also employed by Sir John Mennes, with the screech
owl:

I heard no screech-owl shreek, nor Raven croak.

For the significance of the screech owl see three ancient
references in Aubrey's *Remaines of Gentilisme* and his remark that it was still held unlucky. Webster made good use
of the screech owl when strangling the Duchess of Malfi.
Clouston has some notes on *Folklore of The Raven and the
Owl* in Saxby's *Birds of Omen in Shetland* (privately printed
in 1893).

word. Such was Thomas Cole's fate, the last of sixty victims at the Crane Inn; and in case any other hotel proprietor should be tempted to such practices Deloney says plainly that the wicked host and his wife died by hanging, and in debt at that, proving that crime does not pay.

Another very unpleasant bed was one made of ice, in a house of ice. On this chill couch an aged Russian courtier of the eighteenth century was compelled by the Empress Anne to spend a bridal night with a poor old lady—such was imperial caprice in czarist Russia. It is a curious comment on sleeping habits in some parts of the world that the bride in this story was a woman *whose duty it was to tickle the soles of the feet of the Empress as she was dropping off to sleep.*[15]

A long chapter could, of course, be written for the Horror Section on *haunted beds.* I considered this, but was badly put off the idea at the outset by seeing a photograph in *Time* (December 17, 1945) showing Harry Price—at that time Britain's ace inspector of ghosts— lying in a haunted bed with Dr. Joad. It would be impossible for even the most melodramatic ghost to take the haunting business seriously after seeing that sight; and of course the local wraith did not keep its appointment. How could a howling, moaning, chain-rattling spirit *gae boomp-i'-the-nicht* with any conviction, when confronted with Joad's beard and that infernally rational *It depends what you mean?* They do say that the Great Bed of Ware was haunted by the ghost of Jonas Fosbrooke. Though somewhat overwritten (for there have been many larger), his bed has some claim at least to be

---

[15]*When Lovers Ruled in Russia* by V. Poliakoff, as quoted by C. and M. Gray. The sole-tickling was evidently a common Muscovite custom, as Gogol also refers to it in *Dead Souls.*

mentioned in the teratological department. Fosbrooke
made it, according to legend; and possibly the reason
for all the pinching, beating and scratching which led
to its abandonment by the owners of the Saracen's Head
was the fact that the old carpenter had intended it for
the Royal Family or at least for the Earl of Warwick. I
do not know whether Dr. Joad has asked the permission
of the authorities to sleep in this bed, which is now in
the South Kensington Museum. I should have thought
that an exhibition of the bed with my friend in it would
have proved a profitable undertaking.

The Great Exhibition of 1851 offered a number of
novelties for jaded Victorian tastes. Under *General
Hardware, Including Locks and Grates,* I find that item
56, the inventions of a certain Robert Watson Savage,
included an *Alarum bedstead, causing a person to arise
at any given hour.* How the Savage Bed worked is not
stated, but I have seen a description of such a bed elsewhere,[16] from which it appears that there was first an
ordinary alarm call. If this proved insufficient the bedclothes were automatically removed; and finally the mattress was tilted to an angle of forty-five degrees. It is
said that this infernal machine, though intended for the
Great Exhibition, was never shown there; but one exhibited some years later at the Leipzig Fair, in a booth
on the Königsplatz, evidently resembled it closely. In
this case the *modus operandi* was that after two alarm
calls a notice board with the words *Time to Get Up* was
pushed in front of the occupant's nose. The next step
was the pulling off of his nightcap and finally his delecticulation.[17] The Dresden mechanic who invented this

[16] My authorities are none other than *Tit-Bits* and the *Nord-
deutsche Post.*

[17] My friend, Irene Beeson, who bangs out on the typewriter
the chapters that I write indolently in bed, says that the
correct word is not delecticulation but debunkery.

monstrous bed did, however, show a little humanity, as
the stern robot, whilst ejecting its victim, lit both a
candle and a spirit stove—the latter for his morning
coffee.

Among the French exhibitors of 1851, No. 554 (Kes-
sel, Jean) entered a *Mechanical bed, on a new system.*
What this was intended to convey to the mind I have no
idea. Did it mechanically wash and undress one, as I
have so often wished? Or was it another of those mon-
strosities which mechanically ejected the sleeper with
all the brutality ascribed to scorned women? Stranger
inventions were to follow. U. S. Patent 278, 431, May
29, 1883, was a hammock that swung from an over-
turned tricycle. (The original diagram of this sleeping
apparatus is reproduced by Sigfried Giedion,[18] to whom
I am much indebted for this valuable item of information.) It is, in fact, from about that time onwards that
the strangest and most monstrous beds must be sought
in America. Here is our paradox again, for while American enterprise was developing beds simple, tasteful
and convenient for the ordinary person, American mil-
lionaires and eccentrics were emulating the ancient
world in extravagant and fantastic designs.

In this field Hollywood has, as a matter of course,
assumed the leadership. When Stanley Walker was writing *Mrs. Astor's Horse* the largest bed in Hollywood was,
by repute, that of Carole Lombard, built—so Walker
described it—like an oversized Empire couch. Elsewhere
in his most instructive and entertaining book the author,
having remarked that interior decorators are always will-

---

[18]*Mechanization Takes Command* (New York, 1948), p.
476. I have, unfortunately, no opportunity to search for
myself the records of American patents, which I am convinced would yield a much richer harvest of fantastic bed
designs than one could find even in the British Patent Office.

ing to oblige anyone with a lot of money who wants to go in for conspicuous waste, rules out preposterous expenditure on beds as *vieux jeu*. One would indeed imagine that the possibilities of size and cost had long since been exhausted by the stars. The same authority, however, described the oversized bed *chez* Mae West. No less imposing was her bed in New York when she was playing in *Sex*. And in spite of Mr. Walker's comment the Bed Cult still continues to flourish among the stars.

As late as 1947 I find it on record that a Hollywood manufacturer was specialising in making beds suitable for film personalities. These beds were all handmade to specifications, like the products of a tailor. Double beds averaged between seven to eight feet in length, breadth varying from six feet to nine, showing that maximum beds must have been broader than they were long. Merrill Pannitt, from whom I learn these facts,[19] explained how hard it was to satisfy some film stars. Joan Fontaine proved a tough case, it seems, and Cary Grant wanted one too large to be taken through his doors—he evidently lacked the ruthlessness of Richelieu to knock down the wall. Joan Crawford solved the problem by having her bed hoisted through upper windows; and the manageress of the Bed Store, a Mrs. Gincig, soon took to measuring not only her customers but their windows and doors.

The pre-eminence of Carole Lombard, according to this account, has been usurped by Johnny Weissmuller —unless this information is already out of date. He took the precaution of leaving his house unfurnished until he had installed the *pièce de résistance*. Gloria Swan-

[19] Article in the *Digest of Digests,* September 1947, by permission of *Everybody's Weekly,* magazine of the Philadelphia *Sunday Inquirer.*

son, on the other hand, an old-fashioned lass of quiet
and refined tastes, prefers twin beds. According to *Time*
(January 14, 1946), one of her reasons for wishing to
divorce her fifth husband was a disagreement on this
point, as her husband *pro tem* (William N. Davey)
favoured a double bed big enough to sleep a ball team.
(This may be slightly inaccurate—another account of
the fracas says the bed was large enough to hold eight
people. I am told that is one short, but how should I
know, anyway? All my snobbish *Concise Oxford* says
about baseball is that it's the *U.S. national game, more
elaborate rounders.* . . .)

Parenthetically I should like to remark that Miss
Swanson had, in my opinion, a poor case on the bed
count. An example of what I consider a really serious
case of alleged bad manners was recorded by the Knoxville *News Sentinel* (Tennessee) and it runs as follows:

> Mrs. Josephine Brown, 45, who married her
> husband three times and divorced him twice, has
> filed suit at Chicago (Illinois) for divorce again.
> She charged that her husband, Harry Brown,
> trapped her in an in-a-door bed and then pushed
> it into a closet. . . . Judge Rudolph Desort
> granted her an injunction prohibiting Brown from
> shutting his wife up in an in-a-door bed.[20]

The reasonableness of Judge Rudolph Desort is, I
think, the outstanding feature in this story. I have no
further information, and do not know whether Mrs.
Brown eventually obtained her divorce; still less do I
know if she then remarried Mr. Brown for the fourth

---

[20] I quote this pearl at second hand from *The New Yorker*
of November 25, 1950, where the tag line ran: *Getting
so a man has no rights at all any more.*

time of asking when she became bored with the uneventful monotony of single life.

Reverting to large beds, it appears that in England, lacking the versatile range available at Hollywood, we simply do not know how to bed an outsize man. When Iron Mike Mazurki the all-in wrestler (height 6 foot 4½ inches, weight 245 pounds) came to London in 1949 there was not a hotel in the metropolis which could accommodate him properly—or so he told a London *Daily Mail* reporter. His own cot at Hollywood was seven feet square. In Mike's case this sounds reasonable enough, but the same excuse can hardly be offered for the vogue in outsize beds which was still current in Cloud Cuckoo Land about 1949—even in 1951, to the best of my knowledge. Tyrone Power, Hedy Lamarr, Lana Turner and Marie Macdonald are other celebrities numbered among the addicts and there are rumours that the shapes are in some cases as outlandish as the sizes. One actress who has been married four times has—so I am told—a bed in the shape of a heart.

For an account of another strangely shaped bed I am once more indebted to Mr. Jack York. It seems that when he was a journalist in Birmingham, Alabama (what time he was shyly studying—from without—the safe and unsafe beds of the Deep South), Jack knew a former mayor of Birmingham who combined the means, the generosity and possibly even the tastes of a Maecenas. *Non derunt, Flacce, Marones*—I will myself be thy Virgil, George B. Ward, of Birmingham (Alabama), *atavis edite regibus* for all I know; at least it sounds well. Upon the high peak of Shades Mountain he built his circular residence, modelled (for some reason) upon the temple of the Vestal Virgins.

Now you cannot fit a square bed into a round room, so what did Maecenas do but provide himself with a vast circular bed, which stood on the top floor of his house, that hight *Vestavia*. The household servants were known as Romulus, Remus, Cassius and so forth—with the patient good humour of coloured folk I have no doubt but that they indulged the old man's foibles to the full. He is described as a sound, solid drinker whose head, though often muddy, remained unbowed; and in his seventies he preserved a gay eye and a susceptible heart. His parties at Vestavia, so I am assured by one who was often a guest, were truly Roman. But his bed was his undoing—not the shape of it, even, but the nocturnal habits of George B. Ward. Having married a woman much younger than himself, he was in due course divorced. Most of the court proceedings were conducted *in camera* and the truth was a matter of speculation until a well-founded rumour got around: it seemed that the crime of George B. Ward was that he ate peanuts in his circular bed. The incessant noise of cracking and crunching distressed Mrs. Ward no less than the discarded shells which he scattered inconsiderately among the sheets. When you consider the way the princess in story beefed about feeling a pea through a dozen mattresses you will appreciate the sentiments of Mrs. Ward if she really had to park her moral fibre upon unupholstered nutshells.

When this old reprobate was gathered to his fathers it was found that he had bequeathed Vestavia to a bishop of the Episcopal Church, on condition that he should live there. I have no further information. A bishop in that circular bed, even without the peanuts, is something of a thought.

On reflection I doubt if there is any matter in which well-known or wealthy persons are more prone to assert their personalities than they are in regard to the bed. If they do not demand something extra large or of eccentric design they will express themselves in the matter of night attire or bedding. Thus Caruso would ask for anything up to three mattresses and eighteen pillows; and Madame Chiang Kai-shek, when she was at Washington, let it be known that she wished the sheets on her bed changed every time she lay on it, which was about a dozen times *per diem,* so it was said.

To feed the appetite of eccentricity every imaginable gadget has been devised and marketed. A super hospital bed, operated by thirty electric motors, was designed for the use of Howard Hughes, the millionaire film producer, after he was seriously injured in a plane crash. To remind him, presumably, of his unfortunate experience, the bed was equipped with a dashboard covered with push buttons by means of which he could tour his room, move himself into any position or turn on hot and cold water supplies.[21] Even the British have managed to produce an electrically heated bed (thermostatically controlled) which needs no blankets and folds up when not in use—an exhibit in the *Britain Can Make It* exposition, opened in September 1946. This bed resembles a midget automobile and is made of plastic and aluminum. In 1949 Firestone Plastics announced a mattress that massaged the body; and I myself have invented a combined dressing gown and penwiper for the use of authors when refueling.[22]

Indeed, every aspect of the bed problem appears to

[21]While I am writing this (April 1951) a photograph has arrived of the *Spring Mills* modern bed, on show in New York, complete with a model in a bathing suit to demonstrate the attractions of numerous gadgets; but the only apparent novelty is an oxygen mask for hangovers.

[22]Unlike Hamlet, who evidently typed his letters to Ophelia (*vide* Act II, Scene II: *Thine evermore . . . while this machine is to him*), I do not type and strongly disapprove of typing in bed, anyway.

have received attention in recent years. An electric night light, placed under one leg of the bed, flashes on when the occupant falls out and is not extinguished until the *status quo ante* is resumed. This is an infallible method of showing you where you are. A breakfast tray has also been noted, which radiates infra-red rays, fries bacon, makes toast and boils water but does no damage to bedclothes. At one department in a New York store, known as the Sleep Shop, they were showing in 1948 double mattresses for double beds. Held together by zip fasteners, these mattresses could be divorced by an adroit movement of the arm, indicating a preference for solitude. If the other occupant snored, a neat little mechanism made a noise and emitted air. I am not clear as to whether this meant that the snorer was blown out of bed; but according to information received the effect was to stop the snoring, if necessary by waking up the offending party—no doubt whilst pretending to be asleep one's self.

Further innovations on show at the Sleep Shop were described by Eve Perrick two years later, in the *Daily Express* (September 23, 1950). An improved anti-snoring device rolled the snorer over in bed. A mechanical sheep-rotator saved one the trouble of counting. . . . Electrically heated bedsocks were also available and a biscuit which left no crumbs in the bed. When you think of the late Mr. Ward, whose nocturnal peanuts paved the way to the divorce court, you will realise the importance of that biscuit, a cracker known as *Cheez-It*. Eve Perrick very rightly pointed out that, in a country where reading in bed might be construed as mental cruelty by some courts, one could not be too careful. She concluded that the director of the department, Public Sandman No. 1 Norman Dine, had done his utmost to protect modern American marriages.

With the same object in view, the Sleep Shop apparently offers a Silent Radio (audible only to the one who has it under his—or her—pillow). A waterproof pillow is provided on the sound principle of Mark Antony: *If you have tears, prepare to shed them now. Life* (April 19, 1948) describes a number of similar toys, including an electrically controlled ventilator, which saves one from leaving one's kip to open or shut the window. There is a considerable range of electric blankets now available and a gadget known as the Felevitt is said to enable you to make a bed in one minute. There are Contour Sheets which will not wrinkle and plenty of pneumatic pillows. There is even a bed which is hoisted into the ceiling—the invention of my friend Ralph Erskine in his home at Drottningholm, described in the Swedish journal *Idun* (February 17, 1944). By 1949 research workers at the Air Force School of Aviation Medicine, San Antonio (Texas), had even announced a space bed suitable for tourists to Mars. Constructed with a view to conditions in which the sleeper would be liberated from the laws of gravity, this bed consists of a semicircular trough, with a net to prevent the occupant from floating off when he turns over in his sleep.

I have said little about special hospital beds and bed gadgets, as I hope to say more of such things later.[23] Of strange materials one could write a good deal: beds have been made of solid gold, of glass and of Lucite. Musical beds crop up periodically—generally made with a musical box which is set in operation by the mere act

[23]This must be for another occasion, if ever: see my Epilogue. I see, by the way, that an emergency bed has now been invented to fit into a bathtub. I hope American baths are longer than ours if *Boobus Americanus* is to use this invention.

of lying on the mattress. In one instance of which I have read the occupant was lulled to sleep by soft music, but an alarm apparatus ensured his waking to a march by Spontini, with drums and cymbals. The Maharajah of Baroda, while in New York, had a bed made to fit the opulent contour of his body. The ingenuity of an American inventor (nearly a century ago) produced a bed that was disguised as a piano; and a bed was once invented for a retired sea captain, to give him that undulating motion without which he could not sleep. All that really remains to be marketed is the Z-shaped bed, proposed by Groucho Marx for the accommodation of those who sleep that way.

Design, bedding and bed wear are not, of course, the only media of self-expression. The things that can be done in—or with—a bed are so numerous that I can only hint at possibilities by mentioning in conclusion some examples from the rich experience of the past. Those who habitually move from bed to bed—travelling salesmen and so forth—can always cause a stir if they carry compasses in their pockets and insist upon the head pointing due north. This was a little foible ascribed to Charles Dickens and must have meant more commotion in the days when beds were heavier than they are today—outside of Hollywood. The daring, also persons with low blood pressures (requiring a stimulus to secrete adrenalin), might experiment with a delayed-action bomb. According to *Time* (October 4, 1948), a Frenchman living at Angers, by the name of Jean Pocret, having been uncomfortably aware for four years of a lump in his mattress, opened it up to discover an unexploded booby trap, farewell gift from the German Army of Occupation.

For those seeking to find new uses for beds I also offer a few final hints. In South Africa a hot-dog merchant by the name of Koli Liebenberg found recently that on the mesh of a single bed he could grill thirty pounds of sausages at a time; so the number that Johnny Weissmuller could manage should not be hard to calculate. The possibilities of the bed in the hands of a strong woman were indicated by a Mrs. Alberta Brooks, of Chicago, who dropped her bed on a car parked beneath her window. According to *Time* (January 14, 1946), she explained: *When I shake my bedding, I shake it bed and all. It just slipped out of my hands.* But Ollie M. James, the Innocent Bystander of the Cincinnati *Enquirer* (December 10, 1950), surely points the way to the future. Remarking that he has found a reasonably hard bed useful as a platform for mosquito bashing, Mr. James draws attention to the bleak and slatty appearance of a bed as seen from below.

I doubt if anyone has ever previously considered this aspect, even at Hollywood, from the aesthetic angle; and a completely new field of enterprise is opened up by the suggestion of Mr. James that the atomic menace indicates a need for cheerful chintz or sateen coverings *below the springs.* I have heard that George Moore (or was it some other chap?) kept a snake under his bed[24]; but even a reptile, being (as I am told) susceptible to music, may have other aesthetic needs to satisfy. My own ideal, however, is to emulate a well-known London radiologist who used to have two grapevines growing over him. It meant keeping the room at rather a high temperature, but imagine the luxury of selecting and picking a bunch for breakfast without setting foot to the floor. . . . The peanuts of Vestavia were nothing to such a truly Roman fantasy.

[24]Moore had a pet python, anyway, no matter where he kept it.

Chapter 7

SOME NOTES ON BEDABOOS

BEDABOO. sb. etym.dub. Possibly from
BED + TABOO or by corruption of BUGA-
BOO, cf. O.F. BUGIBUS a demon, perhaps m.
equiv. of Nightmare, a female monster. Some-
thing to be feared or avoided in conn. w. beds;
(colloq.) something not done in bed.
          Reynolds' *Dictionary* (unpublished)

> *Must we to bed indeed? Well then,*
> *Let us arise and go like men,*
> *And face with an undaunted tread*
> *The long black passage up to bed.*
>   R.L.S. in *A Child's Garden of Verses*

ONE OF the most curious things about bed is that, although there is nothing more uncongenial than the prospect of leaving it in the morning, there are few thoughts
more distasteful than the contemplation of going to bed
at night. Robert Louis Stevenson, whose *Child's Garden
of Verses* shows a really remarkable preoccupation with
bed, mainly as a place of pleasurable fantasy (a result,
no doubt, of the amount of time he was himself obliged
to spend there), evidently knew also that sense of de-
pression, almost of despair and terror, which many of us
associate with *the long black passage.*

Like George (Peanuts) Ward, Mr. Stevenson evidently had his own recipe for humanising the situation. The cot of his childhood was a boat for a solitary voyage—

> *And sometimes things to bed I take,*
> *As prudent sailors have to do:*
> *Perhaps a slice of wedding-cake,*
> *Perhaps a toy or two . . .*

Wedding cake (one must assume that weddings were frequent in the Stevenson household), though less romantic than fresh grapes, is much to be preferred to peanuts. The selectiveness of the commissariat suggests comparison with the provisions requisitioned by the Owl and the Pussy Cat. But even wedding cake leaves crumbs and is conducive to indigestion; so the case history provides us immediately with examples of two types of bedaboo—(1) bad behaviour, leading in extreme cases to the divorce courts (*vide* the case of G. B. Ward, *supra*), and (2) bad dreams, the Nemesis of Evil Living.

A standard textbook example of bedaboos involving a whole family, and evidently hereditary, is to be found in Mr. J. Thurber's work, *My Life and Hard Times*. The phobias of Briggs Beall, Aunt Sarah Shoaf and Aunt Gracie Shoaf all belong to one type of bedaboo (well known to psychiatrists), a group of engram-complexes now generally ascribed to prenatal influences such as the grim features of Welfare Workers. Brother Hermann's habit of singing in his sleep may have had a similar origin; but this particular bedaboo is generally considered principally in relation to its social effects. It is, however, impossible to make any clear distinction between different types. A regressive bedaboo (such as kelptophobia, parazombieism, disseminated cacoethes,

syneisaktism, onomatamnesia, pseudometapsychic para-
noia, struthiosity, pathological serendipity[1] or boustro-
phedon somnambulism) cannot, it is clear, be considered
in isolation from the patient's effect upon his environ-
ment—an aspect of the problem which has been neglected in the *vice versa* researches of Pavlov and even by
the Freudians.

A classic instance of the dual problem is to be found
in Froissart (Chron. III:27), where we find a gentleman
getting up in the night, putting on his armour and fighting phantoms all around the house with drawn sword.
All this, being done in his sleep as a result of a surfeit of
lampreys, peaches, malmsey or whatever was available
(or possibly under the influence of prenatal hibber-gibber
about Oedipus), can, of course, be considered primarily
from the standpoint of the somnambulist. But it will be
clear that the social angle should also be considered. A
man blindly waving a naked sword and suffering from
ignoratio hostis should at least be deprived of his weapons pending psychotherapy.

Mr. Thurber's clinical studies, *The Night the Bed Fell*,
The Night the Ghost Got In and *More Alarms at Night*
(op. cit.), all provide valuable examples of the dual
character of a bedaboo. The first rule for the avoidance
of these phenomena is undoubtedly that indicated in
some observations by a sixteenth-century bed in reply to
the poet, Timothy Kendall, who had addressed it, purely
rhetorically, and was no doubt surprised to hear it answer as follows:

> *That I may be a rest of cares*
> *And end of toiling pain,*
> *See stomach thine be not surcharged*
> *When sleep thou wouldst regain. . . .*

[1]Reynolds' Disease, in vulgar usage.

He was also to keep his head free from cares and to deem his feather bed always his grasping grave. I am not sure that the last suggestion is really conducive to peace and comfort, but can endorse the others. As to the grave, there is also Sancho Panza's opinion, in his celebrated eulogy of sleep, when he said that he knew but one thing against it—that it was too much like death.

Indeed, the meanderings of the soul during sleep—a subject which Frazer has so learnedly discussed[2]—are a common source of clinophobia. The dream of the Douglas comes to my mind:

> *I saw a dead man win a fight,*
> *And I think that man was I.*

The thought is not reassuring. False, fleeting, perjured Clarence dreamed his own death, which was coming to him, and found unwelcome leisure in the time of death to reflect upon wealth, wickedness and death in general.

Sleep in poetry is generally lauded for its blessings. John Fletcher's lyric, one of the most happily worded of all the poetic tributes, asks for delight in sweet deceiving:

> *We that suffer long annoy*
> *Are contented with a thought*
> *Through an idle fancy wrought—*

Everyone knows the tortured confession of Macbeth, the praise of Sidney, the song in Tennyson's *Lotos-Eaters*. The same attitude prevails when sleep is viewed objectively—the sleeping figure seen through the eyes of the poet—*As though a rose should shut, and be a bud again.* But even among the poets heads cannot always have been free from care or stomachs from surcharge.

Even Keats, poor harmless John, who was snuffed out by an article, and wrote as kindly as any of the boys about sleep (it was a set subject in those days for poets,

[2] See *The Golden Bough,* Vol. III, passim.

who were not considered to have made the grade until they had produced a rhymed thesis on sleep and on one or more of the seasons)—even Keats begged to be saved from a curious conscience which thrived on darkness. As for poor Wordsworth, he suffered from nightmares about the French Revolution, in which he made long orations before unjust tribunals. How often he must have woken up and struck a light to see if Fouquier-Tinville was under the bed. The dreams of W. B. Yeats caused even the boughs to wither; and Cowper lay awake thinking of burglars, whom probably he found eventually in his dreams.

But if sleep has its terrors, sleeplessness is more feared by most of us. Robert de Brunne, in *Handlyng Synne,* makes it clear that the feudal lords of the Middle Ages kept harpers handy for this reason; but drugs had also been in use from ancient times and Burton gives a good list of them from various sources in *The Anatomy of Melancholy.* Francis Bacon, according to Aubrey, would often drink a good draught of strong beer *to lay his working fancy asleep, which otherwise would keep him from sleeping a great part of the night.* The invocation of St. Vitus was another long-approved remedy— that same St. Vitus who alone would cure the *Chorus Sancti Viti* (St. Vitus' Dance to you), patron of epileptics, madmen, dancers and actors, whose aid was also sought against storms and against the bites and stings of God's problem creatures. But in spite of all recipes fear of insomnia remained one of the great bedaboos. It was among the horrors of *The City of Dreadful Night* that it was *of Night, but not of Sleep—*

Of thought and consciousness which never ceases.

Such was the curse of Macbeth, the murderer; but the condemned man in Reading Gaol slept peacefully—

Wilde's ballad records the endless vigil of his fellow
prisoners, upon whom terror had less pity.

Some few have despised sleep, but they have little
following. In Thomson's *Seasons* it is described as a
gloomy state which could have no appeal to wise men—
nothing but dead oblivion or the feverish vanity of dis-
tempered dreams. But I doubt if even Thomson or Dr.
Thomas Fuller (or any of the anti-sleepers whom I
mentioned in a previous chapter) would have cared to
toss about wide awake in a bed, unless it would be—I
was thinking of Sweet Bessie in Campion's lyric; but
anyway it is specifically stated that all that happened in
the afternoon. Imagine, however, the lives of those miserable Saxons whom the Norman conqueror forced to
extinguish all lights and fires by eight of the clock, under
his dismal curfew law. How they must have twitched and
tossed among the straw and the fleas, of a long winter's
night, waiting for the distant dawn. Or maybe the happy
clods had thick hides for the fleas and no neuroses—
O sweet content! It was, after all, Caliban who said the
last word on the sweetness of sleep, which made a poet
out of that misused drudge. And why, I wonder, did
Bottom give such a poor account of his crowded hour by
comparison with Prospero's moron?

Stories appear periodically in the press of people who
have not slept for years. A recent claimant was Ernest
Lanchberry, of West Ewell, Surrey, who must surely be
World Champion[3] as (at the age of eighty-one) he wrote

[3]The *Daily Express* mentioned an American who had
claimed, in 1930, that he had not slept for seventy-eight
years; but I figure that unless he was entered very early in
life he must be sleeping by now. The South African (also
mentioned) who claimed forty-five years of insomnia in
1934 might, of course, be still going strong. See *Daily
Express* of January 22, 23 and 25, 1951, for the details of
Mr. Lanchberry's case and subsequent correspondence.

to the *Daily Express* in 1951 that he had not slept for fifty years. He asked if any reader knew of a cure, ruling out drugs—for some unspecified reason—and offering £250 to anyone who could guarantee him six hours' sleep per night. The following day there appeared a photograph of Mr. Lanchberry, sitting in an armchair, to prove the story. It seems (from the caption) that Mr. Lanchberry last slept in 1900: it was in Hyde Park and a keeper woke him, which shows how dangerous it is to wake people sleeping in parks. Mr. Lanchberry did not consider that he was disqualified from the championship by forty minutes' sleep in 1930 because that was due to a tablet. He said he'd like to try sleep again, just to see what it was like.

The public response was immediate, though the results —so far as I am concerned—are still unknown. A woman had already rung up when the picture appeared, recommending a pillow stuffed with hops. Another suggested a cat on the counterpane. Letters appeared advocating onions—raw or boiled in milk—or a bottle of stout. One said boil the stout; another said drink it in bed, from the bottle. Hot-drink remedies varied from milk with salt in it to black coffee with a dash of mustard. . . .

Bad dreams and insomnia, however, are but two of the more obvious things to be avoided in bed. Their nuisance value is self-evident; and among such *a priori* bedaboos it is now necessary to add a few words about *Cimex lectularius,* the great pest of the seventeenth and eighteenth centuries, not unknown even in our time. How many must have said (with Clarence), *O, I have passed a miserable night*—and all on account of little *Cimex*. I remember that, when I first walked into the Chelsea Reference Library in search of some general

information about the subject of this book, I turned up
Bed in the catalogue and was impressed to find little but
the following cryptic cross-reference:

BEDBUGS—REFER TO BUGS

Actually, of course, there *was* other information about
bed in our excellent library. I do not want you to form a
false impression, as I am not lacking in local patriotism.
But to find it I had to plod through *Bed Manners*,[4]
Bedale, Beddall, Beddard, Beddington, Beddoe, Beddoes,
Bede, Bedel, Bedford, Bedfordshire, Bedier, Bedingfield
and Bedouin, until I reached BEDS (plural) beneath
which the crock of true gold lay hidden.

Nevertheless, having been so firmly referred to bedbugs at the outset, I did follow up the cross-reference
and soon found myself in a very interesting world. Here
I was, then, with Lin Yutang—and what companion in
all the world could be more agreeable, no matter what
the quest?—considering (*With Love and Irony*) whether
Cimex lectularius exists in China. As every literate person should read that book, and especially this essay on
attitudes in the twenty-first chapter, I will say no more
of it: the quintessential wisdom of Dr. Lin is not to be
digested, distilled, tabloided or otherwise served in concentrated doses for those who are too lazy to seek it at
its source. But whereas, to Lin's mind, the bug is a mere
pawn in a parable, to me it is still a bug.

When I was talking about large beds, not so long ago,
I omitted to mention one that stood, until 1824, at the

---

[4]The treatise by Hopton and Balliol, which I found somewhat disappointing, probably because it deals with aspects
of domestic life of which I know nothing. *From Bed to
Worse* (Robert Benchley) is mostly about Worse, as the
title implies.

Mansion House. Though unequal to the twelve by twelve of Ware and many giants of later days, it was a good welterweight, nine foot by six foot eight. The circumstances of its ultimate eviction were recorded by the *Sunday Times* of December 12, 1824. It appears that a Corporation Committee had been held during the previous week, especially to consider this *grand city state bed,* built to hold the portly lord mayors of London. We are told of its magnificent curtains of rich damask satin, embroidered with gold, and of its original cost—no less than £3000—but its present condition was evidently deplorable.

A certain Mr. Savage had alleged that it was not fit to be seen. *He had examined it as closely as he durst do, and he ascertained that there was living evidence of the impropriety of keeping it any longer in the grand dormitory. . . .*

A MEMBER: Sir, you do not surely mean——
MR. SAVAGE: Indeed, I do; it is almost incredible, but I do assure you that it is the receptacle of all sorts of vermin. . . .

The conditions in which London lord mayors lived do not appear to have been fortunate. (I have remarked elsewhere that—half a century or more after this deplorable discovery regarding the mayoral couch—nematoid worms were found by the hundred in the drinking water at the Mansion House.)

However, as the heavy levity of the *Sunday Times* phrased it, there was a good riddance of the bugbear (italicised as *Bug*-bear, in case Wordsworth or somebody should miss the point). Times had changed. Pepys had once found a bed *good but lousy,* which sounds odd. Indeed, it had, he said, *made us merry.* On the other hand, Sir Thomas Styles (in a later age) had committed *felo-de-se* on account of the bugs in Portugal, during the Peninsular War. Strange tastes, however, are still to be found even in modern times. According to Nina Hamnett, Modigliani cultivated a spider as his companion, and could not even remake his bed for fear of disturbing it or its web. Nothing, *dans cette galère,* should surprise us, and when this book is published I expect to receive numerous letters about some eminent surrealist who makes a household pet of *Cimex lectularius,* on the principle of Oblomov's servant, the man who asked his master (in Goncharov's story): *And what would sleep be without bugs?*

According to a special study of bugs published by order of the British Museum Trustees,[5] their association with man probably dates from the time when bats and men both lived in caves. In the sixteenth century, when men and bugs began to go places and get about, seafaring bugs left the Mediterranean, which had been their home for centuries, and first appeared in England. I cannot tell you under what flag they discovered America, but there is no doubt that they arrived, perhaps in the *Mayflower*—who knows?—and some say in timber; but the Best People are skeptical. Bugs must also have been among the blessings conferred (along with English civilisation) on the people of Ireland. Not that the Irish in those days went in for beds, as we understand them, to any great extent. They made their beds by throwing *brats* on the heather or whatever was handy, *brats* being the woollen mantles then worn, like those which Scottish Highlanders pin to the left shoulder. (It was a far cry from the *O'Dearest* mattresses now advertised so widely

[5]*The Bed-Bug,* by A. W. McKenny-Hughes, D.I.C., and C. G. Johnson, B.Sc., Ph.D. (British Museum Natural History Series, No. 5), 1942.

in the island.) Even in England, of course, it was not unknown for a sturdy rogue to take the measure of a mort beneath a bawdy bush, but the practice was not common and habitual. An increasing number slept in beds, and these very soon became bug-ridden—especially in the seventeenth century.

Remedies were sought in bugbane or bugwort (*Cimicifuga foetida*), in *Agaricus muscarius* or bug agaric, in secret remedies of guaranteed efficacy. It was my pleasant duty not long since to study the records of an institution known as Y^e Friends Workhouse, at Clerkenwell, from which there grew the school[6] at which I received whatever education I ever had. From these records it appears that a certain Christopher Fox had a nostrum which was considered almost miraculous. I quote from the Workhouse Committee Minutes of 1722:

THE STEWARD IS ORDERED TO GIVE A COPPY OF THE FOLLOWING CERTIFICATE TO CHRISTOPHER FOX.

Christopher Fox In Hollywell Lane Shoreditch Undertakes to Destroy Buggs

These are to Certify that in the year 1721 we agreed with him to destroy the aforesaid vermin in 4 Rooms Containing 49 Beds all which was performed with a Liquid so inofencive that the Beds were made use of the same Night and were so Effectually performed that notwithstanding the Beds Walls Ceiling &c were Exceeding full yet upon diligent Observation now the Weather grows warm have not found above three Live Buggs, and any one who pleases to Come to the House under-

[6]The Friends School, Saffron Walden (Essex), where these records are now kept. The school celebrates the two hundred and fiftieth aniversary of its strange origin in 1952.

mentioned may see the Beds and have further Satisfaction

> From the Committee of Y^e Workhouse of
> the People Calld Quakers near Clerken-
> well
>> Signed by their Order 28: ^mo 3: 1722
>> Richd Hutton
>>> Steward

First to be noted is the importance attached to this
exploit, the solemnity with which the Friends, evidently
much impressed, expressed their approbation. Third
month would, of course, have been May (the year still
began in March) which accounts for the warm weather.
The *three Live Buggs* which crawled miserably out, like
survivors of a doomed army, were evidently considered
of small account. In the following November there is a
memorandum of an

> agreement between Richard Hutton Steward and
> Christopher Fox by Order of the Committee that
> the said Christopher Fox shall keep and Preserve
> Friends Workhouse all and every part of the Said
> House and Beds Standing or hereafter may Stand
> therein Clear and Free from Buggs and in Con-
> sideration hereof the said Richard Hutton shall
> duely pay the said Christopher Fox Thirty Shil-
> lings per year. . . .

Marginal rubrics to these transactions include *Proposals
about Buggs and Christ ffox agreed with.* How long this
periodic debugation continued I do not know. Richard
Hutton, the Steward, kept a private notebook, full of
useful information, in which he once jotted down a
recipe for destroying *Buggs*—some concoction recommended to him by a physician—so perhaps he tried to

save the institution the thirty shillings a year paid to Fox. Whatever the explanation, I am inclined to think that the bugs won in the long run. The beds were certainly full of vermin in 1754.[7]

This was in the Augustan Age of *Cimex lectularius*. A much earlier reference to bugs is quoted in my handbook. It seems that in Thomas Moffett's *Insectorum Theatrum* there is a record by Thomas Penny, the entomologist (who had done so much towards the compilation of knowledge which resulted in Moffett's book), showing that two ladies of high degree were much troubled by bugs at Mortlake in 1583. The present bugs of Mortlake may well belong to one of the oldest families of *Cimices* now in England, by this account. The name applied to this insect is believed by some to derive from the Welsh *byg,* meaning a hopgoblin (hence possibly *bogie, bogle* and *bugaboo*)—in fact, if this be the case, the bug is none other than the Boyg, so well known to Ibsen fans. Whichever way Peer Gynt turned, the Boyg always seemed to be there—the identification seems to be almost complete. So this crimson rambler, the new Terror by Night, may well have found a name from existing folklore when it arrived on some captured galleon among the ingots and doubloons. Whatever the truth about this entomic etymology, it is not known when the word was first applied to the invaders. The B.M. pamphlet quotes another early reference to the creatures: it seems that even a Pope (John XXI) had mentioned them in his *Theatrum Pauperum.* And the versatile Welsh physician who did this work into English in 1585 rendered the passage *small stynkinge wormes which live in paper and wod, called Cimices.* They were, it appears,

[7]W. Beck and T. F. Ball, *The London Friends' Meetings* (London, 1869), record this disheartening fact.

used internally as a cure for fever—an unappetising form of therapy.

For some unspecified and hitherto unexplained reason it appears that these *Cimices* rapidly multiplied in the English capital after the Fire of London (1666). Like trade, they also followed the flag: Messrs. Johnson and McKenny-Hughes inform me that *the bed-bug has been carried by commerce throughout the world and is now a cosmopolitan insect.* It was, I believe, one of the few possible points of view neglected by Lin Yutang: so far as I remember, he never considered the line that the bugs of China were brought by the Europeans, which is surely very probable. A few years after the exploits of Christopher Fox in Clerkenwell John Southall's *Treatise of Buggs* (1730), surveying the progress over the past sixty years, said that they were *every season increasing upon us.*

The terminology of entomologists when discussing *Cimices* is fascinating to a layman. The person preyed upon is referred to as the host, as though one threw parties for their benefit. The next moment one is reading about *nymphs;* and after letting the imagination be jolted into a new and startling world of entomomythology one realises suddenly that the term is purely technical, that these are no callipygian naiads, enacting idyllic themes with shepherd hemiptera playing their pipes in the microcosm of the bed. . . . Their habits, as recorded by McKenny-Hughes and Johnson, are equally disconcerting. *They loiter over their meals,* pause awhile (perhaps to say grace?) and then *run away as fast as possible.* As it is also said that they do not survive the winter in most unheated houses it does make one wonder whether central heating is such a good thing after all. It would be worth while, surely, to go without that comfort just to spite little *Cimex.* Perhaps it is just

the cold that keeps them out of my basement—as I survey the decaying woodwork I cannot see much else to
discourage them, unless they do not approve of my blood
group.

The biography of *Cimex* is somewhat horrifying. *On
hatching, the nymph immediately goes off in search of
shelter. . . . It can live at low temperatures for three or
four months without food.* So you can't starve it out by
going away for a spell and shutting the place up. You
merely inflict unnecessary and pointless cruelty, because
the creature cannot moult until it has fed. Naturally it
wants very much to moult. It casts its skin five times
before reaching maturity, *each time getting a little larger
and a little darker.* It is only a plain statement of fact;
but oh, how sinister it sounds. The domestic life has the
same indefinable suggestion of horror about it: *The laying of fertile eggs by the adult females must be preceded
by a feed and mating.* It is that wedding breakfast which
makes one shudder, with the picture we get of a quiet,
well-ordered home life. Though a nocturnal vampire by
habit, *Cimex* will feed by day *if conditions are favour-
able.* What conditions? It makes one look around anx-
iously in broad daylight. As to the bug's preferences or
fads, it is very particular: not only does it feed exclusively on blood, but it will only take it by piercing the
skin. It is absolutely no use to leave some in a saucer
and hope the creatures will lay off.

Of all bedaboos I think *Cimex* is the most terrifying.
Even the other pests cannot compete—the gnat, the
mosquito and the common flea (compared to a *girning
wife,* as the Scottish proverb has it, both *waukrife bed
fellows*). And yet it appears that on one point at least
bedbugs have been libelled in the past. We are assured,
for example, that they have been debited with cannibalism, but bug does not eat bug. Much as they enjoy

going places, bugs are essentially sentimental; and nostalgic longings will take them back to previous haunts. (*Bed bugs,* my authority states, *seem to be attracted to places where they have congregated previously.* It is like Zionism[8] and that sort of thing.) The stories one hears about beds isolated by placing the legs in pails of water or saucers of paraffin, only to be bombarded by bugs dropping from the ceiling, are apparently no myths but well-attested factual records. The authors of this pamphlet seem unable to account for the attraction at a distance, having already stated that *Cimex lectularius* can only be attracted (by heat, and possibly by smell) from a distance of one inch. Personally I am prepared to leave the entomologists to square that for themselves—what bothers me is not the long-distance attraction but the cunning strategy involved in these aerial attacks, of which there are said to be numerous reliable accounts.

Among remedies mentioned, some are not recommended. You can introduce the small Red House Ant, which will prey upon bugs, but few people appreciate ants in their pants, or even in their pantries. An insect known as *Reduvius personatus* sucks blood from *Cimex lectularius* when the latter has fed; but this is not very helpful, and it appears that when *Reduvius* cannot find a well-fed *Cimex* he takes a bite at you instead, which is even more unpleasant than an ordinary bug-bite. Again you can introduce into your house a spider whose monicker is *Thanatos flavidus,* but many people do not like spiders all that much either. Another remedy even less likely to prove popular is *Chelifer cancroides,* described as a pseudo scorpion, of no fixed abode.

[8]Not to be taken too literally. The seacoast now occupied by the Zionists was not among the territory stolen by their ancestors, but belonged to the Philistines and other ancestors of the Palestine Arabs, only recently driven into the desert.

As to cockroaches, it is absolutely useless to keep tame ones in your house in the hope that they will hunt for bugs. There is no truth in the statement, says my handbook: *they may, in fact, live happily together in the same house.* (What we—or rather, the statesmen—might learn from them.) It appears that there is no other way out of it—cleanliness just has to be practised, and a number of insecticides are also recommended. (Certain chemicals, such as orthodichlorbenzene, are apparently not so good: a sinister warning threatens the user with *ill-health, if nothing worse.* And above all, don't use prussic acid on your bedding, or you may regret it.) On the whole, bad cases are apparently best left to the experts. An infallible remedy was, it is true, widely advertised in Ohio many years ago, so Mr. Jack York informs me on the authority of his father. For a mere fifty cents a firm in Cincinnati guaranteed satisfaction on receipt of mail order with cash. In return they supplied two small blocks of wood, on one of which was printed the words *Lay bug on this,* the other bearing the inscription: *Hit bug with this.* This method had obvious drawbacks, and the manufacturer, after making a fortune, was obliged to retire from business owing to the interference of the United States postal authorities with this rugged American individualism. Private enterprise was stifled once more.

Among the Jains of India, whose religion forbids the destruction of life (even the life of little *Cimex*) a method has been perfected of preserving the sacred existence of the bug whilst avoiding his attentions. It is, however, only practicable for the rich by means of a ruthless exploitation of poverty. *Wealthy Jains,* says an authority, *pay able bodied men, who can spare some blood, to sleep in their bug-ridden cots.* When the

Cimices are satisfied the employee is dismissed and the owner of the bed takes his place.[9]

Such meticulous respect for life has always deeply impressed me, although, as a matter of fact, I am not a meat-eater and never kick the cat. But William Cowper, you will remember, remarked in one of his lyrical flights:

> *I would not enter on my list of friends*
> *Tho' graced with polished manners and fine sense*
> *Yet wanting sensibility, the man*
> *Who needlessly sets foot upon a worm.*

He was not, however, a hundred-per-center. He was not a Jain. Elsewhere he qualified the word *needlessly:*

> *A visitor unwelcome into scenes*
> *Sacred to neatness and repose, th'alcove,*
> *The chamber, or refectory, may die:*
> *A necessary act incurrs no blame.*

The distinction is meticulous. We can imagine the poet carefully working it out before his no less laborious statement of the case. With a good conscience he could crush a bug in his bed or take a swipe at a mosquito in th'alcove, and then sit down to cross a delinquent out of his address book for treading on a worm.

There is another type of bedaboo which derives, not from natural and common causes, such as nightmares, insomnia, vermin and the interaction of these, but from custom, religion, fashion, superstition or personal idiosyncrasy. Some of these bedaboos have—or can be given —rational explanations; others are harder to explain. I do not propose to differentiate, but merely to jot down some of the many things which can complicate a per-

[9]P. Thomas, *Hindu Religion, Customs and Manners* (Bombay n.d.), p. 55.

son's bed-life. I list them as bedaboos simply because I
consider most of them are better avoided if the bed is to
be the place of relaxation which it ought to be.

Theophrastus (among many others) has described the
particular bedaboo to which misers are prone—the passage is quoted, with many similar ones, by Burton.[10] We
see the wretch, lying in his bed and asking his wife if all
is made fast. Refusing to be reassured by her, he rises
naked from his bed and searches the premises with a
lantern. The moral of this is to keep your money, if you
have any, in a bank, and to insure any other valuables
you may possess. This particular eccentricity, however,
being among the causes of insomnia, comes properly under that head. The rest of my examples belong to the gay
science of anthropology, the delight of the dilettante,
pasture of the geophagist, playground of the serendip-
itist, and heavenly manna of charlatans such as myself.

You remember that Victorian doctor, Robert Macnish? Among his curious observations about sleep there
is another one worth a moment's attention. He quoted
a fellow physician to the effect that *women who love
their husbands generally lie upon the right side*. The
reason for this belief is not far to seek and will be found
in the Song of Solomon—twice, in fact, so much importance was attached to it—in Chapter II:6 and in
Chapter VIII:3. This is but one of many rules which
might be classified as forms of Bed Ritual. Many apply
only to the double bed, but some are equally concerned
with all beds whatsoever. Thus a friend who has lived
most of his life in Germany and Poland assures me that
great importance is attached in parts of Germany and
eastern Europe to the angle at which any bed is placed:
it must be in line with the walls, and not placed diag-

[10]*Anatomy of Melancholy,* First Partition, Sec. 2, Memb. 3,
subs. 12.

onally, as a bed which does not follow the angles of the room will attract and encourage evil spirits. A similar belief is recorded of some primitive peoples.[11]

In some societies the most complicated taboos surround the bed, making it (one would think) anything but a place of comfort and relaxation. In a radio talk by Dr. Kenneth Little, published later in *The Listener*,[12] we were informed that, among the Mende of Sierra Leone, it is considered incest if a man sits on the bed of his mother or his sister. I don't know if it works the other way round; but when I consider that the bed is almost the only place to sit in this room (even the floor being littered with books) I am very glad that I do not live in Sierra Leone. The stern morality of some primitive societies has not, I think, received sufficient recognition, especially from missionaries, who should have appreciated it. I remember reading somewhere of some people in the New Hebrides whose punishment for adultery was that culprits should be eaten, showing that cannibalism (which has many other demonstrable merits) can also be used as a deterrent, like hanging and other forms of ritual murder. A milder deterrent for the same offence is known among the Arapesh of New Guinea—the yams in the garden show their disapproval by vanishing, like the Baker who set eyes on the Boojum.

For those whose inclinations are humanitarian, the Arapesh method will commend itself and even the stern code of cannibal punishment is dignified by comparison with the behaviour of some civilised people. But one of

[11]According to Raymond Firth (*We, the Tikopia* [London, 1936]), the Tikopia, when sleeping, avoid letting their feet point towards the sacred side of the house, where the dead are buried. There are numerous further examples of the importance attached to orientation.

[12]*Values in Primitive Society, The Listener*, September 14, 1950.

the oddest bedroom scenes in literature, of which this reminds me, is to be found in Malory (Book X, Chapter XXIV). The story goes that the good knight Sir Lamorak de Galis came by night to the dowager Queen of Orkney, sister of Arthur and widow of King Lot. Unfortunately for the queen she had a son, Gaheris, who must have seen far too many Greek tragedies and fancied the rôle of Orestes. Entering without warning and fully armed, Gaheris removed his mother's head with a stroke of his sword. Thus far his behaviour was entirely classical and merely illustrates a bedaboo too well known to be worth discussion—but it was precisely because Gaheris and Lamorak immediately began a tedious argument that I find the incident worth mentioning. With the corpse still lying between them, son and lover (the latter described as being in his shirt—another mediaeval exception) recriminated mutually as here follows, in what I can only describe as low dudgeon:

> LAMORAK: Ah, Sir Gaheris, knight of the Table Round, foul and evil have ye done, and to you great shame. Alas, why have ye slain your mother that bare you? With more right ye should have slain me.
> GAHERIS: This offence hast thou done, notwithstanding a man is born to offer service; but yet shouldst thou beware with whom thou meddlest, for thou hast put me and my brethren to a shame, and thy father slew our father; and thou to lie by our mother is too much shame for us to support. And as for thy father, King Pellinore, my brother Sir Gawaine and I slew him.
> LAMORAK: Ye did him the more wrong, for my father slew not your father; it was Balin le Savage: and as yet my father's death is not revenged.

GAHERIS: Leave those words, for an thou speak-
est feloniously I will slay thee. But by cause thou
art naked I am ashamed to slay thee.[13] But wit thou
well, in what place I may get thee I shall slay thee;
and now my mother is quit of thee[14]; and with-
draw thee and take thine armour, that thou were
gone.

This *post mortem* inquest into the antecedents of the
crime, held on the spot by the murderer and such a
near party to the case, is probably without parallel in
literature. King Arthur, we learn, was *passing wroth* on
hearing of his sister's death and sent Sir Gaheris knight-
erranting somewhere. Gawaine was also wroth: his line
was that Gaheris should have bumped off Lamorak and
not his own mother, who happened to be Gawaine's
mother too. Launcelot, a shrewd, moderate and practical
man, told the king: *I dare say that it was wrought by
treason; and I dare say ye shall lose that good knight,
Sir Lamorak, the which is a great pity*. With an eye to
Dame Guenever, Launcelot may have seen the danger of
letting Gaheris establish a precedent in such highhanded
dealing. The cold-blooded *tu quoque* in which Gaheris
and Lamorak had indulged would have been reasonable
enough if the young man had not struck first and argued

[13]Naked, as the reference to the shirt indicates, only means
unarmed in this context. Gaheris did not, apparently, feel
the same restriction in dealing with his mamma.

[14]English understatement. The filial piety of Gaheris would
make an interesting study, but it is not in my field. He
might be profitably compared with Ptolemy IV, known as
Philopator, who murdered both his parents, no doubt from
motives of duty and affection. St. Julian the Hospitaller
killed both his parents in bed. It was all a mistake, though.
As you can read in Caxton's version of the Golden Legend,
he was *abashed*—no doubt another case of understatement.

afterwards, a point which may have impressed the lover of Guenever. It was certainly the sort of thing that must lead to bad feeling; and it would have tended to make the bed a very unsafe place for the queens of those days. Indeed, Launcelot was soon to have some rather unpleasant experiences himself, and so was Tristan. Their stories are also worth recalling as they illustrate the danger attendant upon untidy sleeping arrangements.

First, as to Tristan. In the castle of King Mark, where the peers of Cornwall lay in the king's chamber, there was no more than a spear's length between Tristan and the queen—indeed, a single bound cleared the distance, for on that fatal occasion when Tristan wanted to say good-bye to Iseult (he was off first thing in the morning and there simply had not been another opportunity to explain) we read of his springing from his sleeping place to that of the queen. This unusual method of approaching Her Majesty was due, as you will no doubt recall, to the fact that an unpleasant creature called Frocin had sprinkled the intermediate floor space with flour. This Frocin was an undersized under-cover man, a dirty little house dick employed by King Mark. Tristan evidently figured he had that jump sewed up; but he never allowed for a wound he had in the leg, which he had forgotten to doctor, the way it dripped blood about. So there it was plain for all to observe that Triss and Iss had been saying good-bye; and a great deal of trouble came of it all.

I can't remember whether Malory used that story—it is certainly all there in the old French romance. But the Tristram of the Morte d'Arthur was in plenty of trouble about the Queen of Cornwall even without that; and anyway Malory's Launcelot was involved in a very similar incident. I can even find the place. It was in Book XIX when Meliagrance put the snatch on Guenever and took her off to his castle, after a fight in which the queen's bodyguard were all badly cut up. In due course Launcelot arrived to rescue the whole party and Meliagrance surrendered unconditionally. Peace was made, in fact, by the intervention of Guenever herself, who was anxious to have the whole business hushed up; and everybody settled down for the night.

It is at this point that we find once more the untidy arrangements noted already at the court of King Mark. The queen, we are told, would in no wise suffer the wounded knights—her bodyguard—to be from her; and she insisted that they should be *laid within draughts by her chamber, upon beds and pillows.* Her intention was entirely kindly, but it involved them all in a most unpleasant scandal. Launcelot, who was not one to lose such an opportunity, must needs pay a nocturnal visit to his mistress, which involved pulling the iron bars out of her window—a feat whereby one of his hands was cut to the bone. Like Tristan, he therefore left a trail, which was naturally attributed to one of the wounded knights; and Meliagrance was not slow to take advantage of such evidence. Any sleuth in a modern whodunnit would have come to the window evidence next, but mediaeval wits were somewhat dim and trial by ordeal took the place now occupied by fingerprints and alibis. The queen was accused of misconduct with one of the wounded knights, and Launcelot was confronted with the awkward situation of being the one person able to explain but quite unprepared to do so. All he could say to Meliagrance, in fact, was that he had no business to be looking at the queen's bed before she was up, which was true enough, but hardly an answer. Of course, everything ended very happily, Meliagrance coming to a bad end in spite of all his skulduggery and scrambunction. Guenever's character was completely vindicated by the one argument really respected in the Age of Chivalry—a variant of the *argumentum a fortiori*.

The moral of these two stories is clear enough: it is to avoid compromising situations, unless, of course, you live in a society which allows you to brazen out the evidence by throwing gauntlets around—and that is not much use unless you happen to be in the Launcelot class. Hence quite a powerful taboo is attached, among the civilised people of England, to the etiquette of the bedroom. A man and woman can be alone together anywhere else at any time of the day or night without scandal. But the mere word *bedroom* is the *Open Sesame* to divorce.[15] Juries shudder, judges wake up and adjust their spectacles, hardened lawyers contrive to appear shocked and a low murmur of excited curiosity among the spectators makes it necessary to clear the court without delay before the witness, under remorseless cross-examination, confesses to wearing bedsocks. In Victorian times it was considered daring to refer to a lady's ankles: it is still a rash move in a British court of law to admit that one goes to bed. *I submit that you went to bed,* rasps Counsel. *To bed, eh?* he repeats with a sinister scowl at the jury box; and the judge makes a careful note as he adds: *In your bedroom, I take it?* The members of the jury, who have been unable to follow anything up to this point, are immediately convinced that you are a Mormon of the *beau temps* convicted out of your own mouth of sleeping in a bed. You are considered capable of anything.

Variations on the bed taboo could, I am sure, furnish quite an interesting discourse by one who was more

[15]Divorce by collusion, though illegal, is the most common practice in England. Young women are well paid merely to make a dent in a bed and play cards for the rest of the night in a hotel bedroom—evidence of *crim. con.*

addicted to the films than I am. My impression is that
Hollywood has a horror of double beds and that in
Anglo-American films generally no two people are to
be seen in bed at the same place and time, unless, of
course, they are Laurel and Hardy. Perhaps I have exaggerated, but such is the impression I have received. The
French film tradition is quite different, obviously, being
uninfluenced by Anglo-Saxon legal bedaboos.[16]

This forensic *argumentum ad lectulum* (with its deriv-
atives among the phantoms of the cave, theatre and
marketplace) may itself be a phantom of the tribe, having some roots in human nature itself, so numerous and
varied are the taboos associated with beds, so wide their
geographical distribution. Even the briefest glance at
The Golden Bough is sufficient to show that when
Learned Counsel dins BED into the ears of the jury distant tom-toms beat to the rhythm of his voice. Mumbo-
jumbo is, in fact, on the move.

Sir James Frazer, in his first volume,[17] tells us that
among the Esquimaux of Aivilik and Iglulik the bedding
must not be raised up while the men are hunting on ice,
lest this should cause the ice to crack. The same authority assures us that if the Bushmen make bad shots when
they are hunting they attribute their poor marksmanship
to the fact that *the children at home are playing on the
men's beds or the like*. The importance of his bed to the
hunter is very clear from other instances cited by Frazer.

[16]Grand opera (especially the work of Wagner) provides
another contrast. My friend Dr. Felix Gross saw a bed collapse on the stage of the Royal Opera at Naples, under the
weight of the *prima donna,* during a performance of *La
Bohème.* The lady was playing the part of Mimi, who was
assumed to be dying of consumption. (Was she Tetrazzini?)

[17]*The Golden Bough* (London, 1917), Vol. I, pp. 121 and
123, where the sources of all the useful information in this
paragraph are to be found.

The wife of a Wagogo must not lie on her face in bed.
If her husband is unsuccessful or is attacked by a lion
he knows she has been unfaithful. An elephant hunter,
in the same part of East Africa, will give up the chase
and return home if he hears of his wife's misconduct—
not, as one might suppose, in order to register his protest, but because his wife's behaviour gives a subtle advantage to the elephant, by whom the hunter will be
killed or maimed if he remains on the spot. In Bolivia
the Moxos Indians are well aware that a hunter whose
wife is unfaithful will be bitten by a snake or a jaguar.
The exacting requirements of the Aleutians, who hunt
sea otters, involve even the beds of their sisters; for a
slip on the part of either wife or sister will ruin the
hunt.

To a mind like my own, accustomed to look always
for a simple and practical reason before dropping a
random bucket into psychic cesspits, the explanation
seems tolerably clear. Surely there must be the Old
Husbands' Tales just as some are attributed to Old
Wives; and I can think of no better or more likely tale
for an Old Husband to have invented than one which
scared his wife into good behaviour when he was away
on business. Men being of one kidney—Esquimaux,
Bushmen, East Africans, South American Indians or
Alaskans—what more natural than a story such as this
among those who lacked that simple device with the lock
and key[18] which was known to the crusaders? Here was
a *ceinture de chasteté* framed from a cultivated inhibi-
tion. But I must confess that Sir James has some further

[18]See the rare and recondite work on this subject by my
friend Dr. Dingwall. It is interesting that the revival of these
mediaeval gadgets was advocated by an Edinburgh doctor
(John Moodie) in 1848 and that they were advertised in
France as late as 1885; but they do not appear in the Kinsey
Report.

propositions regarding the bed which are harder to explain.

Thus we find that when a Dyak of Borneo is away on business (in this case head-hunting) his wife must wear a sword all day. She may neither sleep during that time nor retire until 2 A.M., when she still sleeps with this symbolic weapon, lest her husband should be surprised by an enemy and have his own head collected by misadventure. If the hunter is unmarried, his sister must abide by the same rules. In other parts of Borneo different precautions are taken when the men are away in the front line, these precautions including the opening of the roof before dawn so that the distant warrior may not oversleep in the morning. A similar custom is reported of the Sea Dyaks of Banting in Sarawak (that unfortunate country so recently gobbled up by a gang of crooks at Whitehall, who bleat about justice and liberty—but I must not start on the crimes of the British Labour Government, for there is no end to them). Nearer to my own conjecture, perhaps, is the custom of the Malays, whose pillows and sleeping mats must be kept rolled up while they are away fighting. If anyone else were to use them, says Frazer, the absent warrior's courage would fail and disaster would befall him.[19]

Whatever male subtlety may have contributed to the engendering and preservation of such customs, there is no doubt that Sir James Frazer was right in classifying them under the heading of *Homoeopathic or Imitative Magic*. The Sea Dyak women, like so many others already briefly noted, are taught to believe that the safety of the husband in war depends upon the wife's fidelity. But their anxiety to keep their own limbs supple lest the warriors should grow stiff in the joints at once suggests another form of sympathetic magic, which we have

[19]Op. cit., Vol. I, pp. 127–28. Many similar examples follow.

already considered—I refer to the *couvade,* where the
positions are reversed and man takes his share in the
business of childbirth. It was probably for fear of sympathetic magic—according to Frazer—that the followers of Pythagoras considered it important, when rising
from sleep, to smooth away the impression left by the
body on the bedclothes: much harm could come to a
man from such an impression. A consideration of other
Pythagorean precepts makes it clear enough that similar
beliefs underly them all[20]; though Clement of Alexandria, when discussing what he considered the symbolism
of Pythagoras, gave these maxims a very different interpretation. The bedclothes were shaken, according to
Clement, as an indication of virtuous intentions—sleep
and pleasure abandoned for the toils of working life,
the blanket of darkness and its sweet illusions pierced
by pitiless daylight.

My concluding reflections on bedaboos are concerned
with unpleasant habits and customs which are to be deplored in the bedroom. For example, ever since Roman
times (see Martial, *Epigrams,* XIV, 56) false teeth have
been in use[21] and most people get bored with them

[20]One prohibited eating off a chair, another the stirring of
the fire if a sword was in the house—see Plutarch on Isis
and Osiris and other examples given by Clement of Alexandria (*Miscellanies,* V, Chapter 5). For peculiar mani-
festations of sympathetic magic compare the chapter *De
Stercoris humani usu magico seu sympathetico* in Schurig's
Chylologia, a work with which Francis Barrett was evidently
familiar when writing *The Magus, or Celestial Intelligencer,*
a standard thesis on such arts.

[21]According to Pliny, dog's teeth or pumice were the usual
materials. The art of making false teeth may even have been
known in ancient Egypt. It was lost in the Middle Ages, but
recovered in the sixteenth century, when a set was worn by
a nephew of Sir John Blagrave. King James IV of Scotland
used to pay his subjects to allow him to draw their teeth,

sooner or later. A great-aunt of mine once lost her denture and had the entire household ivory hunting. When it was evident that the teeth were not to be found, my aunt remembered a crust which she had unsuccessfully assaulted and eventually thrown to her little dog. It was possible, she argued, that she might have inadvertently discarded her denture, firmly implanted in the crust (like the sword in the stone) and that the dog . . . She insisted upon the administration of strong medicine, the suspect being kept under close observation, but all in vain. It was not until months later that my cousin Amy, absent-mindedly putting her hand down the side of a large armchair in which she was sitting, was sharply bitten. The explanation was simple enough—somewhere in the back or side of her voluminous skirt my great-aunt had a large poacher's pocket (perhaps several) where she kept oddments; and when disengaging her denture, preparatory to a postprandial dose, she had mistaken that oubliette in the armchair, the home of lost coins and penknives, for her own pocket.

But never mind my aunt. The point is that people who wear dentures, stays and other restricting or galling objects sometimes like to relax,[22] especially when going to

---

as he was an amateur of the art; but he does not appear to have provided them with replacements, which were probably unknown to him. (See Lilian Lindsay, *A Short History of Dentistry* [London, 1933], and Dr. Cabanès, *Moeurs Intimes,* Vol. I, chapter on *La Propreté de la Bouche.*)

[22]Actually the same aunt—I think it was she, anyway—once in her youth slept all night in her clothes because, by some misfortune, she sojourned in a purely male household and there was nobody whom she could ask to unlace her. But apparently some women of that period even slept in their corsets by preference, in the interests of the fashionable figures they wished to cultivate.

sleep, as Herrick said of a contemporary:

Six teeth he has, whereof twice two are known
Made of a Haft that was a mutton bone
Which not for use, but merely for the sight
He weares all day, and drawes those teeth at night.

And of such persons there are still some to be found who think nothing of leaving a denture, perhaps in a glass, to grin at all who enter the room like a skeleton at an Egyptian banquet. This is a bedaboo most emphatically to be avoided, especially by those who like to receive their visitors in a *lit de parade*.

It is probably no longer necessary to warn the reader against the characteristically mediaeval habit of expectoration, though in the British Museum (an institution which naturally preserves all relics of the past) there is a notice on the stairs leading down to the men's lavatories, reminding studious but possibly rather mediaeval (i.e., middle-aged) readers to refrain from spitting. How common this habit was at one time has been shown by Dom Louis Gougaud in his *Anciennes Coûtumes Claustrales* (Vienne, 1930). The unknown author of the *Regula Magistri*[23]—I am afraid this is going to prove a worse hobbyhorse than my great-aunt's denture—this anonymous sage of the seventh or eighth century even felt it necessary to give directions to monks as to how they should spit when singing psalms, presumably in church. In two passages he enjoins them to spit backwards, over the shoulder, and then to cross themselves quickly, for fear of spitting on an angel. As another authority found it necessary to point out, it was particularly undesirable to spit at the altar; and penalties

[23]Capita XLVII (*de disciplina psalmendi*) and XLVIII (*de reverentia orationis*)—see Migne's *Patrologiae*, LXXXVIII, 1009.

were prescribed for this (apparently not unusual) offence.[24]

People who spat in all directions when in church were clearly capable of anything. Before the invention of the cuspidor the most that could be expected was that one should do some smart footwork (*ut quod spuitur*, read an ancient Benedictine rule, *pedibus conculcetur*).[25] At last, and none too soon, spittoons were devised and liberally supplied in the churches. Gougaud (op cit., pp. 42–43) has shown that Benedictines had to be prohibited in spite of these spittoons (*arculae*) from spitting on the church floor whilst at the altar.[26] It is therefore not remarkable that monks should have been addicted to spitting in their dormitories; and as late as 1690 a regulation at Notre Dame de la Trappe forbade brothers to defile the dormitory walls. Some persons of rank even prided themselves on their proficiency in the art of expectoration; and Cabanès, in his essay on *Le Crachoir* (*Moeurs Intimes*, Vol. I), tells of one such, the Sieur Boutard, who visited the Vicomtesse d'Auchy one evening and delivered a lecture on different ways of spitting in society. He distinguished fifty-two separate techniques, which he demonstrated on the lady's carpet, after which he was appointed to an important diplomatic post.

[24]*Si quis emittit sputa, et contingit altare, viginti quatuor psalmos; si parietem attingit, sex.* This from the *Regula Monachorum* of St. Columbanus in Migne, op. cit. LXXX, 217, 222. Curiously enough, the harsher penalty of six lashes was prescribed by Columbanus for coughing at the beginning of a psalm.

[25]This was a thoughtful provision, *ut infirmis fratribus non vertatur in nauseam.*

[26]When in church they were to spit in such a way as to avoid dirtying the floor—i.e., to aim straight at the *arculae* —*at in choro, multo minus ad altare, nunquam spuant in pavimentum aut in tapetas.* Which was reasonable enough.

On savait récompenser, wrote Dr. Cabanès, *en ce temps là, les actions d'éclat.*

Spitting in bed, or even on it, is probably an obsolete custom today, but was so common in the days when no place was safe that it deserves mention, if only as an excuse to drag in these general observations. One of the *caractères* of La Bruyère (Menalque, alias the Duc de Brancas) was accused of using a bed—any bed *dans une chambre où il est familier*—as a cuspidor. As to his own bed, the duc (a perfect example of that much admired French aristocracy, the theme of romantic fiction and film travesties) thought nothing of receiving guests as he lay in it, the familiar *lit de parade*—but let La Bruyère tell the rest of the story: *on lui rend visite, il y a un cercle d'hommes et de femmes dans la ruelle qui l'entretiennent, et en leur présence, il soulève sa couverture et crache dans ses draps.* As late as 1907, according to Emile Barbier (as quoted by Cabanès), it was a pastime and relaxation dear to the inhabitants of Bolivia to lie in bed and practise spitting at the walls and ceiling *des jets de salive multiples et variés.*[27] Notices in hotel bedrooms explicitly prohibited the practice, but nobody took any notice of them. It was customary to keep the bed clear of the walls in order to avoid contact with them.

Obsolescent, but not yet obsolete, is that ancient bedroom utensil, the *vas necessarium*—in Gaelic (if you prefer) the *omarfuail* (of great antiquity), known in eighteenth-century Ireland as a *Twiss* (which was the proper name of a gentleman unloved in Dublin) and in France as a *pot de chambre*. I have said a few things

[27] According to Thedor Sologub, in *The Little Demon* (quoted by Philip Owens in *Bed and Sometimes Breakfast* [London, 1944]), a similar hobby must have been known at one time in Russia.

about this object, the cause of so much embarrassment to Swift's Strephon and Chloe, in my *Cleanliness and Godliness*. I had not, at the time of writing that book, the great advantage of having seen what Cabanès had written upon this and kindred subjects, and I do not propose—since it is so vast a subject—either to repeat my own previous observations or those of the erudite French doctor.[28] But there is one observation which will be found neither in my own work on sanitation nor in the studies of Dr. Cabanès; and this I think sufficiently important to pass on. According to the *Shâhr,* the religious code of Persia, a Moslem of the Shia sect may not pray in a room where there is a *vas necessarium.*[29] The Persians, in this matter, seem to me to show taste and discrimination; but it should surely be clear that a room in which a person cannot pray is no fit place in which to sleep. The moral of this is sufficiently obvious. The *vas necessarium,* in an age of indoor sanitation, is definitely on its way out, and bedrooms are becoming fit for a Shia to invoke the one God, Allah.

Indeed, whatever may go on in distant igloos—as described by Dittmar Bleecken (one of Purchas, his Pilgrimes) by the great Nansen and more recently by Gontran de Poncins—where the *vas* is passed round and (as Bleecken noted) *he is accounted uncivil who abhorreth this fashion*—civilisation marches on, even though it may be marching to destruction. Why, Georg Wilhelm

[28]They will be found in that same volume (No. I) of the *Moeurs Intimes* to which I have already referred in this chapter, under the headings *Vas necessarium, L'Urinal* and *La Propreté de la maison.* The appendices include notes on *Le règne de la chaise percée* and *L'hygiène publique a l'étranger.* Valuable addenda at the end of the sixth edition should not be overlooked.

[29]See S. G. W. Benjamin, *Persia and the Persians* (London, 1887), p. 444.

Steller even said of the Kamchatkans—no, I will not tell you what Georg Wilhelm Steller said of the Kamchatkans. The hour is late, and the British Government is robbing me of one hour's sleep tonight by means of Summer Time. Jack York tells me that a gentleman by the name of Lyons, a citizen of California, has made a fine private collection of *vasa necessaria,* which can be seen at Lyons's Museum, Los Angeles; but I wish to hear no more of them. A museum is the proper place for these objects and proof that a bedaboo in this matter is now firmly established.

I have spoken in this chapter as the *advocatus diaboli.* Believe me, I have ransacked my resources for things to be said in despite and contempt of the bed, but I can think of no more, except for a few observations apropos of hospital beds, which I will save for another occasion.

Chapter 8

OUT OF ZEBULUN, OR FRUITS OF SOLITUDE

. . . out of Zebulun they that handle the pen of the writer.

Judges V:14

John Bunyan
Is not to be confused with Damon Runyon
And furthermore
There is no percentage in the Holy War.

MY CLEVER NEPHEW says he is not so sure about that. He says that Mr. Speakeasy would have been quite at home in some place like Vanity Fair. But first about Zebulun. I know very little about Zebulun except this one remark in Judges, and Joseph's cryptic observation: *Rejoice, Zebulun, in thy going out* (Deuteronomy XXXIII:18). Unless I am mistaken, this means that Zebulun was a literary patriarch; and Joseph wanted to encourage him to get out of his bed. In that case I am entirely on the side of Zebulun. These fruits of solitude would be lost to the world if I rejoiced in my going out.

But notice my emphasis upon solitude. That is why I was thinking about Bunyan and Runyon. Each of these writers has provided us with a glimpse of social life in bed which is terrifying to anyone who values solitude. *My Wife Ethel* is perpetually waking up Joe Turp to tell him something that has just occurred to her. His patience is admirable, but this imposition of sociability must surely be the death of creative art. In just the same way Bunyan's Giant Despair is found discussing the day's work and the next day's plans as he lies abed with his wife, Diffidence. Diffidence, it is true, was not such an incurable egoist as Ethel, but her advice—though well intentioned and entirely concerned with her husband's business as a giant—was very elementary and must surely have been tiresome to any giant who really knew his job.

It is an interesting fact that this chapter in the private life of Mr. and Mrs. Despair is not to be found in the original edition of the *Pilgrim's Progress*. That is because it was probably written in the County Jail, and in bed at that—i.e., in one of those solitary, meditative beds where a man can create such fancies. After he returned to domestic life Bunyan would have been reminded of many things in the rough-and-tumble, the hurly-burly and *brouhaha* of the extramural four-poster. This experience induced him to add some realistic touches to his fantasy. And among these were the famous bedroom scenes at Doubting Castle, which were inserted into later editions of his book.

The first pillow-chat of Despair and Diffidence concerned the two prisoners whom Despair had deposited in his dungeon. Mrs. Despair, of course, wanted to know all about them—who they were, whence they came and whither they were bound. Having obtained all the data, which was entirely irrelevant, the simple-minded woman gave her advice, which was that next morning her husband should beat them without mercy—quite unnecessary counsel, as this was obviously a matter of routine

with guests at the Despairs' establishment. The prisoners
were accordingly given the usual treatment and the next
night another committee meeting took place in the
double bed. This time Mrs. Despair had another inspira-
tion, that the prisoners should be induced to commit
felo-de-se. However, we need not follow all these talks
in detail. The main point is that Mrs. Despair contributed absolutely nothing useful or original. There is, it is
true, evidence of tenderness and affection (*And sayest
thou so, my dear?* the giant replies to one of his wife's
suggestions) but the conversational level is dull and
domesticated.

The formidable Mrs. Caudle can barely be recalled
without a shudder. One is reminded of those lines which
were written when the vestments of the Anglican clergy
were a matter of such hot dispute (in the days when the
Kensitites were lambasting Anglo-Catholics of the Mir-
field Mission in their cassocks and Romish weeds[1]):

> *For me, I neither know nor care*
> *Whether a parson ought to wear*
> > *A black dress or a white dress;*
> *I have a trouble of my own*
> *A wife who preaches in a gown*
> > *And lectures in a night-dress.*

However, that is an old story—as old at least as the
time of Juvenal and probably much older.[2] A more

[1] It was at this time that one of the Kensitites made the
famous declaration: *I will wear no clothes to distinguish
me from my brethren.* Oxford was soon afterwards plastered
with bills showing this zealot as a nude figure, declaiming
from a pulpit.

[2] See Juvenal's sixth Satire, lines 268 *et seq*. As Dryden
renders them, somewhat freely:

> *Besides, what endless brawls by wives are bred:*
> *The curtain lecture makes a mournful bed.*

modern version of the situation came to light in a divorce case, not so long ago, when a gentleman living at Los Angeles claimed that his wife brought several relatives to bed with her every night. Even at Los Angeles, it appears, that sort of relative density is regarded with disapproval, especially if the intruders all want to talk. I know that there is another side to this question, of course, and that the bedchamber has not always proved disastrous to human relationships. Sean O'Neill is even said to have claimed—when taunted with having made peace with Queen Elizabeth—that he made peace with her in her bedchamber.[3] But even so I would not like to suggest that it was a good thing for any Irishman to have come to terms with Elizabeth, whatever the terms were —only that is another story.

As to relatives in bed, Rochester made an even stranger remark apropos of Nell Gwyn (the patron saint of my adopted Borough of Chelsea), though I was surprised to find in Howell's *Epistolae Ho-Elianae* a Spanish equivalent from which the earl evidently borrowed the conception.[4] But I have no mind to discuss rare and improbable cases. The fashion of using twin beds, a typical Anglo-American compromise, shall be our next concern, the more so as it seems to have stirred up some controversy, especially in the United States.

Then when she has thee sure between the sheets,
Her cry begins, and the whole day repeats. . . .

Compare Martial's *sit non doctissima conjux*—coupled with a wish for peaceful nights.

[3] This was Sean an Diomais, not the Great O'Neill (Hugh) with whom Katherine Anthony hopelessly confused him in her *Queen Elizabeth* (New York, 1929).

[4] See the lines beginning *Eres puta tan artera.* The letter will be found in Dent's edition of 1903, Vol. II, p. 251.

Twin beds appear to have been known earlier than one would have supposed. C. and M. Gray refer to an early example.[5] But who cares? Skip all that, as the Bellman said to the Baker; and for once I agree. Early in 1950 researches by the Universities of Chicago and Colgate revealed that double beds were being abandoned in favour of twin beds. The percentage of twin beds purchased in prewar days had been only 25 per cent and it had risen to 68 per cent.[6] The effect upon the birth rate may possibly be estimated from figures published some eighteen months previously, when an investigation had been made of the bedroom habits in a large American city. Although the proportion of double beds in use in this city was unexpectedly high (96.8 per cent in low-income groups), a comparison of the birth rate in the 96.8 class with the rate in the high-income group, where more people used twin beds, showed that the low-income wallahs were leading.[7] Whether this really had anything to do with the bedding arrangements or was merely what you might expect to find in any comparison between the rich and the poor I do not pretend to explain. But for this or some other reason—perhaps some deep and subtle vested interest in double beds—a fierce campaign has been waged, is still being waged, against twin beds.

In 1947, Paul Popenoe, director of the (American)

[5]They were used in the fifteenth century by Charles the Bold of Burgundy and his second wife, Isabelle of Bourbon.

[6]It was only thirty-five per cent four years previously, according to a national survey quoted in the *Sunday Express* of August 18, 1946. These figures refer only to current purchases, and not, of course, to beds already in use. I have been told that the peak figure has been reached and that twin beds are already slumping.

[7]*Magazine Digest*, October 1948.

Family Relations Institute, hurled down a heavy gauntlet:

> This movement towards twin beds must stop.
> It was started by furniture dealers who make twice
> as much money selling two beds instead of one.
> The change from a double bed to twin beds is
> often the prelude to a divorce. . . .

Dr. Popenoe did not give any evidence for his last statement. In all the divorce cases that I have so far recalled, i.e., those—how shall I put it?—where the bed has been a party to the case (such as the tragedy of George Ward and the Swanson Fifth Discord, *supra*), it seems that large beds proved more dangerous than small ones. The nutshells of Mr. Ward would have been innocuous to a wife posted under a separate cover, though I suppose he would still have needed a silencer. And Gloria would never have objected if her fifth husband had been content with a little cot in the corner.

But Dr. Popenoe had at least one predecessor—probably many—in his extraordinary line of reasoning. An article by George C. Ebbert (*Progress*, October 1946) had the alarmist title: "Twin Beds for Divorce." His argument was simple enough. The sale of twin beds is rising in the U.S.A., and so is the divorce rate. *Post hoc, ergo propter hoc*: one must clearly be the cause of the other. But he might in fairness have added that, if the two phenomena were connected at all (and why should they be?) the divorce rate could be the cause of twin beds just as disease is the cause of doctors—we hope— and not *vice versa*. Perhaps the people going in for twin beds are trying to find a way to avoid the divorce courts. Perhaps that's a safe bet. And then again perhaps it's not. Maybe nothing short of separate rooms will do the trick. But more likely it has nothing to do with the case.

If people go on living like lunatics, trying to ameliorate a drab, stupid and precarious existence by drugging themselves with sensations in celluloid, I don't suppose it will make much difference whether they sleep in twin bunks or in a bed the size of Coldingham Common.

The twin-beds-for-divorce theme was taken up again in *Esquire* (July 1948) by Ilka Chase. Here they were attacked as *a self-imposed exile . . . a folly for which there can be no praise*. Single beds, said this writer, were suitable only for hospitals, prisons and insane asylums; and fifty per cent of the inhabitants of these institutions would not be there if they had not used twin beds at home. This article leads up to some special pleading for dual-control electric blankets, enabling each party to maintain any temperature to choice. These dual-control blankets, first put on the market by the General Electric Company in 1946, certainly solve one problem of double bedding—an improved model marketed in 1948 even enabled the sleeper to vary the temperature for different parts of his own body. But electric blankets do not touch such problems as snoring; and even if that can be dealt with by one of the gadgets already described in Chapter 6 there is still the question of solitude. There is absolutely no substitute for solitude. That is where I agree so strongly with Greta Garbo.

The nearest thing to a satisfactory double bed that I know of was the one of which I read not long since. This bed, designed by a South Carolina colonel, resident in California (as described by Ian Mackay in the *News Chronicle* of January 20, 1951), has high soundproof walls of wood and a partition that can be raised and lowered like a centreboard, according to the desires of the occupants—one hopes by agreement, but it is not clear where the winch is situated. One side of this bed is fitted with a perfume spray battery and an electric massage machine, the other being equipped with electric razors—also toothbrushes, which are apparently not required on the distaff side. A ceiling screen enables the restless sleeper to pass the hours watching films or enjoying television. Buttons which, when pressed, release a range of scents call to mind the joys of Huxley's *Brave New World*—though one is surprised to read that *there are even the scents of smoked ham or fresh fish for those who want to feel they are in Maryland or Maine* (an odd way of catering to a peculiar taste). But how is the scent isolated if one party pines for honeysuckle and the other for smoked ham?

Among the advantages of single beds, discovered by two English writers joined in wedlock, was—so I am informed—the pleasure of correspondence. They wrote each other letters, which they afterwards made into a book. This would clearly have been much more difficult in a double bed, except, of course, in that of the South Carolina colonel (with the partition up). The possibility of using one's time well and profitably is obviously increased considerably by twin beds, especially in a literary ménage. It is not that I think single beds in the same room are really much use, but I just want to be fair to them. And incidentally we have had recently a very important legal ruling about twin beds which shows that you cannot take liberties with them. (Where are my cuttings? Under the eiderdown, as usual.) *Evening Standard,* December 13, 1950—the text concerns a divorce case, and I have to admit that here, for once, you have divorce coupled with single beds; but no matter. What interests me is the piece that the judge said—Commissioner Sir Reginald Sharpe, K.C.: *I do not consider twin beds normally occupied by husband and wife are separate sleeping accommodation.*

In the middle of the twentieth century twin beds of the husband and wife are indistinguishable from a bed sawn in half.

Some husbands and wives these days prefer, for reasons probably concerned with fair shares of bedclothes for all, to occupy separate beds. . . .

They are happily married couples. I cannot regard twin beds in a married couple's bedroom as being otherwise than the matrimonial bed.

The implications of this ruling are very clear. In *Beards*—I cannot remember how in the world I gave it some semblance of relevance—there is a reference to the Welsh laws of Howell the Good, in the tenth century. One of these laws was concerned with a runaway wife who leaves her first husband for a second. If (says the Demetian Code) the first husband overtake her with one foot in the bed and the other out, the first husband, by law, is to have her. Now applying the ruling of Sir Reginald Sharpe to a case coming under the Demetian Code (II, XVIII, XXIX), it is clear that *the bed,* notwithstanding and without prejudice, shall henceforward and hereafter be taken to mean any double bed or any two single beds so placed *in loco parentis* of any house, hut or hovel as to suggest that it or they is or are intended for the *usus fructus* of the victims of connubiality.

The importance of separate beds lies partly in the vast difference in personal taste and preference, accentuated sometimes by those conditioned reflexes which we call national characteristics. Suppose, for example, an American marries an English girl. In a very short time all English people will be completely conditioned to hard beds, a result of the devaluation of sterling[8]; and the

[8] See *Reveille,* February 11, 1950, quoting a Board of Trade Utility Bedding Order. In an interview a bedding manu-

English bride, who will have learnt to appreciate a hard mattress (as I do myself), will at once be in difficulties with her hard-currency husband, as hard currency means a soft bed. What are they to do? And again, she may like a short bed, as the hot-water bottle is apt to get lost if there is a No Man's Land of two or three feet beyond your toes; but the husband will want a long bed, because he is a man and anyway American beds are getting longer year by year, according to Arthur D. Little, Inc., whose job it is to know things like that. (It seems that Americans are getting bigger—I hope the boot manufacturers have their eye on this.)

Or suppose—no, there are too many possibilities, like an Esquimau marrying a *hula-hula* girl or an Arab mating with a Maori; or again there's Beverley Nichols. And then some people like their beds low; and I'm told that much of the firewood in America two or three years ago came from sawing off bed legs like they do their shotguns. But others like them high, like Sir Richard Owen, whose bed was right up by the ceiling, so that he could watch the deer at dawn in Richmond Park. He said they behaved differently then. But suppose one had a wife who was not interested in what the deer did at 4 A.M., what then?

> *Wives of Great Men all remind us*
> *How much happier we are*
> *With no waggon hitched behind us—*
> *Just a planet, not a star.*

But even without being great one might still encounter difficulties. What surprises me about marriage is its simplicity. When I sign a contract with my publishers they think of everything and put it all down. But in mar-

---

facturer had attributed the Order to devaluation, and explained that it meant thinner and harder mattresses.

riage there are no clauses and subclauses about beds and things, as you might expect: it is a *carte blanche,* except in countries like France, where there is a great deal of sordid haggling and niggling and pettifogging about a thing called the *dot,* and that is not at all what I mean.

Another thing against the double bed is that it incites silly people to make fatuous remarks and even indulge in fatuous behaviour. (Shakespeare's will would not have been thought funny had his second-best bed been a singleton.) Consider once more that Great Bed of Ware. In the room where it was housed at the Saracen's Head there hung a pair of horns, and on these horns guests were sworn in. Nobody would have thought of that had there been two modest Gemini beds. Of course, I know there is really nothing sinister about horns—that, I am convinced, is just another Gallic notion, worthy of a nation of philosophers.[9] Horns were once highly honourable, and the Fall of the Horn has yet to be investigated. Moses, for example, is described as descending from Mount Sinai (after that exclusive interview) wearing a horn or horns, as we read in the Vulgate, where it says that Aaron and the children of Israel, seeing the horned dial of Moses, were scared of approaching him[10]; and well they might be. But whether they were impressed and awed or plain frightened by the apparition, there is no suggestion that anybody considered the joke was on Moses—nor can any valid comparison be made between this event and the translation of Bottom the weaver.

Now it cannot, surely, be suggested that, while Moses was up aloft, or (as Henry James put it—or was it

[9]*Philosophatur* in silver Latin = *he thinks up a dirty trick.* See *Encyclopaedia Britannica* (14th ed.), article on *Casuistry.*

[10]*Videntes autem Aaron et filii Israel* cornutam *Moysi faciem, timuerunt prope accedere* (Exodus XXXIV:30).

George Meredith? I give you two guesses[11]) *it may well
be that, perhaps, not—and—afterwards—who shall say?
. . . that, in a sense, one might possibly, or no—horrible as the phrase is—think otherwise or not at all.* But
there the horns stand in the text, with the graphic cor-
roboration of certain artists, as Sir Thomas Browne
recalled in his *Pseudodoxia Epidemica*—though Sir
Thomas did his best to explain away those horns by saying that the original word signified *shining* rather than
horned. What matter? The clearer is our proof that horns
and glory were synonymous. Whether Moses and Bacchus were the same person (*as Vossius well contendeth,*
remarks Sir T. Browne) seems very much more doubtful. There was positively nothing gay about Moses,
nothing whatever. But I am myself something of a Haire-
tite[12] and do not greatly care whether *cornutus* implies
the sudden growth of horns or whether it was a mere
dinnacle.[13] What interests me is that in the Bible horns
are invariably symbols or synonyms of honour.

A pentimento of their former glory will be found in
Kit Smart's *Jubilate Agno:*

For I prophesy that we shall have our horns again.
*For in the day of David Men as yet had a glorious horn
     upon his [sic] forehead. . . .*

[11]Wrong both times. It was a man called Frank Richardson.

[12]HAIRETITES, *a sceptical sect among the Mohammedans,
who profess to doubt everything, and to hold their minds
in constant equipoise* (Rev. James Gardner in *The Faiths of
the World,* Vol. II). On any point of controversy Hairetites
say *God knows it, we do not,* as truth is indistinguishable
from falsehood. Some have become *Muftis,* but in their
official capacity they will sign anything with the addendum:
God knows what is best. This is my own attitude when
filling up forms.

[13]The opposite of a miracle—a rare word of doubtful origin
and existence.

*For I prophesy that the English will recover their horns
    the first. . . .*

*For I prophesy that all Englishmen will wear their beards
    again.*

For a beard is a good step to a horn.

I missed that in my own book on beards—the better
justification for this byway. Smart was right about
beards and right in what followed, when he prophesied
that people would go hatless. He even prophesied his
own twentieth-century publisher (*Let Cape, house of
Cape rejoice . . .*[14]). Why should he not have been
right about horns? The very word *scorn* surely signifies
de-horn, to take away the horns of.[15] However, there
is a mass of information on this subject in F. T. Elwor-
thy's *Horns of Honour* (London, 1900), the only notable lacunae being the absence of Christopher Smart's
contribution to the subject and the failure to explain
how horns fell into disrepute. My own view is that it
was due to Waldensian influences, as Odell Shepard
attributes to this source the transformation of the unicorn, in the Provençal Bestiary, from a symbol of good
to a symbol of evil. . . . Perhaps it is time we got back
into bed before those unicorns run away with us again.

A bedroom—though God forbid such a fate should
befall us—may be as villainous as that of Buckingham

[14]At the end of Fytte XXIX. In Fytte XIV there is an obscure reference to another publisher, the Faber-Fish—doubtless Mr. T. S. Eliot. Compare *The fried fish does not dread
the pan,* used *in re* T.S.E. *apud Og* (*Idem and Other Ogres,*
p. 59, line 12).

[15]Murray is equivocal on this point, but admits the obvious
resemblance between the (OF) *escarnir* (also sb. *escarn*)
and the Italian *scornare* (literally to deprive of the horns)
from popular Latin *ex-cornare*. *Ergo,* horns, at least in Italy,
were once objects of pride and worn as such.

*in the worst inn's worst room . . . the floor of plaster
and the walls of dung,* or as stark as the chamber of
Verlaine in that picture of canopied misery drawn by
Francis Grierson. If it afford solitude it has still achieved
its principal purpose. One does not need the bower of
Acrasia to know that sunless cave of sleep which John
Gower (following closely upon Homer) described in his
Confessio Amantis,

> *in a strange lond*
> *Which marcheth upon Chymerie.*

Dan Chaucer knew its joys and described for us:

> *Morpheus and Eclympasteyre*
> *That was the god of slepes heyre*
> *That slepe and did non other werk. . . .*

Non other werk was surely a happy conceit. But where
can this cave best be found?

A bed is, I say and maintain, a place where—quite
apart from bugs or spiders—a normal person normally
prefers to be alone. Here he is relaxed, he is his effort-
less self, his mind wanders without attempt to recall it
to order, until at last it wanders into sleep. There are
but two other places where we can hope to enjoy such
a feast of unself-consciousness—one is the bathroom
and the other a place which has already been the subject of my researches and reflections. The one thing to
which I think that I never fully accustomed myself during my school days was the dormitory system. At the
day's end I wanted no company but my own and I deeply
resented the habits of those who, not being restless like
myself, fell to snoring heavily long before sleep had
closed my ears, so that I was often kept awake most of
the night.

During my last year at school, as a bedroom prefect,

I took a vicious and vicarious revenge upon the enemies of my early days. There were, I informed the boys so rashly entrusted to my care, but two laws in my code—firstly, that they should not snore, and secondly, that in all other matters they should not be found out. Except for snoring—an offence not recognised owing to some oversight in the framing of the school rules—all that I asked was that their misdemeanours should not bring me trouble or embarrassment. But for snorers I kept a squad of four, known as *the navvies*. At a word from myself they would take their places, armed with pillows, two on either side of the bed where lay the offender against Rule I. Each navvy had a number and they struck as I counted, right at the head of the delinquent, while I lay in comfort like an Eastern potentate, whose casual tongue deals death from the cushions of the seraglio. I must have been a singularly unpleasant youth.

But if a twentieth-century school dormitory can be so unpleasant—and I seem to have added my own quota to its disadvantages—what shall we say of those horrible seminaries where supervision was once carried out so systematically that a child could no more escape from the eye of his preceptors than he could elude the eye of God? At the Abbey of Bec a master patrolled the dormitory by night, holding a candle in one hand and a rod in the other. Privacy was unknown to them.[16] I have tasted such horror only in prison—it was but for a week, the alternative to a small fine (for riding a bicycle with-

[16]Details are quoted by the Grays from a translation by C. G. Coulton. In discussing *Cimex lectularius* I have already mentioned the eighteenth-century records of my own school—then at Clerkenwell and known generally as *Y^e Friends Workhouse*—where it was ordained that the boys should occupy a *range of Bedsteads* and that *for the better keeping the Boys in order one or 2 Ancient men to Lodg in the same room.*

out a light) which I was reluctant to pay, whilst I was
consumed with curiosity about the local jail. But next
to the brutality and lack of hygiene in an English prison
I found the lack of privacy the worst thing about it,
and a week was long enough. The sweets of solitude to
which I had looked forward were ruined by the knowledge that, at any hour of the day or night, the eye of a
screw might be peeping through the Judas hole.

The sense of that watching eye and of the temptations
to which it subjects the prisoner will be found in Jim
Phelan's vivid picture of English prison life, *Jail Journey*,
where a Parkhurst ballad is quoted—I have always
meant to ask Phelan for the rest of it:

Down came the Bitches Basterd, to pipe a bitta stuff.
He snooks a balmy Judas and sees him coppa duff;
He snooks it working belty, and nuts the orly mug.
—I want that bleeder chokied. Unauthorised. A plug.

(As Phelan provides a translation it is perhaps possible
to gloss this text: *Bitches Basterd:* the worst type of
screw or warder. *To pipe a bitta stuff:* to catch a convict
with contraband. *To snook a Judas:* to look through the
spy-hole. *Balmy:* a section of the prison used for prisoners supposed to be under mental observation. *Coppa
duff:* apparently to secrete some tobacco. *Working belty:*
stealthily. *To choky:* to put a man in solitary confinement. I hope I have these points correctly, but none of
my expert advisers on jail seems to be handy.) This,
surely, is Hell—never to be sure of solitude.

Is this deep-seated desire a thing of recent growth?
Time was when solitude seems to have been unknown
to men—even hermits were strongly advised to have
companions.[17] C. G. Coulton described the want of pri-

[17]Authorities for this fact, which I found surprising, were
quoted by R. M. Clay in *The Hermits and Anchorites of*

vacy in a mediaeval house as its worst discomfort, to a modern mind. Thus Chaucer, he remarked, though a king's squire, had not a bed to himself; and in the choir schools at Wells they slept in threes—*two smaller boys with their heads to the head of the bed, and an older one with his head to the foot of the bed, and his feet between the others' heads.* This passes imagination.

> *O western wind, when wilt thou blow*
> *That the small rain down can rain. . . .*

Everyone knows the haunting quatrain, fierce in its realism. But how do you imagine the scene? Perhaps shepherds, alone among men, knew the seclusion of a private world withdrawn. (Hence their attraction for the poet.) For such the amorous Silvy would say:

> *Now kiss me and be going,*
> > *My sweetest dear!*
> *Kiss me this once and then be going,*
> *For now the morning draweth near.*

But for those whose wealth could have bought either solitude or intimacy undisturbed the scene might be very different. Even in the sixteenth century and even in the highest circles, as Buckle notes,[18] the bed was not (like the grave) a fine and private place. Buckle's examples included Catherine (*née* Parr), the widow of Henry VIII, later married to Admiral Lord Seymour. When my Lord Admiral was roving the seas or otherwise engaged

---

England (London, 1914). In the introduction (p. xvii) there is another surprise: a system equivalent to licensing, without which one could not, apparently, go into business as hermit or anchorite. Details are given in the appendices of the offices used for such purposes.

[18]*Miscellaneous and Posthumous Works* (London, 1872), Vol. III, p. 531.

Catherine tucked up with a lady called Odell. The admiral himself, with less discretion, would visit the Princess Elizabeth—another bed-sharer—and assist her sleeping companion, Mrs. Katherine Ashley, in tickling the future queen. (*Thei tytled my Lady Elizabeth in bed,* Mrs. A. later admitted, during an investigation which cost the admiral his head.)

Mary Tudor and Mary Stuart both seem to have disliked sleeping alone, though in the case of the Queen of Scots there appears to have been no lack of candidates for her comfort. Buckle thought this common aversion to sleeping alone arose from a desire to keep warm; but there are far too many possible hypotheses.[19] In the case of François I of France, who was also partial to a sea dog, it was by way of conferring a special privilege that he so often shared his bed with Admiral Bonnivet. And then (I do not know whether Spenser in his *Faërie Queene* had the realities of his age in mind) there is that really terrifying scene of two lovers, where

> . . . *round about them pleasauntly did sing*
> *Many faire ladies, and lascivious boyes,*
> *That ever mixt their song with light licentious toyes.*

One might as well, at that rate, plant a double bed on the floor of a *Palais de Danse.*

---

[19]Compare the case of Waring and Gillow (not to be confused with Debenham and Freebody and Deborah and Barak —*vide* Chapter 6) who, we learn,

> *Used to share a pillow:*
> *It was not bonhomie*
> *But sheer economy.*

(And Miss Beeson says, what about Roneo and Duplicate?) One of my great-uncles was temporarily persuaded to abandon the double bed, in which neither he nor my aunt could sleep. But he soon lapsed into old habits, explaining this atavism as a concession to *the opinion of his neighbours.*

Sharing a bed is one of the hardest tests of friendship or even mere tolerance. To those who find even a loving spouse an unwelcome partner in the serious business of sleeping, it must be a source of wonder that for centuries people were packed like sardines between the blankets— a custom still to be found in many parts of the world to-day, and notably among the Esquimaux (under conditions from which imagination recoils). Mere poverty may explain bed-sharing or—in the case of the Esquimaux—the necessity for warmth may excuse it. But these explanations will not serve in many examples that can be cited. The great Percy family was not compelled by either necessity, yet their Household Book[20] records the following obnoxious arrangement:

> For vj Prests, iij Beddes after ij to a Bedde. For x Gentillmen of the Chapell, v Beddes ij to a Bedde. And for vi Children, ij Beddes after iij to a Bedde.

Burd Helen in the old ballad apparently shared her bed with her entire offspring of seven sons. When her cruel husband said she was to learn to make her bed and to *ly her lane* she replied (with what seemed to her devastating logic) that how could she make her bed

> *Unless I mak it wide,*
> *Whan I have seven o' your sons*
> *To lie down by my side?*

But even stranger things are to be found in the prosaic pages of English history. Imagine, for example, how English citizens must have felt in the early seventeenth century, when the saltpetre men—having a commission to dig where they pleased—heaved up the floors of churches and private parlours in their zeal, operating

[20]Quoted by C. and M. Gray, *The Bed*, p. 53.

even *in bedchambers, and under the very beds.*[21] Having dug beneath one's bed and used much base and uncivil language, these preposterous intruders apparently departed without, as a rule, so much as filling up the holes. However, no doubt gunpowder was badly needed and it was all part of the armaments race—proleptic of guns for butter, our present (quote) socialist (unquote) diet. In modern times a bomb through the roof leaves a bigger hole; but public opinion does not resent the intrusion so bitterly because the whole business is so much less personal.

Even in the seventeenth century the privacy of a single bed was appreciated by such a connoisseur as Pepys. On one occasion he stayed in a place where he and his wife *had two beds in the room and so lay single.* The event impressed him: *Of all nights that ever I slept in my life,* he wrote, *I never did pass a night with more epicurism of sleep.* Dorothy Osborne, the gallant wife of Sir William Temple, was another whose tastes in this matter correspond with my own. During her long courtship and correspondence with her future husband, she recorded sharing a bed one night with two companions—*which was all one to mee as if wee had not gone to bed at all.*

And yet not even the sick were (in those days) spared the horrors of multiple bedding. Who has not seen illustrations of hospital life in the Middle Ages and right down to the end of the eighteenth century, showing the overcrowded beds in which the patients were housed?

[21]The words are quoted from a committee established in April 1630 to enquire into this matter. C. and M. Gray are much to be congratulated on the discovery of this astonishing information in the Calendar of State Papers. The saltpetre men were accused of *placing their tubs by the bedside . . . even of women in childbed and of sick persons lying in their deathbeds.*

Max Nordau is quoted[22] as describing a hospital bed during the late eighteenth century: *In it lay four, five or six persons beside each other, the feet of one to the head of another, children beside grayhaired old men . . . men and women intermingled . . . individuals with infectious diseases beside others only slightly unwell . . . a woman groaned in the pangs of labour, a nursing infant writhed in convulsions, a typhus patient burned . . . a consumptive coughed . . .* Dr. Saul, in quoting this account, gives insufficient reference to enable me to check its accuracy, even if I had a mind to do so. But the account merely repeats with variations a familiar theme—I think I remember some such stories in H. W. Haggard's *Devils, Drugs and Doctors.* If not they should be easy enough to find.[23]

The stern Dr. Macnish has this at least to his credit, that he considered it *more wholesome to sleep single than double.* But plural bedding continued in England in many very unpleasant forms throughout the nineteenth century and up to very recent times. When Kingsley

[22]By F. W. Saul in *Pink Pills for Pale People* (Philadelphia, 1949). In happy contrast Dr. Saul quotes the *New England Journal of Medicine* as saying that *in the Pacific was once the most perfect quarantine against disease ever known— cannibalism. . . . Social intercourse was reduced to a minimum.* I have already noted the efficacy of cannibalism as a punitive measure; and I take the liberty of adding here a third advantage. According to a brochure by F. A. Pearson and Don Paarlberg (*Starvation Truths, Half-Truths, Untruths,* N. Y. State College of Agriculture, Cornell University), *Cannibalism has been an adjuster of the food supply to the population and of the population to the food supply. It is the only adjuster that has this double distinction.*

[23]A false trail, I fear. I see that Haggard only refers to the same description, evidently of the *Hôtel Dieu.* Harvey Graham uses it in *Eternal Eve;* but I still do not know its source or value as evidence. (Query: Ambroise Paré?)

wrote *Cheap Clothes and Nasty,* in 1850, the tailors of
the London sweat shops lived in unbelievable conditions.
In one case which he mentioned the sweater, together
with his wife, sister-in-law, four children and six men, all
lived in two rooms, of which the *larger* one was eight
feet by ten. There was no chimney or ventilation, and
the six men slept three in a bed in the smaller room,
estimated at six feet square. Turn-up beds were used, the
room being in use all day as a workshop.

I am not sure when the so-called rope beds were abandoned in certain cheap lodging houses. Strictly speaking, they do not qualify for inclusion as beds at all. The
plan was that people sat huddled on benches, set in rows,
with a rope stretched behind their backs to lean upon. In
the morning—so I am told—the sleepers were woken
and the house cleared by the simple expedient of releas-
ing the rope at one end. But I am beginning to weary
of these horrors. Let us consider something more cheerful.[24]

I do not propose to discuss here the many stories
which deal with the Box-cum-Cox theme or with The
Wrong Bed. For those interested a good selection from
the available literature on the latter subject will be found
in the Grays' anthology. Their repertoire includes one of
the adventures of Don Quixote, a misfortune which be-
fell Mr. Pickwick, a well-known story by Boccaccio and
the same story as recounted by Chaucer in *The Reeve's
Tale.* There is also a story from the *Morte d'Arthur* in
which, as the editors remark, Sir Launcelot's behaviour,
on finding himself in the wrong bed, is *suggestive of the*

---

[24]I am considerably omitting all the evidence relating to
accommodation shared with pigs and poultry. Though commonly told of the Irish, there is evidence enough that in the
nineteenth century such stories were equally true of many
English families. But I find the subject tedious.

manners and customs of Groucho Marx. I will only add, at this point, that Groucho Marx had, as a matter of fact, already given to the public, many years previously, his own considered views on this very question. In *Beds,* Groucho divided men into *monobedders* and *polybedders,* a useful form of dichotomy ignored by earlier scholars. He pleaded for tolerance on the part of the *monobedders* for those who, *equally earnest and sincere, prefer a variety of beds.* His view was that *polybedders* should not be compelled to jump out of any window above the second floor, and that even so they should be given two minutes' start.

My final thoughts (for the moment) on the sharing of beds are concerned with the *Jus Primae Noctis*—partly because I am not sure under what other heading I could legitimately include it, and it would surely be very wrong to omit the subject altogether in such a treatise as this. After all, it has much more to do with beds than many of the observations which have somehow intruded in these pages. But there is really not very much that is worth saying about it. Montaigne was among the first scholars to draw attention to certain mediaeval practices, later discussed briefly by Bayle in his *Réponse aux Questions d'un Provincial,*[25] with reference to observations by François de la Mothe-le-Vayer and other writers. Montesquieu and Voltaire also had something to say; but the fury of controversy did not begin until the middle of the nineteenth century, when the famous French advocate, A. M. J. J. Dupin (known as Dupin the Elder), read a paper on the *Droit de Seigneur* before the *Académie des Sciences morales et politiques.*

Dupin's paper was published in 1854. Its appearance, about the same time as a study by an antiquarian, Bouthors, on local customs in the bailliage of Amiens, stirred

[25]Chapter XCVI, Vol. II, p. 694 in *Oeuvres,* 1727.

up the bile of a choleric journalist, Louis Veuillot, then editor of the Catholic paper *L'Univers*. After publishing a series of angry articles Veuillot came out with a book (*Le Droit du Seigneur au moyen âge*) in the same year —1854. He said that the *droit* had never existed: all that had been said about it was pure invention, pure lying, pure ignorance. This right had not existed *ni toujours ni quelquefois, ni partout, ni quelque part; il n'a jamais existé!* Veuillot's arguments, which showed more zeal than judgment, were demolished by a provincial scholar, Jules Delpit, whose *Réponse d'un Campagnard à un Parisien* appeared in 1857. A second edition of Veuillot's work occasioned a further reply from Delpit (*Le Droit de Seigneur . . . ou seconde réponse a M. L. Veuillot* [Bordeaux, 1873]).

This is but a brief sketch of the controversial background of clericalism and anti-clericalism, supplied out of sheer goodness of heart because it is almost the only aspect of the matter not discussed by Westermarck— indeed, he altogether omits to mention, in his *History of Human Marriage,* the contributions of Dupin and Delpit, though referring to Veuillot. But, by the time Westermarck wrote, the subject was being regarded in a much broader way; and the politikirkality of a nineteenth-century controversialist such as Veuillot had actually little relevance to the anthropological discussions which were to follow.

Since then the *jus primae noctis* has been discussed this way and that. Some say the bridegrooms asked for it, others attribute it to the preference of the brides, while some old-fashioned folks still think, in spite of everything, that the seigneur had a large vested interest in the matter. Sir John Lubbock regarded the *droit* as a survival of promiscuity, a symbolic token of sexual communism; and (though it appears to have been discarded) this view might yet become fashionable once more if the press could only discover that the old custom had been revived behind the Iron Curtain. Whatever the origin, the custom implies remarkable tolerance and is generally coupled by anthropologists with that of lending one's wife (or one of them) to the stranger, as an act of hospitality.[26] Westermarck mentions, on the authority of Bishop Egede, that those Greenlanders who lent *without pain or reluctance* were esteemed *the best and noblest tempered*.

Of these same Greenlanders Hans Egede also said that husbands were so honoured by the attentions of any *Angekokk,* or Prophet, to their wives that they would even pay him a fee rather than risk disappointment. Equally friendly is the application of the *jus primae noctis* as a common war-right in cases of marriage by capture or—to use Westermarck's phrase—as a *reward for a good turn done*. Priests, naturally, have been among the successful claimants, and Westermarck says cryptically that *Sugenheim believes even that in certain parts of France, a similar right was accorded to the higher clergy during the Middle Ages*. The anti-clerical reader's curiosity being thus aroused, he is referred to Sugenheim's *Geschichte der Aufhebung der Leibeigenschaft und Hörigkeit in Europa;* and we will leave the matter there, in spite of a promise of some good stories relating to the Bishops of Amiens. Actually it only takes us back to Monsieur Bouthors and the original controversy.

It must therefore have caused widespread disappointment when Carl Schmidt, in 1881, came out with his work on the *jus primae noctis,* endeavouring once more to prove that it had never existed in Europe. Schmidt's

[26]Such customs were twice noted by Marco Polo and have been claimed with regard to various peoples (e.g., the Circassians, by P. S. Pallas) on innumerable occasions.

conclusions, in a studious survey which had none of
Veuillot's blatant prejudice, seemed tantamount to a suggestion that the French Revolution has been based upon
false premises. Pro-Jacobins must have resented the im-
plication of fake propaganda, whilst the *ci-devant* aristocracy doubtless felt virtue depart from their ancestors.
Westermarck originally did something to re-establish the
authenticity of the legend, pointing out that the *droit
de seigneur* had obtained in Russia in the nineteenth century; but later editions of his *History of Human Marriage* showed a marked retreat on the European front.
The very phrase *droit de seigneur,* however, should remind us that our chief difficulty lies in discovering exactly where the *jus* was vested. Was it, in fact, a *droit de
seigneur* or a stranger's privilege, or a priest's prerogative? Or did the right lie with the wife or bride? Or was
it, perhaps, really vested in the husband himself?[27]

Two things appear to be clear: first, that the power of
a feudal lord over his serfs, in this matter, existed in
fact, if not in law. Secondly, that the distinction between a legal and an illegal authority is quite unim-
portant and unreal so long as the generality of people
(be they feudal serfs or colonial subjects) have neither

---

[27]This last explanation could have been true in one of two
senses. Either, as many instances suggest, the husband may
sometimes have had the right to invoke the aid of (e.g.)
the priest, upon whom the custom would—in that case—
have imposed a duty rather than conferring any privilege;
or the *jus* itself may have been, as Frazer has suggested, the
conjugal right assumed to exist in the husband. It seems
that an alleged canon of that so-called Fourth Council of
Carthage (the doubtful records of which gave rise to so
much controversy, as I showed in the matter of *Beards*)
ordered that the newlywed *eadem nocte in virginitate per-
maneant.* The Church may at one time have attempted to
enforce this ruling, later accepting financial compensation
for the breach of it.

the making of the laws nor the power to enforce them. If the feudal lords exercised a propriety right in respect of the *adscripti glebae* (particularly in respect of the *adscriptae*) and treated them like cattle—which they were in effect—but presumably with more familiarity, what compensation was it for the serfs to know that the *jus* did not exist on the Statute Book, if in fact a denial of it meant challenging a master who was judge in his own case, with no right of appeal? Slaves, for the matter of that, have in most slave-owning communities had certain theoretical rights; but there can have been few slaves in history who were ever bold (or foolish) enough to claim their mite of justice with the scales of retribution weighted so heavily against them.

A parallel to many of the classic cases of the *jus* (especially in its variations as a form of courtesy to strangers) will be found in the odd behaviour of that surly and singularly unpleasant old Roman, Cato the Censor. Hortensius first asked him for his daughter, though she was already married. On this point the *jus* seems to have been in doubt, proprietory rights being claimed, no doubt, by Cato's son-in-law. But when Hortensius changed his mind, asking for Cato's own wife (on the grounds that she was young and that Cato had enough children), the old boor handed her over with no more ado than obtaining the consent of her father. Roman history must be a feminist's nightmare. The action was the more odd in view of Cato's emphatic opinion on the subject of adultery: that a woman who committed it was no better than a poisoner. Having legalised the poison by his consent, Cato survived Hortensius and received his wife back once more when she became a widow—a very eligible relict and a good investment (as Caesar did not fail to point out), since Hortensius was a leading barrister and very well to do.

It was interesting for me to find that Westermarck
had mentioned the case of King Concobar (who ruled
Ulster in the heroic days of Cuchulain) in connection
with the *jus primae noctis*. I had been thinking about
Concobar in this connection myself, before I came upon
the passage in *The History of Human Marriage*[28]; and
to check my own conjecture I had written to my learned
friend, Michael J. Lennon, who has often advised me
in matters relating to Gaelic texts. Concobar, said Mr.
Lennon, exercised no *droit de seigneur,* and nobody ever
thought of such a thing until some modern scholar tried
to pin the idea onto the Concobar story. Now the Concobar story—and I see that Westermarck himself half
admits this by speaking of King Concobar's so-called
droit as perhaps *a duty incumbent upon him*[29]—this
story makes it clear enough that the *jus* lay with the lass
and not with the king. It was, in fact, as Mr. Lennon
puts it, a *droit de vierge*. Women in Ireland have always enjoyed a high status.

The nature of the case is made explicit in the instance of Cuchulain's marriage to Emir. There would
have been no difficulty about this if Conobar had merely
possessed a right, because a right, like a privilege, need
not be exercised. The text, on the other hand, makes it
clear enough that Concobar was bound by a duty; and
what was to be done about it with Cuchulain liable to
those sudden and very destructive attacks of uncon-
trollable fury? With much tact Concobar sent the hero
to drive home the royal herds which were then on Sliav
Fuait. This Cuchulain did, and quite exhausted himself
—a good beginning. While he was away it was arranged
that Concobar should formally share a bed with Emir, in

[28]London, 1921, Vol. I, p. 179 et seq.
[29]Op. cit., Vol. I, p. 194, where Westermarck quotes *Leabhar
na h-Uidhri* on this point quite conclusively.

company with a fighting man called Fergus and a druid by the name of Cathbad—the equivalent, Mr. Lennon comments, of a modern archbishop—so that everything was highly respectable.

By this procedure (not unlike that which was used on occasion in a marriage by proxy) the king's *devoir* was considered to be accomplished, even to the extent of Concobar making what appears to have been the usual payment, gratefully accepted by Cuchulain. Clearly the king was not concerned, in this *lit à quatre,* with any royal prerogative but with the rights of the young lady, which were considered to have been satisfied by this elaborate arrangement.

This at least makes clear the distinction between a *jus primae noctis,* which may be vested in one of many possible claimants, and a *droit de siegneur,* which is specifically just what it is called. The two expressions should obviously not be used interchangeably, one being a subdivision of the other. A very similar case to that of King Concobar was cited by Alfred Marche,[30] who said of the king of the Ballante, *Ce n'est même pas pour lui, à proprement parler, un droit, mais une obligation.* The failure to keep this distinction clear has contributed no less to the general confusion than the factitious distinction between *de facto* power and *de jure* right. Funk and Wagnalls' *Standard Dictionary of Folklore,*[31] which does not distinguish between the *jus* in a general sense and the right of the lord, actually quotes the case of Concobar as its principal instance and further confuses the whole position by claiming that Catholic authorities *are vehement in their assertion that this* (i.e., the *jus*) *is a fable of modern date.* So far as I can discover, this is not true of Catholic authorities as a whole. In spite

[30]*Trois Voyages dans l'Afrique Occidentale* (Paris, 1879).
[31]New York, 1949–50, article on *Jus prima* [sic] *noctis.*

of the bilious propaganda of Veuillot, Catholic opinion generally has only maintained that the particular form of *jus* known as the *droit de seigneur* was never officially condoned by the Church in Europe—and that is clearly a different matter altogether.

What we do find unquestionably in the mediaeval records is an assumption that the Master of the King's Bedchamber had a right to the bridal bed after a royal wedding. Whether this was originally a substitute and represented a commuted vassal's right I am unable to say. If so there was a further commutation as a rule, for the M.K.B. was generally bought out by a cash payment. Such was the case with the Earl of Oxford, who put in a claim for the bridal bed used by Edward III and Philippa of Hainault, the king replying very reasonably that, although the wedding was over, he still required his couch, and offering a hundred marks in compensation.

August Bebel considered that such words as *Bettmund, Hemdschilling, Jungfernzins, Schürzenzins,* and *Bunzengroschen* were sufficient evidence that the *jus primae noctis* had existed in Middle Europe, the right having been commuted into a cash payment. This argument, however, is today considered quite inconclusive as evidence of any legal recognition of the *jus*. What the payment represented was, as Westermarck shows, a compensation to the lord when he was deprived of some human livestock, which was probably the explanation of the ancient bridal taxes recorded of Scotland and Ireland (the *mercheta mulierum* of English law.)[32] I must

---

[32]This was the explanation of the *merchet* given by Carew Hazlitt in an addendum to Brand's *Popular Antiquities* (London, 1870), Vol. II, p. 116. A similar example of a story invented to explain a custom may possibly be found in the changing of the traditional Jewish wedding day from

admit that I have never myself found any explicit statement of a seigneurial right in English law, in spite of all
those very odd tenures which Blount records in his
Fragmenta Antiquitatis. You may read of the Barony
of Burgh, held by Cornage (*which meant to blow a horn
when any invasion of the Scots was perceived*[33]), and of
other strange tenures, such as that of Geffrey de Lyston,
who *held lands in Witham, by the service of carrying
flour to make wafers for the King's birthday, whenever
his Majesty was in the kingdom.* But the old *droit* does
not get so much as a mention among these charming
and not too exacting feudal customs. (*Cornage* puts me
in mind of Moses again—but let that pass.)

But the true, the most blessed *droit de seigneur* was
surely that of which we read in Montaigne, who (as
Florio has it) loved *to lie hard and alone, yea and without a woman by me, after the Kingly manner; somewhat
well and warme covered.* I cannot, of course, agree to
all that the old philosopher had to say. He would never
have his bed warmed, which I should call plain maso-
chism. But though he recommended activity and vigilance
to youth, reproaching himself for his *lumpish heaviness
or drowzy dullnesse,* repenting his long sleeping (and
particularly that he would fall asleep again after first
waking in the morning), where would one find a better
product of better habits? The mind of Montaigne was
surely the quicker for bodily rest, more humane and
social for long solitude, more volatile for occasional

Wednesday to Tuesday—allegedly to outwit the Gentile of-
ficials who once exercised this right over Jewish subjects.

[33]Blount's own footnote. See edition of 1815 (London), p.
96. Why has no enterprising publisher ever produced an illustrated edition of this fascinating work? Surely Mr. Osbert
Lancaster would have been right in his natural element.

heaviness, more luminous for its periods of dullness; in short, even more than Dr. Johnson, he practised better than he preached. For his preaching he could cite Plato —a heathen, a blackguard and a bore—but in his practice, like Swift in the Battle of the Books, he disproved his own case by his own example. And (like many true bed-lovers) he was quite as hesitant to seek his bed as he was to leave it. Even so do swimmers often hover long before taking the delectable plunge, as though they feared their own happiness.

Few moralists have had a good word for sloth and somnolence. They are coupled by Gower as things to be avoided:

> *And he is cleped Sompnolence*
> *Which doth to Slouthe his reverence. . . .*

And often—sometimes even when they are most intent upon abusing this blessed pair—the poets and preachers, like Milton when portraying Satan, have betrayed their real esteem for the object of vilification. James Thomson's *Castle of Indolence* must surely make any normal reader think with affection of a solitary pillow. But what deep wells of sympathy are stirred by that unknown genius—another solitary, I avow—who wrote:

> *Sleep is a reconciling,*
> *A rest that peace begets. . . .*

That passage in which Thomas de Quincey described with such exact detail each movement which Kant would make after entering his bed (in order to ensure that he could enjoy the maximum of comfort and the optimum of warmth) shows us that philosophy can be usefully applied to this subject. It is strange that Kant should nevertheless have regarded the bed as a *nest of diseases* —another example of preaching versus practice. But no system, not even that of Kant, can settle a problem so essentially personal if a second person or (heaven forbid) a whole trinity or a multiplicity of bedfellows should be tugging, heaving, rolling, pushing, squeezing and making sudden, impulsive movements—especially, as we know, when these movements are made in sleep. Can anything place a greater strain upon human nature than the outrageous selfishness of a partner who—without even having the decency to wake up—rolls to the off side with the entire complement of bedding?

And how, again, can one read in bed with that timeless sense of the whole night to waste, if need be, when the gnawing claims of altruism demand that the light be switched out, or when the critic on the neighbouring pillow is there to remind one of the hour? Reading in bed is essentially a solitary pleasure. Tastes may vary. For Mr. Ivor Brown[34] *The Corpse in the Ash-can* is, on some occasions at least, an essential. He recommends detective fiction (as I do myself) for all cases of illness and convalescence and (when more than usually sceptical of his own doctor's attentions) likes to imagine the feelings of Dr. Watson's patients during those brief intervals when he was not serving as a foil for the brilliant deductions of Mr. Holmes. Others have sterner standards; and Mr. Huxley has told us of a holiday spent with a volume of the *Encyclopaedia Britannica*. I cannot remember which it was, but I know that there is a place in that *Encyclopaedia* where one passes abruptly from Marx to Mary, from the masses to the Mass, from the materialist conception to the immaculate. It is that volume which I think I should choose, for its bewildering variety—or would I? That would not be a bad literary competition: Which volume would you choose and

[34]Article on *Medicine and Murder* in *The Observer*, January 14, 1951.

why? (Answer in a sonnet to your favourite volume.) Do you begin to feel lumpish and drowsy already?

I will pass over the solitary art of dreaming, that *pas seul* of the liberated fancy, where

> *ever with dim consuming fire*
> *Swirl the slow eddies of desire.*

The quotation is from *Abnormal Psychology*, containing some heartening reflections by Barrington Gates upon the Unconscious Mind. It is but one of the many aspects of dream and fantasy which receive attention in Walter de la Mare's anthology, *Behold This Dreamer*. Here, if you would follow the wanderings of the soul in sleep as an underlying experience of mysticism, you may read all that I have omitted to tell you, such as the findings of Frazer, the reflections of Anna Robeson Burr. An anthology of this sort is not to be duplicated, and I have no mind to attempt the task. But I could add at least one point to the discourses upon divination by Pantagruel, Sir Thomas Browne and others—even, it might be, a cud for the Freudians to chew—and that is an observation of my old friend Verrier Elwin regarding the dream life of the aboriginal Gonds of central India. Whether it is still true I do not know; but in 1937 Mr. Elwin recorded this fact: that the dreams of the Gonds were preoccupied with anxiety (mainly regarding food) and fear—chiefly of the police. The police, said the Gonds, were symbolised by the bear—the only animal which attacks without provocation.[35]

Heureux qui peut dormir sans peur et sans remords
Dans le lit paternel, massif et vénérable,
Où tous les siens sont nés aussi bien qu'ils sont morts.

[35]*British Journal of Medical Psychology*, XVI (1937). The Gonds have not a very high opinion of the police, or had not

Not upon all of us did the bees swarm what time we
lay in our cradles, as they settled upon the mouth of
Plato (if you believe it) and upon the lips of the blessed
St. Ambrose, in token of future eloquence. I have no
words to describe the pleasures or the horrors of this
other world, except to say that a quiet conscience, a good
digestion and a mind free from anxiety, released from
fear—in short such a recipe as Burton and so many
others have offered—can turn the solitary bed of torture into the scene of our happiest memories, be they
waking or sleeping. But taste is an unaccountable thing,
concerning which we are wisely warned that *non est
disputandum;* and we may look long to find another who
completely shares each fad or fancy of our own. To
good Sir Thomas Browne and to Richard Hooker sleep
appeared as Death's younger brother,[36] and so like his
senior that neither dared trust him without prayer. But
to King William IV, as one might expect, the whole thing
looked very different. *I will not detain you any longer
from your amusement,* he said one evening to his guests,
and shall go to my own, which is to go to bed.

Or consider our eccentrics—and who is not guilty of
eccentricity in some form or other? Take by way of example one Thomas Bushell. A spectacular figure in his
time (both as courtier and as inventive engineer), he
did not—so John Aubrey tells us—*encumber him selfe
with his wife.* He was certainly married, a fact which
Aubrey himself mentions; so I construe this to mean that
he did not let Mrs. Bushell interfere overmuch with his

at that time. I recall Mr. Elwin explaining to me that, according to their story of the Creation, when the gods had
made all other creatures, out of the excrements of these they
fashioned policemen.

[36] An old dodge: Homer worked it. So did Beaumont and
Fletcher, and Sam Daniel, Uncle Tom Cobley and all.

way of living—which was as well for them both, as the ways of Thomas were somewhat irregular. Some of his exploits are but hinted in the *Brief Lives. He had the art,* wrote Aubrey (the *art,* mark you), *of running into dept, so sometimes he was attacqued and throwen into Prison; but he would extricate himselfe again straingely.* (He must certainly have practised his art successfully, as he died £120,000 in debt.) But the best reason for not encumbering himself with his wife was surely that she would never have agreed to share his bed or even his bedchamber, the way he preferred to appoint it. When in hiding from Cromwell's men he lay in a garret at Lambeth *hung all with black, and had some death's heads and bones painted.* At one end a recumbent skeleton was painted. *Here he had severall mortifying and divine Motto's . . . and out of his windowes a very pleasant prospect.*

Even the pleasant prospect from the window would hardly have reconciled most wives to the rest of that bedchamber—

> *Lay her in lillies and in violets*
> *And silken courteins over her display,*
> *And odoured sheets and Arras coverlets. . . .*

Spenser's bridal fantasy would suit better the minds of most women. Not that I greatly envy Mr. Bushell myself. But his case illustrates the necessity for separate sleeping arrangements where tastes differ, which they so frequently do. Think of Nebuchadnezzar. And Thomas Bushell's tastes were not so unique as you might imagine: they were but a dramatisation of a common theme. Thus Henry Vaughan the Silurist welcomed sleep as *death painted in a night-piece . . . a prelibation of that deep slumber . . . which nature never made nor meant to fright us with . . . giving us the fruition of this resemblance of death, lest we should grow impatient with delay. . . .* In a single phrase, he found that the very purpose of sleep was *to strengthen our hope of dying.* (Yet he would never sleep the sun up.)

It is in bed that one is best able to appreciate the truth of those ancient mythologies which gave precedence to darkness and death, for Dusky Dis was the All-Father and there is plenty of evidence that this was general in all the great mythological systems of Europe. This belief is echoed in the words of Mephistopheles:

I am part of the part which at first was the whole.[37]
Into that primeval Whole we sink, deeply satisfied to feel the end of feeling, to know that knowledge is gliding from the tired cells of the brain, conscious only of oncoming unconsciousness. But to revoke the step, as Virgil said, *superasque evadere ad auras,* to accept the awful impact of consciousness and the shock of its responsibilities is something which all normal people must necessarily dread. Leigh Hunt, in one of his essays—it is a wonder that I never noticed it when writing of beards —would lie abed thinking of the razor (*how totally opposed to every sensation of bed—how cold, how edgy, how hard!*) and admiring those who had the courage to go unshaven.

We, then, whose little life is rounded with a sleep, may do worse than those who have esteemed the treasures of oblivion. Sir Thomas Browne, the best of philosophers, seeing that the night of time so far surpassed its day, was content to welcome the brother of Death without feigning; and who shall deny that Thomas Bushell, Sarah Bernhardt and others have provided possible models for us? Yet for my own part I think of a bed as,

[37]See Goethe's *Faust: Ich bin ein Theil des Theils, der anfangs alles war.*

before all things, a place of unself-conscious idleness. But this same habit of idleness, said Burton, is the bane of body and mind, the nurse of naughtiness . . . the chief author of all mischief, one of the seven deadly sins and a sole cause of this (i.e., melancholy) and many other maladies. He summed it up as the Devil's cushion, and in another context he recalled among the terms of abuse heaped by Cicero upon that scoundrel Verres that in winter he was never *extra tectum—vis extra lectum,* making his lying abed into one of his crimes. I remain utterly unmoved by all such rhetoric. If it is a sin, it is a darling sin, and let each bear his own bundle: *Sed nisi peccassem, quid tu concedere posses?*[38]

I will even put in a word for bed at midday (or of a summer afternoon)—whether it be to sleep or to lie as I do now, reading and putting one's idle thoughts upon paper. *Sit brevis aut nullus tibi somnus meridianus*—so ran the stern ruling in the famous *Regimen Sanitatis Salernitanum,* Englished thus by Thomas Dekker:

> *Short let thy sleep at noon be*
> *Or rather let it none be.*

So also we find in John Russell's *Boke of Nature* that *moche slepe is not medcynable in myddis of the day.* Plautus had the same idea and probably a hundred others. What matter? And as for the hours we spend in this place:

> *Nature requires five,*
> *Custom takes seven,*
> *Laziness nine,*
> *And wickedness eleven.*

---

[38] I hoped this was said by the Bishop of Hippo to his Maker, but it seems it was only a remark made by Ovid to one of his girl friends.

I would be wicked could I only get me to bed in time. By cheating myself at that end I achieve grace in spite of myself. But give me the opportunity, and I will compete with the best. By the way, the word *dormeuse* is disappointing. I thought it meant a sleeping princess— at least she might be a princess, but I wouldn't have been particular about that. Murray says it might mean (a) a nightcap (to wear), (b) a travelling-carriage, adapted for sleeping in, or (c) a kind of couch or settee. Ouida is cited as the authority for this last usage: even Ouida omitted the sleeping lady, but the idea of anyone making a full-time profession of sleeping attracts me considerably. When Byron referred to sleep as *awful* (in *Don Juan*) he must surely have been thinking of the celebrated occasion of his own wedding, when he lay abed with his bride remarking: *Now, indeed I am in Hell.* Surely no solitary sleeper has ever felt that way about his bed.

Dream noble deeds, don't do them all day long. The world would be a happier place if all its would-be saviours could only be persuaded to take that advice. If only all the politicians, the generals and their armies, the sleepless editors, journalists and compositors, the advertising racketeers, the financiers and brokers and bankers, the tax collectors, the salesmen, pimps, lawyers and everybody (in a word) except those who grow food, make clothes, build houses or try to make this world a little less ugly, a little more amusing—if only all but these would retire to bed and stay there, daydreaming their wars and empires, their fortunes and scoops and booms and slumps, their laws and speeches and public antics—THIS WORLD WOULD BE A GOOD PLACE, AND FIT TO LIVE IN.

The Gull's Hornbook should be their breviary, as it

has so long been my own. Sleep, says the author, till you hear your belly grumbles. Never rise till you hear it ring noon at least. This custom he found venerable and princely, though the physicians damned it lest it brought too much health to mankind and an end to the trade of medicine. Sleep, the poor man's wealth (as Sidney has it), is not to be bought by tyrants. And Dekker, in reminding us of this, adds very aptly that *of so beautiful a shape is it, that though a man lie with an empress, his heart cannot be quiet till he leaves her embracements to be at rest with the other.*

This is the very core of my own doctrine. And as to the hour of rising:

> By the opinion of all philosophers and physicians it is not good to trust the air with our bodies till the sun with his flame-coloured wings hath fanned away the misty smoke of the morning . . . which work questionless cannot be finished, till the sun's car-horses stand prancing on the very top of highest noon. . . .

My father-in-law, a simple man, put it more tersely. He said one should not get up till the streets were aired. And in England the whole day may pass us by before those flame-coloured wings have done their chores. But if one must rise at all, surely it should be at noon, the hour (according to Dekker) when lords and ladies rise, and simpering mechants' wives, the fairest liers in the world. In this practice (*vide* the case of Robert, Duke of Normandy) he discovered much thrift—the saving of food, the preserving of our clothes.

No wonder that Zebulun (murmuring, *Où est la plume de ma tante,* as Joseph tried to pull off his bedclothes) preferred to remain where he was. Zebulun and I are of one mind.

There's something less than just and more than human
In early rising. When the Trumpet blows
To call us sluggards from our last repose,
I shall just yawn, and say (with J. H. Newman)
The night is dark and I am far from home:
Let them write ABSENT in the Judgment tome. . . .

But my state must be in the kingly manner—in the
manner of Montaigne

Chapter 9

STRANGE BEDFELLOWS

*To the Greek canonists of the 12th century
the name Syneisaktos means no more than the
housekeeper of a clergyman. Syneisaktism must,
therefore, have undergone a transition.*

Hans Achelis

*It isn't politics that makes strange bedfel-
lows. It's matrimony.*

Groucho Marx

He WAS WRONG, of course—I mean, Groucho. It is
murder, miracles and religious eccentricity, as we shall
see. Or there was Herman Melville's story of sharing a
bed with a head-hunter (the Grays quote it at length)
but I'll leave Melville till I get to Jonah's whale. I've a
few other things to get off my mind first; but that whale
is worrying me—the enormous whale, to which (for
some reason) Kit Smart likened the man of prayer.

I seldom finish a chapter without a few afterthoughts,
and one occurs to me right now on the text that *Coals
are not so necessary as husbands warme in bed.* The
quotation is from *The Mid-wives just Petition . . .
which said complaint they tendered to the House on
Monday last, being the 23 of Jan. 1643.*

This pamphlet purports to have been printed in London in the year 1643,[1] when both coals and husbands were no doubt scarce in the capital owing to cruel civil wars. In 1646 the pamphlet was reprinted, with a few small alterations, as *The Mid-wives just Complaint*—this time alleged to have been brought before the House of Commons on September 22, 1646. There are some odd things about this little squib, which I observed when reading up seventeenth-century midwifery, for some reason that I have forgotten. I noticed that the Thomason Catalogue treated the two editions as separate works, calling the second edition a satire, as though the first was a serious account of an actual petition. And a recent writer on the history of obstetrics[2] actually cites the edition of 1646 as a genuine document issued by the London midwives. At this rate it will not be long before some scholar pins a musty thesis onto my own rambling thoughts.

But about coals and husbands: among all the bright thoughts on bed and bawd to be found in *The Midwives just Petition* I know of no more spurious demand than this, which treats of husbands as though they were no more than warming pans. If natural warmth is to be a commodity of exchange, it is my considered opinion that women are in this matter better equipped than men; for most men of my acquaintance would die of cold if they

[1]The copy in the Thomason Collection has a manuscript correction, stating that the year should be 1642. This is immaterial, as the petition was in any case quite fictitious. The original pamphlet is E.86 (14) in the B.M. catalogue, the pressmark of the 1646 edition being E.355 (20).

[2]Harvey Graham in *Eternal Eve*, p. 189. The writer takes at face value the statement that this Complaint was actually presented to the House, as claimed. Would that such frivolity were possible; but if it were we must assume that this obvious satire was twice tendered to Parliament; and there is no record, alas, of either occasion.

were compelled to wear the clothes which the tougher sex finds sufficient in midwinter. The warming-pan theory, for what it is worth, is therefore a male argument,[3] showing that this seventeenth-century pamphlet must have been written by a masculine hand.

And yet I doubt if men, in spite of such notable exceptions as King David, have often sought the company of women for warmth. A wife cannot be thermostatically controlled; and even in the most primitive times more effective methods must surely have been available—at least in the post-Promethean period. Perhaps it is not too improbable to suppose that Prometheus was punished for that very reason. If the gods, so exemplary in their own married lives, felt as some modern writers do about double beds, they may have regarded the Promethean patent as the first step towards the divorce courts.

What did exist in times past, however, was a common belief that elderly people, by sharing beds with the young, acquired from them not so much heat as *vitality*. I am not sure to what extent such bed-sharing was practised by the elderly with this object, though there is a suggestion in I Kings I:3–4 that Abishag the Shunammite had something besides calories. The transference of vitality, however, was chiefly noticed by those who were concerned with the loss of it by the active partner. An example of this argument will be found in A. H. Japp's *Industrial Curiosities*,[4] where the author, who was among

[3]*Bonnie and Buxom in bed and at board* was what the old Anglo-Saxons expected their wives to be; but whoever heard of a buxom husband?

[4]London, 1880. Japp had a number of interesting observations on the beds and bedding habits of his time. He found the box-beds of Scotland *intolerable,* denounced wooden beds as unhygienic and spoke of the plank beds used in English prisons as *unenviably notorious.* They have not greatly changed.

the early opponents of the double bed (he quoted a certain Dr. Richardson in favour of single ones), was particular upon the point that the young were *enfeebled* by sleeping with the old.

Whatever the facts may be about this transference of vitality, we do know that there was a sound practical reason for prohibiting mothers and nurses from sharing beds with infants. Thus, in the *Concilia Scotiae*[5] there are several references to this prohibition, which occurs frequently in the canons of the Scottish Church. Number 56 (*De Baptismo*) warns women against keeping babies near them at night lest they should overlay them —which all goes to show how ably celibate priests can give their minds to domestic matters. Such regulations were not peculiar to Scotland, and the learned editor of the *Concilia Scotiae* quotes references showing that, in the thirteenth century, similar admonitions were considered necessary in England, and in the Isle of Man and the Sudreys (i.e., the Southern Hebrides).

The matter is mentioned again under the heading *De teneris infantibus custodiendis* (No. 84) and—curiously enough—under No. 108, *De vita et honestate clericorum*. When Calvinism had swept the country the Reformed Church debated the matter at its General Assembly in 1565. It was decided that *sik as oppressis children* (the meaning seems to have been restricted to the literal sense of lying on them) should be secluded from the sacraments until they had satisfied the Kirk. A ruling of 1568 defined the nature of the required catharsis: penance in

---

[5]Published by the Bannatyne Club (Edinburgh, 1866). See Vol. II, p. 31: *Femine moneantur ut pueros suos . . . juxta se de nocte non collocent* (etc.), and p. 42: *prohibemus ne matres aut nutrices teneros infantes in cubilibus secum collocare presumant* (etc.). See also p. 52 and the Preface (Vol. I), pages cxc and cclxxxi.

sackcloth, barefoot and bareheaded, so oft as the Kirk might appoint.

Kirk sessions at Glasgow in 1586 and 1589, according to Joseph Robertson, ordered that *smoorers* (smotherers) should be punished as adulterers. The continued recurrence of this theme and the appearance, on occasion, of the husband with his wife in the place of penance (*as art and part in smooring the bairn*) make it clear enough that the Kirk was not merely concerned to prevent accidents. The truth was that *smooring,* if countenanced at all, would have provided an almost perfect alibi for deliberate infanticide; and it was against murder that all these admonitions and penalties were really directed. In short one does not need the elaborate engines of Deloney and Wilkie Collins or the Archbishop's bed (was that Conrad? I can't trace it) to make sleeping a perilous thing: a bairn's worst bane, argued the Kirk, is its ane mither. At least, the Kirk was taking no chances.

To *smoor* is apparently quite a respectable word in the dictionary. Murray, among many instances of its use, cites Coverdale's version of I Kings III:19, where it appears that, in one of Solomon's celebrated court cases, a woman was alleged to have *smoored* her child and stolen a neighbour's baby to replace it. My ever resourceful friend Mr. Ben Vincent (who has just sent me II Corinthians II:9 as an indication of his willingness to read the proofs of this book) comes in at this point with a story that might well provide a case of *smooring.* He says that he is assured (on the impeccable authority of his much-travelled and very observant sire) that certain polygamous Bantu dispense altogether with beds by the simple expedient of sleeping on a row of nice fat wives. Like so many Pantagruelian fantasies, I should imagine that this would in actuality be very unsatisfactory, even for the husband. But few of my readers will know that

Jonah was nigh *smoored* on his second *voyage en pois-son*. I don't suppose you even knew he did make a second trip that way; but he did, and I had intended to deal with it in discussing *wagons-lit* (*wagons-lits? wagon-lits?*) and other travelling accommodation. However, as it is clear now that we shall have no room for that, here is the story apropos of *smooring*.

It seems that, according to rabbinical accounts, which are somewhat confused, Jonah was either of Zebulun (the literary set) or again he may have been the son of that widow at Zarephath, who took in Elijah as a lodger. (At this point I could, of course, digress at length about landladies and boardinghouse beds; but the whole matter has already been covered by Philip Owens in a compre-hensive anthology.[6]) If the latter account is to be cred-ited, Jonah must have been familiar with cruses in early youth (see I Kings XVII:9-16). It will also be recalled that the landlady's little boy (query Jonah) died while Elijah was there, and that Elijah made himself very use-ful by restoring him to life and one thing and another about the house. The method of restoring this boy may be mentioned *en passant*, because it is important that Elijah placed him upon his own bed, doubtless relying on some form of sympathetic magic—though this form of therapy is not universally approved.[7]

So if the widow's boy was indeed none other than Jonah, the future prophet had also an early acquaintance with the miraculous. By one account he is furthermore to be identified with that young prophet whom Elijah sent in order to incite Jehu to revolt—this seems a likely

[6]*Bed and Sometimes Breakfast.*

[7]Whatever the virtues of a prophet's bed may be, some have maintained that it is taboo to sleep on the bed of a saint. See Stith Thompson's *Motif-Index of Folk Literature,* under C.93.1. For Elijah's use of the bed, see I Kings XVII:19.

guess, as the rather coarse speech made by the young prophet in II Kings IX shows a strong resemblance to Jonah's choleric style of rhetoric. Be that as it may, when Jonah grew up and was duly taken on board by the large fish ordained for that very purpose from the beginning of time, he was quite used to improbable adventures and settled down very comfortably.

Now it appears further that the destiny of this large fish was to be eaten by Leviathan, and that he had an appointment with Leviathan for this purpose. Unwilling to embarrass his passenger by involving him in an incident which could easily have proved a *casus belli,* the fish explained the situation to Jonah, who was by no means travelling *incognito.* The resourceful prophet, however, gave Leviathan the shock of his life by popping out and displaying an Israeli passport—nothing less than the Seal of Abraham. This so impressed Leviathan that he agreed not to operate on Jonah's large fish, which expressed considerable gratitude. In fact Jonah proved as lucky to that fish as he had been unlucky to his previous transport; and the fish, to express his thanks, took the prophet on a lightning tour of the world.

At this point it is necessary for me to record my own apology to Herman Melville. In *Beards* (how in the sea did it ever get into *Beards?*) I threw some doubt on Melville's suggestion that Jonah circumnavigated Africa in three days, long anticipating Vasco da Gama and establishing a submarine record never since equalled. But the rabbis say that among the places visited on this sightseeing *rundfahrt* was the place where the Israelites crossed the Red Sea. As the Suez Canal had not at that time been constructed, this clearly means that Jonah made it the long way round within the three days, which is very good going.

We now come by an equally roundabout route to the

real point of this story. The accommodation on this fish
was excellent. It even ran to artificial light and central
heating.[8] In fact Jonah became so comfortable that he
thought of taking up that sort of life as a career. And I
regret to add that he did not even say his prayers; for the
more comfortable people are the less they are apt to
pray, as experience shows. It cannot have been at this
time that the bowels of the monster resounded with the
psalms of his food (that pleasant conceit of Sidonius
Apollinaris) but during Jonah's short trip in Fish No. 2,
who is at this very moment approaching.

Fish No. 2 was much larger than Jonah's fish, which
we will now call Fish No. 1. No. 2 was sent because it
was clearly necessary, if Jonah was to be induced to say
his prayers and to get on with that job at Nineveh, to
make him less comfortable. Fish No. 2 was a hijacking
female who delivered an ultimatum to Fish No. 1 (a
male, by the way) to the effect that she held a warrant of
extradition[9] for Jonah ben Amittai, described as a
prophet, and that furthermore, if Fish No. 1 did not
immediately hand over the goods, the result would be
very bad for Fish No. 1, as he would be eaten, with con-
tents, by this aggressive female. At this point there appears to have been some sort of conference, at which
Leviathan was subpoenaed and came alongside to give
evidence; but I think this was only to give a cloak of
legality to what was really a question of *fish majeure*.

In the upshot, so to speak, the prophet was depiscisated

[8]See the *Jewish Encyclopedia,* Vol. III, p. 227, Col. 1. The
lighting is clearly specified. I deduce the heating from the
state of Jonah's wardrobe when he arrived at Nineveh. The
fish—or possibly this was the second fish—was evidently
overheated, as his clothes were somewhat scorched on dis-
embarking.

[9]Or it may have been a writ of *habeas corpus:* the rabbis do
not specify.

by No. 1 and taken on board by No. 2. Here he had a thoroughly bad time, as this female fish was *enceinte,* and he found the accommodation crowded and inconvenient. The pregnancy of No. 2 certainly suggests that she was no true fish at all, but a whale—in fact the question as to whether Jonah was swallowed by a fish or a whale can now be regarded as answered: he was swallowed by each in turn. In the female whale it appears that Jonah—I have reached it at last—was all but *smoored* by baby whales waiting to be born. It was on this second (and most uncomfortable) voyage that the prophet remembered again to say his prayers and promised to live a better life, etc., if only he could be released. A bargain was made, Jonah was ejected onto the good earth, and the captain and crew of that Joppa–Tarshish coaster (his original vessel) were so impressed—they happened to be on the quay when he made his spectacular landing —that they all went at once to Jerusalem to be circumcised. As to Jonah, he lived to a fine age and eventually —like his godfather, Elijah—was translated (assumpted?) to heaven without the inconvenience of dying.

However, the strange partners of the *proud plumpe bed* which concern me tonight are not embryonic whales. Nor will I write of *incubi* and *succubi,* though my witchcraft files are full of stories strange enough, complete with the most elaborate confessions in courts of law.[10] No: our discourse shall be, oddly enough, of

[10]The Benedictine Abbot of Senones, Augustin Calmet (uncle of that great pogonologist, Dom Fangé, who wrote his biography), said that the Jews in post-biblical times used to write in the four corners of the bedroom the words, *Adam, Havah, Chutz, Lilith* (Adam, Eve, scram Lilith). They had every reason to fear Lilith, who was chief of the *succubi.* Witkowski says that *l'intarissable Dom Calmet passe pour avoir été un peu crédule;* but Ulrich von Hutten

ascetics. We know, from the story of St. Anthony, to
what torments ascetics have been subjected. Whoever
has seen Anthony as Goya saw him—and didn't Goya
himself run off with a nun?—will remember the contrast
between the tortured saint and the cold cruel effeminacy
of the Spanish Bourbons in the Prado. Here, then, was a
problem real enough. But Anthony did not go in search
of temptation; and I now propose to consider, in place
of the common theme of saints assailed by *succubi,* the
unusual saga of saints in search of trouble.[11]

No one, perhaps, ever proposed to himself a more
singular reason for sharing a bed than the Blessed St.
Aldhelm of Malmesbury, who would spend his nights
(so Giraldus Cambrensis informs us) *inter duas puellas,
unam ab uno latere, alteram ab altero.* This peculiarly
uncomfortable arrangement he favoured not for any
carnal reasons but rather for the pleasure of self-mortification; and not merely for that alone, but in order that
people should speak ill of him—*ut ab hominibus diffam-
aretur.* Whether the girls were consulted on either
point we are not informed; but one way or another,
whatever sort of a man Aldhelm was (and it is my con-

---

quoted a very similar incantation and I make a guess that
the familiar appeal to the four evangelists has a very old
history and is connected with this very matter.

[11]All the same it reminds me of another way to get murdered
in one's bed. According to Southey's *St. Romuald,* a good
method is to get named as a saint in any place where they
value the bones of one. St. Francis was all but torn to pieces
before he was dead, such was the piety of the people of Assisi; and in Southey's ballad the good people, having a saint
among them,

> . . . *thought it prudent to secure*
> *His relics while we might;*
> *And so we meant to strangle him one night.*

jecture that he was no matinée idol), it cannot have been a very pleasant experience for his companions. Moreover, whilst the saint exposed himself to censure, the *puellae* must surely have laid themselves open to ridicule. Perhaps it was to compensate them that Aldhelm wrote his treatise, *De Laude Virginitatis*.

This is but one of many examples mentioned by Dom Louis Gougaud in an article entitled *Mulierum Consortia, Etude sur le Syneisaktisme chez les Ascètes Celtiques*.[12] The classic case of syneisaktism appears to have concerned a lady by the name of Crinog, to whom an anonymous Irish ascetic wrote a poem, of which a translation is given in Kuno Meyer's *Selections from Ancient Irish Poetry*.[13] The poet, who had apparently occupied a portion of Crinog's bed when he was seven years old, recalls more recent events, or at least the talk of the town:

> *Since then you have slept with four men after me,*
> *Without folly or falling away:*
> *I know, I hear it on all sides,*
> *You are pure, without sin from man.*

Meyer, in a note to this poem, definitely claims Crinog as a *conhospita*—a nun who lived with a priest, monk or hermit as his *uxor spiritualis*. This practice, suppressed or abandoned elsewhere, is noted as a curious survival in the Irish Church of the tenth century, to which the poem *An Crinog* belongs. The ninth-century story of Liadin and Curither indicates a similar custom, worth a moment's attention.

Liadin was a poetess. On one of her travels she met a young poet called Curither, in Connaught. Curither sug-

[12]In *Eriu,* the Journal of the School of Irish Learning, Dublin, Vol. IX, pp. 147–56.

[13]London, 1913, pp. 37–38 and note on p. 112.

gested they should get together, using more or less the same argument that Isadora Duncan tried on Bernard Shaw, some years later. Liadin seemed to find the idea quite agreeable, but pointed out that it would interfere with her programme just then. She suggested that they should make a date later, and this was agreed.

In the meantime, however, Liadin had (for reasons unexplained) become some sort of a nun; so the lovers sought the advice of King Cummine the Tall, who was by way of being a saint. He offered them the prospect of soul-friendship (*hamnchairde*) with the alternatives of being allowed either to talk or to see one another but not both. Curither chose talk; he said they had seen quite a lot of one another already. The result was that they spent some rather bleak hours talking through closed doors. Liadin, in the poem, says a sad piece about this, and how there would never be a thigh bone at the right hand of the man who used to be a poet.[14] She says also that she herself cannot sleep.

The next thing is they are back talking to Cummine the Tall, and Liadin is complaining rather bitterly. In reply Cummine makes the curious proposition that the lovers shall sleep together for one night, with a student between them to see fair play. The Cummine compromise is accepted and the following day the student is cross-questioned by Cummine, who threatens to kill him if he does not come clean. What follows is a little obscure. We are not told what the youth said about the matter, because somebody (Curither?) had evidently threatened him with death if he confessed. There is no

[14]The right hand indicates a reversal of Solomon's prescription, already mentioned (Cant. II:6, and VIII:3). But the Irish always liked to be different—compare their practice in the matter of Easter and the tonsure. Even today English Catholics shake their heads about Irish liturgical usage.

record of what the student said, faced with such a di-
lemma, or of what happened to him as a result. We pass
straight on to Curither, who is now practising celibacy
among the scholars and later on the open road, deeply
bemoaned by Liadin. She even goes after him, but he
books a passage in a coracle and is not seen again.

What was the meaning of the strange ordeal proposed
by Cummine the Tall? We have, of course, the authority
of the *Catalogus Sanctorum Hiberniae* that the saints in
those parts did not (in Ireland's Golden Age) decline
the company of women, being so firmly grounded on bed-
rock that the winds of temptation had no terrors for
them. But they do not always appear to have been so
self-confident. St. Ciaran, who went to a co-educational
school run by St. Finnian of Clonnard, studied alongside
of a princess—but he affirmed afterwards that he could
never have recognised her, as he saw no more than her
feet. It must have been somewhat gloomy for the girl.
Peculiar as it may seem, the original arrangement made
for the lovers by Cummine was one not so unusual in
Middle Ages. I mean talking without seeing each other—
not that bed business.

For example, Thomas Walsingham (*Gesta Abbatum
Monasterii S. Albani*) tells of a good monk who left St.
Albans to live in a hermit cell near Dunstable. There he
had a next-door neighbour called Christine, a virgin
whom he indoctrinated for four years without once setting eyes on her (*Non tamen consensit ipse faciem videre
virginis*) by means of which extra precaution, for he was
already of a great age, a good time was enjoyed by all.[15]

---

[15]It was by no means unusual for a female recluse to be
found living at or near a mediaeval monastery, whilst some
men preferred to practise their austerities (says Dom Louis
Gougaud) *dans un monastère de femmes* (*Ermites et Reclus*
[Vienna, 1928], p. 76).

But Cummine may have had special reasons of his own, as he was himself the incestuous product of careless bedding arrangements in the royal household of King Fiachna. He had every reason to believe that things should not be left to chance.

Such somewhat cautious *consortium* hardly concerns us, however. The *Catalogue of the Saints of Ireland*—an eighth-century work—recognises decline in all such timidity. The original meaning of *consortium* was quite simply and explicitly this: *the association of a woman vowed to perpetual chastity with an ecclesiastic, both occupying the same house and living together as brother and sister*. I quote the definition given by the Rev. T. Olden in an article on this subject.[16] Such a relationship as that of Dame Margaret Kyrkby, disciple of the famous mystic Richard Rolle, with the austere Richard does not belong to this category; she lived twelve miles away in her own cell, mindful (no doubt) of her master's own dictum: *Fugito feminas, qui Christum amare voluntarie vovisti*.[17] To a hermit of those days (early fourteenth century) a woman could be nothing but a temptation: and innumerable stories are concerned with the devices of the Devil to snare the recluse by means of women or even by personal appearance in the guise of a wench, that is to say, as a *succubus*—but I must try to keep off that subject.

The practice which many saints had emphatically condemned (as we shall presently note) lingered long in the ecclesiastical anarchy of Ireland—and that in spite, also, of official efforts to suppress it. Even among the first

[16]*Proceedings of the Royal Irish Academy*, Third Series, III (1894), 416.

[17]Richard had very good reason. A devil disguised as a young woman once invaded his bed and was only with difficulty put to flight by prayer.

generation of Irish Christians the conflict had begun. A bishop in St. Patrick's time—his name was Mel—set up house at Ardagh with a lady who has been described as his aunt,[18] but it seems that St. Patrick had his doubts and personally investigated the matter on the spot. His conclusions were evidently unfavourable to Bishop Mel, for he issued a decree forbidding this sort of thing. Thomas Olden noted that the wording of this decree corresponded closely with the ninth canon of a famous early synod of the Irish Church:

> Let not a monk and a virgin from different places dwell together in one house.

St. Patrick, as Olden pointed out, was not a man to stand any trifling. This was made clear in the case of Lupait, said to have been the saint's own sister, though in fact he had no sisters in Ireland. (*She was one of those sisters I am treating of,* says Olden.) Believing her to be guilty of misconduct, Patrick drove his chariot over her, not merely once but three times in succession, to make sure. He was a savage old man, by all accounts. And Olden's problem, writing in 1894, was to reconcile Patrick's attitude—confirmed by the synod already quoted—with the statement in the *Catalogus Sanctorum Hiberniae* that the first and holiest saints *rejected not the service and Consortia of women.* There seems to be a good deal of confusion, in fact; and one of the few things which emerges very clearly is the symbolic fire test. The woman who was really playing this game according to the rules could carry fire—neither she nor her clothing was combustible. If this proved to be wrong she was no good woman; and the sooner she was turned adrift the better for the reputation of the monk, clerk or

[18]See Dr. J. H. Todd, *St. Patrick, Apostle of Ireland* (Dublin, 1864), pp. 90–91.

hermit.[19] Curiously enough, the question of the inflammability of the male partner is never discussed, because (apparently) it did not arise.

Another reference to the *consortium* in Gaelic literature occurs in the *Calendar of Oengus* (c. A.D. 800) where the habits of an ascetic by the name of Scothine were described[20] in the course of an enquiry similar to that conducted by Patrick into the *Affaire Mel*. Scothine, like Aldhelm, evidently had two partners for his purpose, which was quite simply (I quote from the translation by Whitley Stokes) *that the battle with the Devil might be the greater for him*. The ecclesiastical inspector, St. Brendan, who was sent to look into this matter was invited by Scothine to take his place in the bed, where the young women arrived carrying glowing embers and nonchalantly threw them on the floor before they lay down beside the horrified Brendan. His companions soon advised him to adjourn to the bathtub, observing that Scothine found cold water helpful.[21] As we have already observed, this custom was not uncommon among mediaeval ascetics, even when enjoying the comparative comforts of solitude; and even the heroic Aldhelm used

[19]Chastity tests by magical means are very common in folklore. Sometimes they are made by means of the bed or the pillows. See Stith Thompson's *Motif-Index*, H.411.10.

[20]*Avec une extrême crudité d'expression,* as Louis Gougaud puts it (*Eriu*, IX, p. 152). See previous reference to Scothine, supra, p. 92.

[21]*Félire Oengusso Céli Dé,* edited by Whitley Stokes; Notes to January 2 (Henry Bradshaw Soc., Vol. XXIX [London, 1905]). In the notes to November 25 the curious case of Findchu is mentioned. This saint, when not suspending his body between two sickles, placed beneath his armpits, would share his bed with any corpse that had been brought to his church for burial. Cold water was very mild medicine by comparison.

cold water or tumbles in the snow as a specific for such purposes, according to William of Malmesbury.

That this custom of bed-sharing among Christians, as a means of flouting the Devil, had an ancient history (though hardly to be called reputable) is attested by the denunciations of the Early Fathers. Thus St. Jerome, in his celebrated epistle *Ad Eustochium* (Ep. XXII), mentions the custom—blushing to do so (for all the world like Macaulay in that coy passage where he refers to Clive's forgery). What says St. Jerome? *Pudet dicere, pro nefas!* But all the same these are the sad facts, says he. Whence came this plague of *agapetae*[22] into the Church? Whence these wives *sine nuptiis*, this *novum genus* of concubines . . . these monogamous harlots? They share the same house, the same *cubiculum*, often the same bed—*et suspiciosos nos vocant* if we jump to conclusions. Against these *agapetae*—Beloved Ones— the saint hurled Solomon's warning, out of Proverbs VI:27:

> Can a man take fire in his bosom and his clothes
> not be burned?

Well, apparently there were once women who could literally do that thing—in Ireland. But St. Jerome was naturally, perhaps, of a sceptical nature. Even the chaste widows he suspected of sleeping off their dinners by dreaming of apostles; and one may more easily believe it after reading the erotic passages in which the saint himself describes the rewards of chastity (Ep. XXII, 25), quoting the Song of Solomon but surpassing it in the voluptuous quality of his own imagery. His views on

[22]*Erant igitur* Agapetae *virgines aut viduae, quae specie caelibatus ac virginitatis nuptiis nuntium mittebant et cum Clericis in eadem domo habitabant, ac, ne qua pravi consortio suspicio esset, sese invicem* dilectos *ac* dilectas *appellabant, vel etiam* fratres *aut* Sorores (Du Cange).

woman in relation to man were simply and succinctly stated—no one was safe who slept near a snake: it might bite or it might not, and there was no more to it. Woman, said this saint, burns up the conscience of her consort. Irenaeus is more vague. Attacking the Valentinians, a heretical sect (*Adv. Haer.*, Book I, Cap. VI, 3), he accuses them of false and deceitful forms of syneisaktism, but without making clear his views on the genuine article. Epiphanius, who spoke of the matter as common talk, was very definite in his condemnation of such a source of scandal (*Panar. Haeres.*, LXIII). Generally speaking, we shall observe that the later writers are more vehement than the early ones.

And yet, although even in Cyprian's days[23] these curious practices were definitely being denounced, they evidently died very slowly. The Benedictine scholar, Dom Louis Gougaud, who was skeptical of the exaggerated importance given to syneisaktism by Hans Achelis and others, himself considered that remains of it were traceable in England and Wales as late as the twelfth and thirteenth centuries. Gougaud was nevertheless right in contending that the practice never received official approval. As often as it crept into the Church it was denounced, until eventually it disappeared. St. John Chrysostom found syneisaktism rampant at Constantinople when he became Patriarch there, and is said to have begun by sweeping the stairs from the top[24]—a new

[23]*I.e.*, during the third century, between the time of Irenaeus and that of Jerome. I will quote Cyprian later, but I cannot keep this up without another story, and nor can you.

[24]Thus Palladius in his *Dialogus*. The opinion of this saint regarding women was sufficiently comprehensive. They were, he said, a necessary evil, a natural temptation, a desirable calamity, a domestic peril, a deadly fascination and a painted evil. (Note to publisher: what about a book on antifeminist literature?)

broom indeed. He forced the Byzantine priests to give up their unlawful companions, though it lost him popularity.

A German legend might throw some light on this, if there were a grain of truth in it, though I fear there is none at all. According to this story (published by Richard Benz in his *Alte deutsche Legenden*), St. John of the Golden Mouth, while living as an anchorite, was visited by the emperor's daughter, who was blown there in a great gale. The same wind separated the princess from some other young woman, with whom she had been picking flowers. What was the good man to do? He could not let the girl starve or send her out to be eaten by some beast of prey. So he took her in.

At first, so the legend tells us, all went well. John made a line across his cell, and each lived as a recluse for all the world as though the line had been a wall ten feet thick with no door nor so much as a window. But fasting and prayer proved insufficient to keep away the Father of Evil. It was John himself (indeed this is a most scurrilous story, for which the saint has, I hope, pardoned both the author of the libel and myself for repeating it *in nomine ben trovato,* as they say in Macaronia), it was John, I repeat, who first crossed that line and—once more, what was he to do? Terrible remorse followed. John felt the risk of allowing the young woman to remain, for what had happened once might happen again. He could so easily be led into sin again. To obviate this the holy man took drastic steps: he led his companion to the edge of a cliff and pushed her over.[25]

Not until this was done did it occur to John that it

[25]I seem to remember a similar story about St. Kevin of Glendalough; but in that story the woman did rather ask for it.

was, after all, he himself who had crossed the frontier. The unfairness of his behaviour struck him with remorseless logic. He observed that he had now committed yet another sin, laying upon his soul, with which (as you will observe) he was more concerned than with anything else, the crime of murder. Actually he was quite mistaken about this, for the story ends as happily as any stage play, where the dead can always be counted upon to take a bow and receive the plaudits due to them. To keep you no further in suspense, it appears that after various adventures John was captured by the emperor's huntsmen, who mistook the unkempt hermit for a strange beast of unknown species. This curious specimen was naturally brought before the emperor himself, whose wife had recently produced another child.

Now this child was such another as those whom we met in Chapter 1, the type that answers back from its earliest youth. It is not on record that the little sister of the unfortunate woman whom John had launched into space (and eternity, as he believed) actually held conversations in the womb. But this babe certainly knew her own mind, for when the Pope had offered to baptise her himself, which is considered quite an honour in some parts, what had she done but tell him flatly, plainly, in simple, straightforward language, that he should do nothing of the sort. The unusual fact of a newborn child having spoken at all had been eclipsed by the unorthodoxy of her observations: indeed, they appear to have caused so much distress that the legend passes over the really important fact, the irrelevant miracle, with an impatience that recalls the reply of the man in the story— you know it, of course—to the effect that his dog was not very clever because it had just lost three games of chess. It is indeed in old legends that we should seek for the origin of such stories, in legend that we may hope to find the true and original shaggy dog, for which the Greeks must undoubtedly have had a word.

But I promised to bring my Chrysostom Apocrypha to a happy ending, and it shall be done. The Pope, it seems, had condescended to argue with this precocious infant, who had replied that she would be baptised by none other than the holy St. John. This was Dutch to His Holiness, who had no idea what the child was prattling about, though in fact John had once been quite a pet of his—but there were so many Johns and nobody at the emperor's court could think of one, just then, who could have been called holy or a saint. It was not until the huntsmen returned with their strange find that the infant, instantly recognising John in the baboon or gorilla, or whatever it was they took him to be, began another conversation, which ended with John standing up suddenly, all couth and kempt, and baptising the child according to her wish.

Soon afterwards the story of the cliff incident appears to have leaked out—apparently via the confessional, as we are only told that John confessed it to the Pope. But the emperor, coming to hear of it one day, asked John just where it all happened. And the most remarkable thing is that when John went with some of the emperor's men to find the place and identify the body, what should he be finding at the bottom of the precipice but his old *syneisaktos,* the emperor's older daughter, alive and in excellent health, and she as beautiful as ever, provided miraculously with a suitable trousseau. As for John, he was down for a bishopric.

All the same, if you think of it, an experience like that would make any Patriarch think twice about the wisdom of syneisaktism. Perhaps the story was invented in order to explain John's attitude to the practice.

Du Cange, under *subintroductae,* has an interesting

entry regarding this practice, mainly concerned with
official efforts to prohibit it. He explains that the word
is the equivalent of *Extraneae* but that *Subintroductae*
was the word more commonly used—hence the Nicaean
ruling that *Presbyteri vel Diaconi Subintroductas mulieres nullo modo secum audeant habitare nisi forsitan
matrem suam, aut proximitatem generis sui habentes.*[26]
These *subintroductae* are by no means to be confused
with *Superinductae,* who were merely plain concubines
(dog bites man). There is a wealth of information on
this subject, as it affected the Eastern Church, in the
volumes of Migne's *Patrologiae* and various scholars
have dealt with the practice in the West.[27]

One story of Joannes Cassianus[28] tells of a holy man
named Paphnutius, who made the discovery that he
could still burn his hand in the oven. This made him reflect upon the weakness of the flesh; and in a subsequent
vision he was properly put in his place by an angel who
invited him to experiment in syneisaktism if he really
imagined himself to be beyond all human weakness.
(Paphnutius wisely declined to accept this challenge.)
Cassian himself, in a remarkable passage, suggested that
a monk should by every possible means fly from women
and bishops (omnimodis monachum fugere debere mu-

[26]H. C. Lea, in his *History of Sacerdotal Celibacy,* built up
a strong case that the authority for the Roman practice in
this matter derives entirely from this canon of the Nicaean
Council, and that the canon was never intended to prohibit
the marriage of the clergy, which had, in fact, never been
specifically prohibited in any General Council at that time.

[27]The footnotes on pp. 86–88 of Gougaud's *Christianity in
Celtic Lands* (London, 1932) constitute almost a complete
bibliography of this subject.

[28]Collatio XV, *De Charismatibus Divinis,* Cap. X, *Revelatio
de perfectae castitatis experimento.* The story is told on the
authority of Abbot Nesteros.

lieres et episcopos[29])—the juxtaposition is of some interest. Cassian cited it actually as a *sententia* of the Fathers which still held good, but admitted to some personal weakness, as he could not escape either his sister or his bishop.

Syneisaktism was condemned by a synod held at Elvira (A.D. 305) and at Ancyra (A.D. 314), also by the Council of Nicaea. Pope Zosimus is also listed among those who considered it necessary to condemn the practice explicitly. The extent of such customs among Christians, particularly during the first four centuries, has been much debated, and the frequent condemnations of syneisaktism by the Fathers of the Church have been cited as proof that it could not have been a common practice. This argument is surely somewhat distorted— the Early Fathers would not have wasted so much time in condemning habits which affected very few people. Indeed, the language used by St. Cyprian makes it reasonably clear that he condemned something well known to everyone in Carthage and most other places. There were, he specifically tells us, certain Confessors of the Faith who blotted their own brave record by sharing their beds with women.[30] The context makes it quite clear that this sharing was a form of syneisaktism. The

---

[29]*De Coenobiorum Inst.*, Lib. XI, Cap. XVII, *Quod monachus mulieres et episcopos vitare debeat.* See Migne, *P. L.* XLIX, 418.

[30]*Epistle to Rogatianus the Presbyter,* and others (No. VI in Migne and No. XIII in the Oxford edition). Those accused were among the *élite*—the *illustrata.* In another letter Cyprian speaks of this practice and explicitly forbids not merely sleeping but even living together (i.e., a modified form of *consortium*), the former practice being described in the strongest language as *turpis et foeda dormitio.* This is in the *Epistle to Pomponius* (No. LXI in Migne), a letter devoted entirely to the evils of syneisaktism.

Confessors were, in fact, showing off—and Cyprian reproved them for endangering the salvation of their neighbours (presumably the *subintroductae* in question).

Pierre de Labriolle, in a long article on *Mariage Spirituel* among the early Christians,[31] quotes from a document of unknown authorship, *De singularitate clericorum,* in which some bishop once found it necessary to warn priests against such practices. This priest made it clear that delinquents against whom he directed his rhetoric regarded syneisaktism as a daily triumph for chastity (*cotidianus triumphus pro castitate*[32]). With the devastating logic of the extremist, some apparently argued that—if the sexes were really of such danger to one another—the whole co-educational basis of religion should be revised. Where, in short, was the line to be drawn? The scriptural precedents were numerous—a whole range from Elijah, who lodged with a widow (see my observation on Jonah), to that mysterious passage in I Corinthians VII (36–38) where Paul discoursed of some unknown practice:

> But if any man think that he behaveth himself uncomely toward his virgin, if she pass the flower of her age, and need so require, let him do what he will, he sinneth not: let them marry.
>
> Nevertheless he that standeth stedfast, in his heart, having no necessity, but hath power over his own will, and hath so decreed that he will keep his virgin, doeth well.

[31]*Revue Historique,* Tom. 137 (1921), 204–25.

[32]The case of Leontius and Eustalia, mentioned by Athanasius, is sometimes cited in this connection; but the facts clearly do not fit the case, for Leontius was not concerned with the *cotidianus triumphus.* As Bayle says, *il se fit mettre en état par de bonnes mutilations de coucher avec cette amie, sans qu'on le soupçonnât d'impudicité.*

So then he that giveth her in marriage doeth
well; but he that giveth her not in marriage doeth
better.

I should be rash to comment on a passage of apparent
hibber-jibber that has puzzled wiser heads than mine.

There is a curious passage in *The Shepherd,* that
elaborate allegory written by Hermas, brother of Pope
Pius I, about the year 148 or earlier. I quote it from the
translation by William Wake, later Archbishop of Can-
terbury, as published in 1693. This passage is to be found
in the third section of *The Shepherd,* known as the
Similitudes, in which the Shepherd (who is the Angel of
Repentance) takes Hermas to a place where a tower is
being built by a multitude of men, apparently assisted
(in a manner not very clearly specified) by some good-
looking young women. In the ninth *Similitude* (Chapters
X and XI) the Shepherd leaves Hermas with these young
women, remarking, *I have at present a little business;
but I will suddainly explain all things unto thee. Tarry
here for me till I come.*

> I said unto him: Sir, What shall I do here alone?
> He answered, Thou art not alone, seeing all these
> virgins are with thee. I said; Sir, Deliver me unto
> them. Then he called them, and said unto them; I
> commend this Man unto you till I shall come. So
> I remain'd with those Virgins; Now they were
> Chearful and Courteous unto me, especially the
> four which seemed to be the Chiefest among them.
> Then those Virgins said unto me; that shepherd
> will not return hither today. I said unto them;
> What then shall I do? They answered; Tarry for
> him till the Evening, if perhaps he may come and
> speak with thee. But if not, yet thou shalt con-
> tinue with us till he do's come. I said unto them,

I will tarry for him till Evening; but if he comes not by that time I will go home, and return hither the next Morning.

Thus far the story continues on a very practical level, what with the Angel of Repentance being called away on a *little business* and the very sensible discussion with the girls as to whether one should wait till he returns. It is also quite natural that Hermas should accept the invitation to stay on for tea and maybe supper. But at this point the allegory takes quite an unexpected turn:

> They answered me; thou art delivered unto us, thou mayst not depart from us. I said, Where shall I tarry? They replied; Thou shalt sleep with us as a Brother, not as a Husband: For thou art our Brother, and we are ready from henceforth to dwell with thee; for thou art very dear to us. Howbeit I was ashamed to continue with them. But she that seemed to be the chiefest amongst them, embraced me, and began to kiss me. And the rest when they saw that I was kissed by her began also to kiss me as a Brother; and led me about the Tower, and play'd with me. . . .
>
> And when the Evening came on, I would forthwith have gone home, but they with-held me, and suffered me not to depart. Wherefore I continued with them that Night near the same Tower. So they spread their Linnen Garments upon the Ground; and placed me in the middle nor did they any thing else but Pray. I also pray'd with them without ceasing, no less than they. Who when they saw me pray in that manner, rejoyced greatly; and I continued there with them till next day.

Here again there appears to be a suggestion that the practices of Aldhelm and Scothine may have had very ancient precedents. If we include heretical sects there is perhaps some similarity to be traced between the synei-saktism of certain Catholic enthusiasts and the customs of the Abelians or Abelonians, who took their name from Abel. Unlike his father Adam, and determined not to repeat the mistake which had occasioned his own birth, Abel took a wife—so it was said—but rejected the tree of knowledge. In order to return to this state of innocence, for which Eden was intended, the sectaries who followed Abel's example made marriage compulsory, whilst placing all procreation under a rigid taboo —a restriction which, as Bayle remarks, was in no way calculated to make the sect lasting. Such, in fact, was the logic of their own tenets that the Abelians died out some time before the days of St. Augustine. They were, while they lasted, to be found around the saint's home town and Augustine makes mention of them.

These Abelians did, it is true, endeavour to perpetuate their own ideas by availing themselves of the human frailty of less enlightened persons, just as a celibate clergy must recruit perpetually among (e.g.) the nephews of the hierarchy. Each pair of sectaries was intended to adopt two children—one boy and one girl—whom they thereby saved from poverty in this world and damnation in the next; and the adopted children were intended to inherit jointly on the same basis of partnership. Whether the Abelians subjected themselves to the ordeals already described is not known, but even without such a test there may well have been practical disadvantages in this form of housekeeping which accelerated the collapse of the Abelian system. Abbasa, the sister of Haroun-al-Raschid, when married to his favourite, Giafar, under similar conditions (imposed by her tyrannical brother) certainly found such a marriage intolerable, and so did her husband. They took risks, were betrayed by a fine pair of twins, and paid the penalty which one might have expected—he with his life, and she with her liberty. If such risks are taken by those who live within peril of a caliph's whims one may reasonably ask whether there were not sometimes lapses among the Abelians and a landslide on occasion.

Other heretical sects practised various forms of syneisaktism. Hans Achelis[33] cites Eusebius on the case of a Montanist who was said to have been united in spiritual marriage with a prophetess.[34] Another heretic—the ex-Marcionite Apelles—had a couple of spiritual wives, if Tertullian is to be believed.[35] But in none of these heretical instances is the relationship defined closely, as it was in some of the classic cases already mentioned—the statements are suspiciously vague in many cases; and one may reasonably suspect that syneisaktism was often used as a term of abuse or to discredit an opponent, much as we have seen such words as bolshevism, fascism, nazism, communism or anarchism used in our own time.

When Paul of Samosata, Bishop of Antioch, was condemned as a heretic by a synod of the Church (about A.D. 266) it was natural enough, surely, to pin on him and his presbyters and deacons the charge of keeping in tow a number of *subintroductae*, including two of ex-

[33]Article on *Agapetae* in *Encyclopaedia of Religion and Ethics* (1908).

[34]Eusebius, *Ecclesiastical History*, Book V, Cap. XVIII. Apart from the *ex parte* nature of the statement, however, the text itself is obscure. See Dr. Lake's comment in the Loeb edition.

[35]*De Praescriptione Haereticorum*, Books VI and XXX (see also Eusebius, Book V, Cap. XIII). Tertullian had his own version of syneisaktism: see *De Exhort. Castit.*, Cap. XII, where he attacks second marriages and suggests living with a poor and holy old woman as an alternative.

ceptional glamour for the bishop's personal delectation;
with whom he always (so it was said) went places. The
wonder is, on reflection, that the good Catholics who tortured and murdered Priscillian and his followers in the
fourth century (a novelty in those days, which disgusted
St. Ambrose and aroused the indignation of St. Martin of
Tours) did not use the same label to discredit Priscillian-
ism—for did not these *Abstinentes* hold that the relationship between the sexes should be purely spiritual? Propaganda came near enough, however, for it traced the
Abelonians to Priscillian, and threw in the Adamiani,
reputed to worship in the altogether, in promiscuous
steam baths. . . . Similar stories have been told of the
Apostolici or Apotactics and the Encratites.

I am not sure whether or not I should include among
my examples of syneisaktisms the lady mentioned by the
Chevalier de la Tour Landry. He was writing, I may remind you, for the instruction of his daughters; and in
Chapter XXV of his book we come across this gay lady,
society hostess and patroness of tournaments, who used
to share her bed with one of the gentry, the Seigneur de
Craon—*mais ce fut sans villennie et sans y mal penser.*
On the whole there seems no reason to believe that the
practitioners of syneisaktism behaved otherwise, in spite
of instances to the contrary, because they were obviously
exceptional men and women.

Nevertheless, a writer in the *Saturday Review* of July
13, 1867, commenting on some passages in Joseph Robertson's *Concilia Scotiae,* went so far as to suggest that
the *subintroductae* of the early Church in Ireland and
the Scottish Highlands were

> not nuns, bound by the vow of chastity. On the
> contrary [sic] they were all young and beautiful,
> and were selected not only for their natural

charms, but for their power of seductiveness, and their freedom from all virtuous scruples. The use they were put to was to test the purity of the saints —to try, by the sound Baconian method of experiment, whether those who aspired to hagiological honours really possessed the superhuman asceticism of which they boasted.

The writer found such practices *more picturesque than edifying*. He did but follow the line already taken by such learned prigs as Gibbon. The author of the *Decline and Fall* in his famous fifteenth chapter (see Bury's edition, Vol. II, pp. 36–37) noted some whimsical codes which, said he, *would force a smile from the young and a blush from the fair*. O, the coy, the smug, the preposterous Mr. Gibbon on his eternal seesaw (scribble, scribble, scribble . . .). See how he swings:

> Some were insensible and some were invincible against the assaults of the flesh. Disdaining an ignominious flight, the virgins of the warm climate of Africa encountered the enemy in the closest engagement; they permitted the priests and deacons to share their bed and gloried amidst the flames in their unsullied purity. But insulted Nature sometimes vindicated her rights, and this new species of martyrdom served only to introduce a new scandal into the Church.

There is not a word about the honest efforts of the Church to suppress these peculiar practices—efforts which were, at last, successful. But a footnote informs us that *something like this rash attempt was long afterwards imputed to the founder of the order of Fontevrault*. On this delicate subject, said Gibbon, Bayle had amused himself.

Gibbon's reference to Bayle and Fontevrault leads us
to the *Nouvelles de la République des Lettres* (April
1686) where Bayle reviewed a work on the Order of
Fontevrault, founded by Robert d'Arbrisel in the year
1100. The order included both monks and nuns; and it
appears that at different times a cardinal and a bishop
had written to Robert d'Arbrisel, urging him to give up
sharing his bed with the *religieuses* of his establishment.
One of these letters had been published by the Jesuit
scholar Sirmond in 1610, causing no small embarrassment and annoyance to members of the Order of Fontevrault; and the Père de la Mainferme had taken it upon
himself to answer the charges on behalf of this order.[36]

In reviewing this apologia Bayle explained that *l'on
n'accusoit pas Robert de se mettre au lit avec des filles
pour satisfaire les desirs de la Nature; c'étoient seulement
pour se mortifier davantage, & pour livrer à ses sens une
guerre plus cruelle*. The founder of Fontevrault wished to
triumph over women (that is to say, the Devil) *dans le
même lieu qui est le champ & le théâtre continuel de
leurs triomphes*. For this purpose he was accused of having selected the most beautiful of his nuns, *pour passer
les nuits avec elles dans un même lit tout déshabillez,*
though Bayle points out with commendable fairness that
there is absolutely no evidence that he chose good-looking lasses.

Once more it may be necessary to emphasise the fact
that this practice at least received no official contemporary approval. Geoffrey, Abbot of Vendôme, stated
the charge quite bluntly (*Faeminarum quasdam, ut*

---

[36]*Clypeus nascentis Fontebraldensis Ordonis, contra priscos
& novos ejus calumniatores*. This was the second edition of
a work previously published under another title. The first
volume of this second edition had appeared in 1684, published in Paris.

*dicitur, nimis familiariter tecum habitare permittis, &
cum ipsis etiam, & inter ipsas, noctu frequenter cubare
non erubescis*). But note the *ut dicitur:* the abbot does
not seem quite certain of his facts, and proceeds with:
If you now do or have ever done this you have found
out a new, unheard-of, but fruitless kind of martyrdom.
The Bishop of Rennes was equally vague, but no less
clear in stating the official view. He had heard that
Robert allowed women to share his bed at night and
took a poor view of it.

Here was smoke enough; but the eventual conclusion
of Pierre Bayle was that the story was untrue—a legend
built upon a slander—and the impartial sceptic rejected
it, in spite of the able presentation of the case by the
French wit and *savant,* Giles Ménage.[37] The most that
can be conjectured from such a story is that the idea of
syneisaktism was still in the minds of those who invented
the calumny. But, for the matter of that, the idea was
still alive when Léon Bloy introduced it into his novel
Désespéré, as Pierre de Labriolle pointed out. Here the
heroine deliberately defaced herself, in the best mediaeval manner, rather than remain a source of temptation.

According to one account, the origin of *Bundling* in
America was that same urge towards Works of Su-
pererogation which led ascetics of the Adlhelm type to
subject themselves to temptation. An old Quakeress,
Hannah Whitall Smith, claimed that the practice began
at Brimfield, Massachusetts, where a group of young
women *attempted to increase their spiritual virtue by
killing the sense of shame which had been put as a
curse upon Adam.* To this end they are supposed to have
devised the custom of bundling, *which consisted in entering the bedroom of a young preacher in the middle of*

[37]See Bayle's *Dictionary* (English edition of 1734-41),
article on Fontevrault in Vol. V.

the night and putting themselves into highly compro-
mising situations . . . and the greater the scandal and
opprobrium the better they were satisfied that they were
making an acceptable sacrifice to the Lord.[38]

How wrong, how very, very wrong this statement was
we shall see in the next chapter. My notes on the subject are enormous; but we have spent so much time daydreaming (and so much of the publisher's paper), what
with Jonah and the Whale and one thing and another,
that I shall have to cut the matter somewhat short. Perhaps after all I shall have to make a separate book of it
some day.

[38]Hannah Whitall Smith, *Religious Fanaticism,* edited by
Rachel Strachey (New York, 1928). Curiously enough, this
is the only passage, out of all the vast store of Bundling
Literature, which is quoted by C. and M. Gray in their
anthology. The more is my regret that I shall have to curtail
my own notes on the subject, which is surely due for further
investigation.

Chapter 10

THE ART OF BUNDLING

Art consists in drawing the line somewhere.
G. K. Chesterton

BUNDLE . . . to sleep in one's clothes on the same bed or couch with (as was customary with persons of opposite sexes, in Wales and New England).

Murray's *English Dictionary* (1887)

QUEESTEN: an odd way of wooing usual in some sea-towns on Isles of Holland, after this manner: when the wench is gone to bed, the fellow enters the room and lays himself down, in his clothes upon the blanket, next unto her, and thus he talks with her very innocently, as it is reported.

Willem Sewel's *Large Dictionary English and Dutch* (Amsterdam, 1708)

SUPERFICIALLY, I suppose that nothing could be more similar than certain aspects of syneisaktism (left-wing syneisaktism) and the practise of bundling. Actually the gulf between the two is as broad as that which separated Dives from Lazarus. In one case we have ascetics wilfully

mortifying themselves by exposure to temptation: in the
other we have young couples, with an eye to matrimony,
using a bed as a rendezvous for sweet converse. Bundling in this sense must therefore be strictly distinguished, on the one hand from the self-torture of the
ascetics and on the other hand from less restrained uses
of the bed with which it has often been confused.

It is true, of course, that established usage justifies
the employment of this word for one other purpose.
Thus Captain Grose, in his *Dictionary of the Vulgar
Tongue,* defined bundling as:

> A man and a woman lying on the same bed with
> their clothes on; an expedient practised in America
> on a scarcity of beds, where, on such occasions,
> husbands and parents frequently permitted trav-
> ellers to *bundle* with their wives and daughters.

We must grant this seconday meaning. Indeed, it may
have been, perhaps, the primary meaning, from which
the more familiar use of the word—with a more familiar
practice—eventually arose. What was permitted to the
stranger might, *a fortiori,* have been claimed by the
lover, ever eager to make use of all opportunities. If so,
then time and custom eventually restricted the application of the word; and it is with bundling in the amorous
sense that I am now concerned.

Fortunately the whole subject was carefully surveyed
in 1869 by Dr. Henry Reed Stiles, an American antiquarian who wrote at a time when memories of bundling were still sufficiently green in America to assist
him in his survey. I have, at the moment, no complete
information regarding the various editions of his book.
The first edition appears to have been published at Al-
bany in 1869. Before me at the moment are two editions.
The first bears a preface of 1871. It was obviously pub-

lished much later (privately issued for subscribers only), but indicates neither a date nor its place of publication. My other copy was published by the Peter Pauper Press (New York), undated, but I think in 1937—if I rightly identify it with the edition mentioned in the Cumulative Book Index (New York) for 1938–42. However, I do not pretend to be a bibliographer—someone with more patience and less fond of his bed must sort out these undated volumes. I only mention the matter because I shall be referring to Dr. Stiles a good deal and *my references will all be to the Peter Pauper edition,* as the least unlikely one for the reader to have handy.

It is, of course, improbable that you will have *any* edition at hand. The book is for some reason almost unknown in England. There was not even a copy in the British Museum until one was presented by Mr. George Shively of Doubleday and Company in 1951, at my suggestion. . . . The American editions appear to be rare—they were limited and never achieved the popular success which the book deserved. Perhaps Americans are sensitive on this subject, like the Welsh scholars from whom I made roundabout enquiries, receiving in reply an indication that they were most unwilling to supply gunpowder for more squibs against Welsh Wales. I can't blame the Welsh, though I solemnly affirm that I meant them no mischief. But the Americans, since they now rule the earth, ought not to mind being laughed at. I would like them to know that this is a good safety valve for us (the subject peoples) that we should laugh at them—for which reason mediaeval kings employed court jesters, who had license to be as offensive as they pleased.

As to Dr. Stiles, I do not wish merely to give you a digest of his entertaining book, so I shall quote it only where necessary, presume to correct the doctor upon certain points and add some scraps of further information or indications as to where it is to be found; but always with the hope that a new edition of *Bundling: Its Origins, Progress and Decline in America* will appear and have a better reception. Indeed, as I cannot possibly share all my own material with you now, I am most willing to edit a new edition of Stiles, with additional notes and corrections, for the public of America and England—and Wales and Holland. (*Advt.*)

As recently as the year 1941 a newspaper correspondent[1] reported the continued existence of bundling in the Orkneys as one of the discoveries of British troops stationed in these islands. According to this writer, parents in the Orkneys tied *a special, traditional and very complicated knot round the ankles of the girl for bundling purposes*. The explanation given for the custom was that the houses were mere shacks and that it was impossible for courting couples to find a room in the house where they could be alone, except in a bedroom. Cold and snow would make *walking out* impossible of an evening, so that logic indicated the bedroom as the only possible place. The writer was careful to note that bundling was carried out *in the most decorous manner,* and recalled that three or four years previously a play had been performed in London which dealt with the American version of the custom, indicating that a long wooden plank had been used in New England to separate the courting couples.

This play must have been *The Pursuit of Happiness,* a comedy by Alan Child and Isabelle Louden, first produced in New York (1933). The theme is that Max Christman, a deserter from the Hessian troops employed by the British in the American War of Independence, seeks for life, liberty and the pursuit of happiness as

[1]*Daily Mail,* January 6, 1941.

laid down by the famous American declaration. On his way to join the colonial army he falls in love with a young woman and dates her for bundling. After some complications, including threats of scandal and the interest of another man (the sheriff, no less) LOVE PREVAILS. However, before we come to New England bundling I propose to say a few things about the less famous (but no less honourable and ancient) practices in the British Isles and some other places.

The Scottish custom of *hand-fasting*, which was a form of probationary marriage, has sometimes been confused with bundling. This is a libel on bundling proper, which never assumed such liberties in theory, however much its opportunities may have been occasionally abused. It is also only fair to the Scottish kirk to remark that *hand-fasting*, though common enough until modern times, never received any blessing from the ministers—who, indeed, lost much trade by it.[2] But the reason for it is quite simply stated by Halliday Sutherland in *The Arches of the Years:* the necessity of being certain of children. A small crofter could not afford to have a childless wife; and he made sure of children, as the best old-age insurance, before he married. A similar custom was once found in Ireland.

But this is not the purpose of bundling, in spite of

[2]For ecclesiastical condemnation of *hand-fasting*, see the long footnote to Vol. I (Preface), p. clxxxvi and clxxxvii, of the *Concilia Scotiae*. It was denounced by a synodal statute before the Reformation, in the time of Archbishop Forman, but was still flourishing under the nose of John Knox, and was deplored in 1562 by the minister and congregation of Aberdeen as a common practice, though it was *manifest fornicatioun and huirdom*. According to the Rev. W. Gregor, in an article on the Folklore of N.E. Scotland (*Relics of Pop. Antiq.*, Folk Lore Soc., No. VII), the practice of *hand-fasting* was justified by an interpretation of Job XVII:3— which seems a long shot.

Washington Irving's hint that it helped the early settlers
to produce in record time

> a long-sided, raw-boned, hardy race of whoreson
> whalers, wood-cutters, fishermen and peddlers; and
> strapping corn-fed wenches, who by their united
> efforts tended marvellously towards populating
> those notable tracts of country called Nantucket,
> Piscataway, and Cape Cod.

More to the point is a reference by Halliday Sutherland to the customs of Lewis, the most northerly island
of the Hebrides. Here, as in the Orkneys (and for a very
similar reason), it is evident that bundling has been
practised in our time. I am informed that this is still
the case in Lewis, but that the people are far too shy
of foreigners to tell them anything—which, of course,
is quite as it should be. In their low, rectangular black
houses (built of drystone with thatched roofs) there is
little accommodation. Retiring from the one living room
to the girl's bedroom, the lovers seek warmth in bed. In
place of the Orkney ankle-knot we read that the girl's
legs *are inserted into one large stocking, which her
mother ties above the knees.* What is perhaps most important is the fact that, according to Halliday Sutherland, this practice is called bundling.[3] It seems unlikely
that the Hebridean islanders should have borrowed from
America a name for what must surely be an ancient
custom of their own. If not, then both the American
custom and its name must surely come from Scotland
or both from a common origin.

The anthropologists have, in fact, given insufficient
attention to this phenomenon, leaving the origin and
cultural track of bundling for anybody's guess. The significance of the mere word, for example (this fact that

[*] *The Arches of the Years* (London, 1933), p. 291.

the people of Lewis and those of New England call the same sport by the same name), automatically disposes of one important point—bundling, it is clear, is not an autochthonous development in America and the Hebrides. We must look for an explanation in the diffusion of culture—probably in some Calvinistic Culture Complex which might include (say) chapel-going, psalm-singing, fuel economy, canny lads, braw lasses, thrifty parents and bundling.

Evidence regarding the Scottish mainland seems to be somewhat inconclusive. Dr. Stiles, who devoted some space to *hand-fasting* (plus a considerable Appendix dealing exclusively with the Royal Commission on the Marriage Laws, in 1868), completely failed to establish any case whatsoever for bundling in Scotland, apart from the islands, which he apparently ignored. There is said, however, to be a reference in Walter Gregor's *Echo of the Olden Time from the North of Scotland* (which I cannot trace) indicating a form of true bundling on the mainland.

Campion's slanders (those English Catholics were always so charitable to their fellow Catholics of Ireland) went too far to justify any charge of bundling against the Irish.[4] Of course Irish sleeping habits have, in every generation, been a matter of stock humour in England.

---

[4] C. S. Wake in his *Evolution of Morality* (London, 1878), Vol. I, p. 401, vaguely includes *Celtic peoples* among his bundlers and suggests that bundling arose from *such a condition of things as that which was prevalent among the ancient Irish*. It need hardly be added that Wake's authorities for Ireland and its customs were persons violently prejudiced against the Irish—a criticism which applies (*mutatis mutandis*) to almost the whole of this absurd and pretentious book. With the same credulity he accepted at face value the opinion of Caesar on the ancient Britons (*De Bello Gallico*, V, 14)—another conqueror's verdict on the conquered.

What, after all, is more exquisitely funny than the sight of people living in poverty when one has stolen their best land? Whether they shared their cabins with their livestock at any time I do not know. It is quite certain that in the seventeenth and eighteenth centuries they commonly made use of one room for man, wife, children and guests—for the very sufficient reason that a one-room cabin was the total accommodation available.

In this they resembled the ancient Britons, whose practice in this matter so shocked (and misled) the Roman invaders. But the Rev. Caesar Otway (whose *Sketches in Erris and Tyrawly* is one of the authorities often cited for the existence of the communal sleeping room in Ireland at the end of the eighteenth century) was very definite in his statement that there was *great propriety of conduct*.[5] Moreover (in spite of statements which have been made on this subject by Dr. Stiles and others), there appears to have been no true bundling (i.e., in the amatory sense) at any time in Ireland. One point of general information regarding the beds used in the seventeenth century—and much later in some parts of the island—is that they were evidently mere bundles of straw and that it was customary to burn the bed of a person who had died, as a preliminary to the Wake; but that hardly helps us and we will look next at Wales, where there is plenty of evidence.

It is, in fact, curious that so much has been said and written about bundling in New England, whilst *caru yn y gwely*, that is to say, courting in bed (the similar custom which so long prevailed in Wales), has received

[5]Edward Maclysacht, in *Irish Life in the Seventeenth Century*, shows that the same opinion was expressed by another English writer, Philip Luckombe, who toured Ireland in 1779. Very similar arrangements were common in Iceland in the early nineteenth century.

so little attention. William Wirt Sikes, in his *British
Goblins*,[6] is particular on the point that the Welsh words
sopen (a bundle or squeezed-up mess) and *sypio* (to
bundle or squeeze together) are not used for courting in
bed, especially as *sopen* can also mean a baggage in
the old English colloquial sense of the word. The phrase
honoured by time and custom in Wales is *caru yn y
gwely*. It was originally regulated by laws of some severity, and a slip could literally send a careless young
woman over the edge of a precipice. For the man the
courting bed was little but a trick, if Mr. Wirt Sikes is
to be credited, for there was no turning back and marriage was all but inescapable.

Stiles has several quotations on the Welsh theme,
which need only be summarised here. Welsh sleeping
arrangements in the twelfth century were similar to the
somewhat promiscuous arrangements to be found at
that time in any European country; yet Dr. Stiles—quite
unwarrantably—deduces that *these habits . . . were con-
verted . . . into amatory custom*. This will hardly do,
as the doctor argues on the false assumption that the
conditions in mediaeval Wales were unique or unusual.
By the eighteenth century the evidence of S. J. Pratt
makes it clear that bundling was then practised by Welsh
courting couples—*and what would astonish more pol-
ished lovers . . . carried on honourably*.[7] Pratt wrote
from personal observation and evidently made careful

[6]A single paragraph on pp. 301–2 of this book (published
in 1880) appears to have suggested the theme for *The
Black Venus*—a fact which I offer gratis to future biog-
raphers of my friend Rhys Davies, to whom I am much indebted for permission to use quotations from his entertaining novel. See below.

[7]*Gleanings through Wales, Holland and Westphalia* (London, 1797), Vol. I, pp. 105–7.

enquiries. The Rev. W. W. Bingley confirmed this account a few years later[8] with reference to Caernarvonshire, Anglesea and Merionethshire. He explicitly compared the Welsh custom with American bundling, assured his readers that the Welsh lover retained *an essential part of his dress* and gave the usual assurance that it was all due to shortage of fuel. Perhaps the reverend gentleman's most choice remark, however, was that

> Since this custom is entirely confined to the labouring classes of the community, it is not so pregnant with danger as, on a first supposition, it might seem.

Further confirmation is provided by Stiles from J. T. Barber's *Tour throughout North Wales and Monmouthshire* (London, 1803, pp. 103–4) and Sir John Carr's passages on Wales in *The Stranger in Ireland* (London, 1806, p. 11). Barber described the bed as a mere heap of straw or fern in a lonely Welsh hut and was careful to note that the courter was admitted as *consors lecti* but not in *nudatum corpus*. Carr mentioned a device not unlike that already noted in the Orkneys and in the Isle of Lewis—the fastening of the girl's petticoat at the bottom, though he hinted at sliding knots. (Sir John was a professional tourist and raconteur.)

The publication of Carr's book evidently caused relief in America, where bundling was already the occasion of rude comment by visitors from Europe. Stiles quotes a review of the book from the *Connecticut Courant*, which found *no small gratification* in the thought that bundling was probably an import from overseas. More

[8] *North Wales, including its Scenery* (*etc.*) (London, 1804), Vol. II, p. 282.

astonishing, however, was an article by John Neal, over twenty years later.[9]

Neal's case—and he was evidently out to defend the honour of America—was that many travellers had written about American bundling, but that careful research on his own part had only revealed one single admitted case within living memory. As to the value of that statement, we will deal with it presently: the really preposterous thing is that John Neal, who discounted all travellers' tales regarding his own country, and demanded proved and attested instances (rightly enough), adopted quite the opposite policy when discussing Wales. Here it was sufficient that a lady (*a Welsh woman whose word is truth itself*) had told Mr. Neal not only that bundling was common in her country but that it was not carried out with New England propriety. On this single charge and without further investigation the sober, cautious, shrewd Mr. Neal condemned the entire Welsh nation. Indeed, after stating very categorically that *they bundle in Wales; bundling there is a serious matter,* the Yankee champion went on to say flatly the opposite:

> Bundling, however, is known in other countries, where they have less excuse, and in Wales where they do *not* bundle, as I have said before, it is no reproach for a woman to have had a child before marriage. . . .

The Welsh case for bundling has been brilliantly stated in recent years by Mr. Rhys Davies in his novel,

[9]See Stiles, p. 24, for *Connecticut Courant* and Appendix One, pp. 77–84, for Neal's article and later editorial note. Neal was then editor of *The Yankee* (Portland, Maine) and his obnebulations on bundling appeared in 1828, August 13 (p. 258) and August 20 (p. 271).

The Black Venus (London, 1944). Here the theme is that of a handsome young woman, Olwen Powell, heiress to rich farm lands, who is determined to use the old and accepted practice in order to find the right husband. Urged on by an Englishwoman, the local vicar attacks bundling from his pulpit and directs his attacks principally against Olwen, as a notorious practitioner. The Chapel faction, composed of old-fashioned bundlers for the most part, becomes very uneasy. Bundling has hitherto been a matter of one man and one woman; but Olwen, by sampling in turn every eligible man in the neighbourhood, has aroused the anger of the men and the jealousy of the women. The story opens at an unspecified date, but presumably in the early years of the twentieth century.

The minister of the Chapel decides to hold an enquiry and Olwen agrees to put herself and her conduct on trial. She is an ardent feminist, willing and able to justify herself. This tribunal (all male), presided over by a local justice of the peace (Moesen Rowlands), meets *in camera*. It would be impossible, and most unethical, to reproduce the wealth of evidence that is brought forward. The fact is that everyone should read this delightful novel. *Well, stop it,* says one man. *Then what happens, hey? Pneumonia caught in the damp and chests bad at thirty.* Even in the summer there were gnats. Adam and Eve had been turned out of Eden for courting in the open. . . .

Another speaker refers to progress. To him bundling is an antiquated custom, doomed like the horse by the toot-toot of the automobile. But his is a lone voice. Another replies that there has been progress in bundling. His point is important, as it suggests a possible derivation of this custom from the *grossesse d'essai,* to which I shall refer later. It had been a hard test, with the woman cast aside in scorn if not fertile she proved. The present custom was both moral and humane—a great improvement. For proof there were now less hurried weddings than there had been at one time.

One reference of some interest is genuine, so the author assures me, though neither he nor I can trace the source from which he obtained it. This is an account of stitching the courters up together in a sack—a practice attributed to the people of Merionethshire. More to the point, perhaps, is the proposal of Moesen Rowlands, J.P., that there should always be a bolster between the courting couple—the equivalent of the plank attributed by some to New England. This he describes as an old seventeenth-century remedy, long fallen into disuse. A strong and healthy flavour of Welsh nationalism pervades the discussion, distrustful of English criticism and innovations. (*A new and foreign race the English are and have not yet had time to settle successfully in Britain* . . . they are without background and look like lost orphans, though it is true they have a language of their own, like hens, crows and wasps . . . *our guests, the English.*)

Olwen is agreeable to the use of the bolster, but points out with pride that the dead feathers and stale wool of civilisation do not make such a bolster as a woman with a will can raise. Actually, as we learn later, Olwen has her own private rearmament programme—a sharp hair-prong which she keeps under her pillow.

Though some of Olwen's suitors are silent and embarrassed, *caru yn y gwely* provides opportunities for others to discourse eloquently. I don't propose to say any more here about pillow chat, but those who take my advice and read *The Black Venus* (if they have not already done so) will be delighted with the courtship of John Damsons, the undertaker, who talks of

beds and coffins. I was particularly interested in one
of Rhys Davies' courters who leaped from the bed during a thunderstorm and hid underneath until the storm
was over. His behaviour, peculiar as it may appear in
any circumstances, and particularly as an interlude in
such an intimate method of wooing, had a precedent in
the behaviour of that lady of whom the Duc de Saint-
Simon tells in his *Mémoires,* for she not only took
refuge under the bed at such times, but caused her servants to sit on top, apparently in the capacity of shock
absorbers. (Incidentally, Edward I was nearly killed
by lightning when sitting on his bed with his wife, so
Ollie James of the Cincinnati *Enquirer* was right in suggesting that beds should be decently upholstered underneath.)

According to Brand's *Popular Antiquities,*[10] bundling
was at one time customary in Westmorland and Cumber-
land, but already obsolescent in 1839. No evidence is
supplied, but the strong Celtic tradition of the English
Lake District (long part of the ancient British Kingdom
of Strathclyde, even in Saxon times) suggests that the
story is not too improbable—the more so as the mountainous nature of the country would have created
conditions similar to those which encouraged Welsh
caru yn y gwely, and—as we shall see—bundling in
Norway.

So far as England is concerned there is no more to
say except for two observations, neither of which can
be taken to imply the existence of any established custom. The great William Harvey (according to John
Aubrey, who is by no means a very reliable authority)
was perhaps a bundler, in some sense. *I remember,* wrote
Aubrey, *he kept a pretty young wench to wayte on him,
which I guesse he made use of for warmeth-sake, as*
[10]Vol. II, p. 56.

King David did. (Aubrey also credited Dr. Harvey
with the view that *we Europeans knew not how to order
or governe our Women, and that the Turks were the
only people who used them wisely*.) Whatever may be
the truth about Harvey's pretty wench, the author of
the *Brief Lives* makes it clear that the poor man suffered as much from heat as he did from cold: *He was
hott-headed, and his thoughts working would many
times keepe him from sleepinge; he told me that then
his way was to rise out of his Bed and walke about his
Chamber in his shirt till he was pretty coole, i.e. till he
began to have a horror, and then returne to bed, and
sleepe very comfortably*. Perhaps it was then that Dr.
Harvey found the need of warmth again. As he is generally credited with discovering the circulation of the
blood[11] it may be that these alternations proved of
empirical value in his researches.

This is one isolated case. Another is a mediaeval instance (fiction at that) mentioned by Stiles (p. 27)—
the incident from *Blonde of Oxford*, an old romance in
which a young lady called Blonde apparently bundles
with a gentleman known as Jehan. (We are not told
if he eventually married a brunette.) The English evidence is admittedly thin—an important point if we are
to apply diffusionist theories to the origin of American
bundling.

The idea, if not the actual practice, of bundling ap-

[11]This discovery was first made by Servetus—that great and
enlightened genius, who was burnt for heresy by the
Calvinists at Geneva (Calvin seeking the co-operation of
the Holy Inquisition in the same spirit that made Herod
and Pilate friends). This discovery by Servetus is mentioned
by H. W. Haggard in *Devils, Drugs and Doctors* (New
York, 1929), p. 147, but he is not correct in identifying the
views of Servetus on the circulation of the blood with the
heresy for which he was judicially murdered.

pears to have been known to Marguerite of Navarre, who introduced a bundling anecdote into her Heptameron; which caused Montaigne to remark (I quote him in Florio's English) that:

> I think it not a wonder . . . nor doe I deeme it a matter of extreame difficultie, for a man to weare-out a whole night, in all opportunitie and libertie, in companie of a faire Mistresse, long time before sued-unto, and by him desired; religiously keeping his word, if he have engaged himselfe, to be contented with simple kisses and plaine touching.[12]

Bayle in his *Dictionary* (article on *Fontevrault*—Remark O.) speaks of having heard tell of men being so tried by maids. It is—the idea occurs to me at this moment—perhaps the most important distinction between bundling proper and certain practices superficially similar to it that in bundling *it is the maid who tries the man*. In *hand-fasting* and in the *grossesse d'essai* it is the woman who is tested. In bundling the man's behaviour is on trial; in these older customs it is the woman's fertility. Thus, if one developed from the other, there must at some point have been a feminist revolution of the greatest importance. It is for that triumphant feminism that Mr. Rhys Davies' heroine speaks so eloquently.

C. S. Wake's statement that the Kafirs of his time had a custom *allied* to the bundling *of the Celtic peoples* is too typically vague to be considered seriously.

[12]*Essays*, Book II, Chapter XI. In Chapter II of the same book Montaigne spoke of his own father, who *would often report strange familiarities, namely of his owne, with very honest women, without any suspicion at all*. This might be a form of bundling, but there is unfortunately no proof of it.

As the only Celts of whom we can positively say that they practised bundling in any true sense were the Welsh and some Scottish islanders, it may well be that there is a confusion here with *hand-fasting*. The expression *allied to* also allows of too much latitude. Wake's reference to the Dyaks of Borneo (also mentioned by Stiles in the same connection) is equally inconclusive. No less nebulous are Wake's hints of similar practices among Indian aborigines.[13] His reference to Afghanistan is more fortunate; and here the evidence of Mountstuart Elphinstone (*Account of the Kingdom of Caubul,* [London, 1815], pp. 182 et seq.) can be supplemented by Charles Masson's *Narrative of Various Journeys (etc.)* [14] where a bundling system is mentioned, said to be called *namzat bezé.*

The theme of trial marriages to ensure fertility is only indirectly relevant to the present subject. Havelock Ellis, in a book to which I shall refer presently, gives several references to the work that has been done in this field, showing that fruitfulness was considered the test of a sound marriage in the Middle Ages, and especially by peasants. In England the trial marriage, as a recognised institution, survived longest in Portland, as John Hutchins showed in his *History and Antiquities of Dorset* (London, 1861–73, Vol. II, p. 809).

Trial marriage in Brittany was described by Dr. Marcel Baudouin in his work on *Le Maraichinage* (Paris, 1917), where he compared the practices of the *Pays*

---

[13]Compare p. 269 (footnote). References to C. S. Wake are to the same work, Vol. I, pp. 118 (trial marriage among the Todas), 124, 179, 390 and 401. Another doubtful reference to bundling is cited from the Abbé Fortis (*Lettre . . . à Mylord Comte de Bute sur les moeurs . . . des Morlaques,* 1778) regarding the Slavonians of Dalmatia.

[14]London, 1842, Vol. III, p. 287.

de Mont (Vendée) with similar customs in many parts of the world.[15] The matter has also been discussed by M. A. Potter in *Sohrab and Rustem*.[16] On the other hand, there are many apparently allied customs which are neither true bundling nor tests of fertility. Verrier Elwin's fascinating study, *The Muria and Their Ghotul,* describes a system (there are many similar) which could have been classified by C. S. Wake as *allied to handfasting,* though in fact its purpose is entirely different; and both nature and purpose are very remote from bundling. The *Hlobonga* of the Zulus (described in recent works by E. J. Krige, E. D. Earthy, I. Schapera and Monica Hunter) provides another instance, which probably accounts for one of C. S. Wake's unjustifiable generalisations.

Very similar again is a practice described by Kenyatta in *Facing Mount Kenya,*[17] a form of love-making known among the Gikuyu—and the only reason that I mention any of these various amatory customs is that I have seen them all described as variants of bundling or again as forms of trial marriage, when they are neither the one nor the other. One might as well say that bundling is practised by the Mundagumor of New Guinea, because a father will sometimes share a sleeping basket with his daughter—a practice due to the extreme jealousy with which daughters have to be guarded among those people.[18]

---

[15]See Chapter VI on *L'Essai loyal ou Grossesse d'Essai avant le Mariage en France* and Chapter VII on *La Grossesse d'Essai dans le Monde.*

[16]Grimm Library, No. 14 (London, 1902), pp. 129–42.

[17]London, 1938, pp. 157 et seq.

[18]See *Sex and Temperament in Three Primitive Societies* by Margaret Mead (London, 1948). Apparently a daughter or sister has to be traded for a wife, and this occasions rivalry

The bona fide trial marriage certainly deserves some attention, because of the possibility that bundling is a survival from it. But all enquiry here is complicated by the hopeless confusion of those who have so far attempted to sift the evidence. I have even seen Plutarch's description of a Spartan custom(in the fifteenth chapter of his Life of Lycurgus) quoted as an example of trial marriage, though there is absolutely nothing to justify this assumption. By appearances the custom described may have been a survival of marriage by capture, but there is no suggestion of trial or experiment in Plutarch's account, for what it is worth, which is not much.

Among modern scholars Havelock Ellis suggested a connection between such customs as *Probenächte, fensterln, kiltgang, hand-fasting* and bundling.[19] Havelock Ellis' information was admittedly somewhat inadequate. He relied upon the doubtful evidence of Richard Twiss that *it* (i.e., a confused mixture of all these very different customs) *existed in eighteenth-century Ireland* —a statement entirely without confirmation and meaningless as it stands. And he described the New England variation as *tarrying*—presumably on the authority of Burnaby or Anbury, whose use of this word as a synonym

---

and mutual suspicion between fathers and sons, who both draw cheques on the same bank account. The author has further interesting material about these sleeping baskets, from which it appears that girls do sometimes sleep alone in them. An illicit lover runs considerable risk (shared by the girl) as an irritable parent is liable to secure the opening of the basket, roll it down a six- or seven-foot house-ladder (almost perpendicular) and prod it with a spear before looking to see who is present.

[19]*Studies in the Psychology of Sex* (Philadelphia, 1910), Vol. VI, pp. 380 et seq.

for bundling is rightly queried by Stiles.[20] The super-
ficial resemblance between bundling and trial marriage
was noticed also by M. A. Potter, who, however, accepted the slanderous suggestion (on the authority of
G. L. Gomme) that in Wales the test of fecundity was
universal. If that statement is correct categorically, as
quoted,[21] then the statement on the next page, that
Welsh bundling has a *resemblance to the experimental
unions,* is meaningless. The two become identified. There
would, in fact, have been no scope for bundling in any
country where trial marriage was still universal.

Such a custom is said to be still known in Norway.

[20]See Stiles, pp. 49–50, quoting T. Anbury's *Travels through
the Interior Parts of America* (London, 1781), Vol. II, pp.
87–88. It is true that Murray gives this meaning for *tarry,*
citing Burnaby and Anbury; but it is not found in contemporary American literature, though William Weeden
and others used it later, having fairly obviously adopted
the word from one or both of these two English authors.
The explanation appears to me to be simple. The word, as
used by the A.V. translators, was still so used in America
(see R. H. Thornton's *American Glossary* [Philadelphia,
1912] under *Tarry*) but was unfamiliar to an Englishman at
least in 1819, if not earlier. Hence, if an American spoke of
tarrying (meaning simply sojourning), an English traveller
might confuse this with the object of *tarrying*: e.g. (perhaps), bundling. But it is curious that the *American Glossary* under *Bundling* quotes Burnaby on *tarrying* quite un-
critically and without reference to Stiles's comment. It is even
possible that Anbury himself originally picked up this use
of *tarry* from Burnaby's *Travels*. An anonymous American
writer, quoted by Stiles (pp. 44–45), used the word in 1815;
but this quotation also makes it clear that the American did
not regard the words as synonymous.

[21]Op cit., pp. 131–33. Gomme is quoted in *Sohrab and
Rustem* as saying that in Wales *they do not engage in marriage until they have previously tried the disposition and
particularly the fecundity of the person with whom they are
engaged.*

Havelock Ellis mentioned it[22] in 1910, with the comment that it was called night-running, on account of the long distances travelled by the courter. In the Scandinavian variation (according to Havelock Ellis) the girl wore several extra skirts. The practice was continued in spite of clerical opposition—I mean to bundling, not to the extra precautions. Potter gives a number of references for the custom as it is said to have existed in Germany, but I am not clear that the German practice was bona fide bundling: indeed, there are far too many indications to the contrary.[23] A few other European examples of what might possibly be termed bundling are to be found in Brantôme's *Vies des Dames Galantes* and in the nine volumes of *Historiettes* by Tallemant des Réaux, but none indicative of a national custom. Stiles (pp. 27–28) quotes some doubtful evidence relating to Switzerland, from which it is by no means clear as to whether *lichtgetren, dorfen, kiltgang* or *strubetegetren* is true bundling or not.

Apart from Norway, it is only in Holland that we find any established custom on the continent of Europe corresponding to the known method of courtship in Wales, the Scottish Islands and New England. At the head of this chapter there is an early reference to *queesten* (or *kweesten*), a term which indicates the former existence of such a custom. The definition of the old Quaker historian, Willem Sewel (who shows cautious

[22]Op cit., Vol. VI, p. 380.

[23]See *Sohrab and Rustem*, pp. 134–35, and Havelock Ellis, loc. cit., also C. J. Fischer's *Deutsche Probenächte*. There are at least three French editions of Fischer's work (*Les nuits d'épreuve des villageoises allemandes avant le mariage*) but no English edition and this book is evidently very rare. Has anybody seen a copy of *Le Lit* (Henri Lavedan)? It ought to be helpful.

scepticism), is confirmed by J. H. van Dale's *Groot Woorden Boek* (1914), though most modern Dutch dictionaries are discreetly silent on this subject. Even some earlier dictionaries (e.g., H. Hexham, *A copious English and Netherdutch Dictionary* [Rotterdam, 1672–75]) gave nothing away, and Calisch's *Dutch-English Dictionary* (edition of 1892) dismisses the word with: *v.n.* (*vulg*) *see* VRIJEN. *Vrijen* merely means to court, to woo, to make love to—all very vague. Nevertheless, the bundling sense of the word is accepted by P. Weiland in a *Woorden boeck* published at Amsterdam in 1799–81, the islands of Texel and Vlieland being named as places where *the lover woos the woman under the coverings.*

Stiles naturally connects this word with our *questing* —i.e., seeking, in this case for a wife. In view of my hypothesis of a Calvinistic Culture Complex, with its probable concomitants, a remark by Dr. Stiles (p. 25) is of possible interest. He attributes Dutch *kweesting* to *the parsimony of the people.* In a note to Stiles, a former United States minister at the Hague said that this form of bundling was customary in Holland, to a limited extent, in former times, but that he had not heard of it while he was in the country. I have enquired as to whether the custom has survived in South Africa, among the Boers, and am informed that it has not. This seems odd, as it would have come so easily to people who slept in their clothes *en tout cas.* . . .

Some echo of the Dutch variety is surely to be traced in that story of the Prince of Orange, father of our William III, and his marriage to Mary Stuart. The princess was a child, not ten years old at the time, but a sort of formal bundling took place—apparently in the presence of a good-sized audience, as we are informed

that Charles I had some difficulty in conducting his
son-in-law through the crowd to the bride's bedside.

> Solemnly, in the sight of many courtiers, the
> two children were placed in bed side by side. This
> was the Orange guarantee. The hems of the little
> bride's nightgown were carefully sewn together.
> This was the guarantee of the Stuarts.[24]

Here again is the formal precaution, so frequently noticed.

In view of the Dutch evidence it is a matter of importance, duly noticed by Dr. Stiles, that Washington
Irving, when describing early incidents in his *History of
New York,* should have mentioned that *purest of Dutch-
men* (Stiles) Anthony Van Corlaer

> passing through . . . all the border towns, twang-
> ing his trumpet like a very devil . . . and stopping
> occasionally to . . . *bundle* with the beauteous
> lasses of those parts.

However, Stiles himself showed the evidence of *Diedrich
Knickerbocker* to be unreliable and self-contradictory;
and we must look elsewhere for more reliable evidence
of American bundling.

In discussing this matter it is almost inevitable that
one should mention the Rev. Samuel Peters.[25] This
inevitability is very unfortunate, as there is no doubt

[24]G. J. Renier in *William of Orange* (London, 1932). While
looking this up I recalled that G. J. Renier's brother, my
good friend Fernand, had produced the most recent and up-
to-date Dutch-English and English-Dutch Dictionary. I
looked in it for *kweesten*—in vain. The very word has followed the custom into oblivion, during the sixty years since
Calisch's edition of 1892.

[25]See McCormick's edition of Peters' *General History of
Connecticut* (New York, 1877), pp. 224–28.

that Peters was a liar, a scoundrel and a Quisling. In 1774 his house was invaded by a mob and not only was he charged with un-American opinions (enough to have landed him into serious trouble today) but positively and with good reason he was alleged to have engaged in anti-American activities. It is true that England was then the enemy and that a hostile crowd is not a court of law, but allowing for the time and the circumstances, Peters may be said to have been in quite as ill odour, and with at least as good reason, as any modern Russophile ever branded in a judicial heresy hunt. He was, in addition to this, an incurable romancer —one to whom lying was not merely a utilitarian mechanical craft but a high art, in the service of which he competed, upon occasion, with Mandeville and Münchhausen. I shall therefore pass over, for the most part, the evidence of the Rev. Samuel, to which Stiles devotes so much space, except to remark that he affirmed the strict morality of American bundling and compared rural bundling in this respect very favourably with the urban habits of the sofa—that apparently innocent engine which provided the dreary Cowper with a theme for the blankest of blank verse.

Also—and this may be of importance—Peters declared that

> The Indians, who had this method of courtship when the English arrived among them in 1634, are the most chaste set of people in the world.

This statement, though from so doubtful a source, cannot fail to arouse curiosity. Did the European settlers in America, in fact, learn bundling from the Red Indians? Unfortunately the evidence is thin. The testimony of Peters is too unreliable; and a passage which Dr. Stiles quotes from Lahontan's *New Voyage to North*

America is quite inconclusive.[26] I am myself inclined
to attribute the custom, as it existed among the settlers,
to Dutch influence, in spite of the views of C. F.
Adams (to which I shall refer later). The fact that a
custom lingered longer among English settlers is no
proof that it was not originally introduced from Holland.
After all, nobody has suggested that bundling is an inherited characteristic—it is merely a cultural symptom,
and culture can be passed on as easily as measles. But
at this point somebody will be querying the validity of
my assumption in even attributing bundling to the American settlers, and something must be said upon that point.

In the years 1759 and 1760 the Rev. Andrew Burnaby,
Archdeacon of Leicester and Vicar of Greenwich, travelled through the Middle Settlements of North America
and published his observations on the state of the British
colonies for a very laudable purpose.[27] A rupture between Great Britain and her American Colonies was, he
perceived, seriously apprehended. Foreseeing calamitous
consequences from so disastrous an event (I do but
quote his own words in the preface to his third edition),
the Rev. Burnaby, flattered by his friends, and perhaps a
little also by vanity, presumed to hope that the publication of his tour . . . might, in some degree, conduce to
this desirable end . . . i.e., to prevent this breach.

His intentions were good—or were they?—but his
methods were deplorable. The English always have said
the wrong things to, and about, their colonies. Look
at the Mayo-missionary mixture they served out to
Mother India. It had the double effect of insulting and
irritating the Indians whilst arousing a strong anti-

[26]See Stiles, pp. 29 and 37, for the evidence relating to the
indigenous customs of America.

[27]*Travels through the Middle Settlements* (*etc.*) (London,
1775), pp. 141, 144 (American ed., New York, 1904).

Indian feeling in Britain. In the same way the Rev. Burnaby's remarks were often unfortunate even when they happened to be correct in fact. His brother minister, the Rev. Peters, in a sudden frenzy of patriotism, took offence—and again I am sorry to bring him up, but it shows how ticklish this subject really is. Peters did not, as we have seen, deny the existence of bundling. Far from it—he gloried in it. His objection was that Burnaby slighted the custom and attributed it to the *lower class* of Americans. Peters maintained that it was prevalent *among all classes, to the great honour of the country*.

But this was by no means a usual American reaction. There was plenty of British provocation. Even the schoolboys of Westminster lampooned bundling in Latin verse (Stiles, p. 43) and in 1815 an anonymous American wrote bitterly upon the subject of English superciliousness (Stiles, pp. 44–45), with a wealth of *tu quoque*—even the Irish and their pigs were the subject of a hint. But—and again this is important—there was here no categorical denial of the charge. The most extraordinary apologia, however, was to come from John Neal, whose unprovoked detraction of the Welsh I have already noted. I will remind you that Neal was writing in 1828 —within living memory of what is generally considered the Augustan Age of American bundling.

Curiously enough, Neal had himself deplored bundling, treating it as a Dutch custom, in 1825.[28] In *The Yankee* his defence was strange and confused, apart from the Welsh digression. First he noted that everyone disowned bundling but said it was practised by others somewhere else—which is more or less what somebody said about the *couvade* (I think among the Basques). Having all but denied that it existed in New England,

[28]*New Englanders* by *Brother Jonathan* (John Neal), 1825 Vol. I, p. 118.

Neal then said that, *though bad enough,* it was not a
twentieth part as bad as things that went on in other
countries.[29] The defence is rather like that which one
often meets in an English suit for slander: (a) the
words were never said; (b) if they were they did not
mean what they were supposed to mean, and were not
defamatory; (c) if they were defamatory, the occasion
was privileged and (d) in any case they were true, and
should have been said if they were not.

Neal, for some reason, charged the Marquis de Chas-
telleux [sic] with having charged the New Englanders
with bundling. It is a case of he said that you said that
I said . . . the fact being that Chastellux never even
mentioned the subject. It was his English translator, a
certain Mr. Kent, who threw in a footnote (see the first
volume, p. 154, of the English edition, 1787). Mr. Kent
was distinctly offensive. He had even, he said, seen a
grave Quaker and his wife sitting on their bench at the
door—an old Philadelphia custom—whilst a 'prentice
boy and a domestic servant within their sight proceeded
to such familiarities as would shock the modesty and
draw down the vengeance of the virtuous citizens of
London. . . . Americans resented the suggestion that
this was another old Philadelphia custom and that
they were less virtuous than the London cits. They also
—those of the upper classes—objected to Mr. Kent's
suggestion (perhaps following the Rev. Peters) that
bundling, though *particularly striking amongst the mid-
dling classes and common people,* was nevertheless
prevalent *amongst all ranks.*

On the whole, however, the reputation of Chastellux
stood high, in spite of his translator. When J. K. Paulding
wrote *John Bull in America* (London, 1825) he counted
Chastellux among those Utopian romancers against
[29]Stiles, pp. 77–84.

whose radical eulogies of America the *Quarterly Review*
had warned him. Under better instruction he had learnt,
before ever sailing to the United States, that the people
were *a bundling, gouging, drinking, spitting, impious
race*—and indeed, he seems to have learnt little more
while he remained in America, except to add the words
*arrogant, self-sufficient, guessing, dirking, chewing and
pig-stealing*.

So, then, bundling was accepted, at least by outsiders,
as characteristically American. But indigenous sources
of information are not lacking, to keep a check on the
possible prejudice of some foreigners and the hundred
per cent ill will of others. There is some reference to *a
little peaceable bundling* in an early play, *The Contrast*,
by a New Englander.[30] Writing many years later, but
with all the advantage of access to numerous local records, Charles Francis Adams said that the prevalence of
bundling could be assumed throughout New England
and especially in southeastern Massachusetts. He did not
think it was practised in Boston itself, but was convinced
that Weeden's remark about bundling having *lingered
among the lower orders . . . prevailing in Western
Massachusetts as late as 1777* was thoroughly mislead-
ing. It had, in fact, continued up to the close of the
eighteenth century.

Adams maintained that American bundling was

---

[30]M. C. Crawford, in *Social Life in Old New England* (Boston, 1914), p. 197, says that this play, by Royall Tyler, was
produced in 1787 at the John Street Theatre, New York. On
p. 200 Mary Crawford makes the interesting observation
that (according to an ancient belief) a child born on the
Sabbath had also been conceived on the Sabbath. Hence it
was that baptism was often refused to children born on a
Sunday—a ban vaguely connected with the fact that week
ends were the usual times for young men to visit their
friends and spend two nights bundling.

autochthonous, quoting Dr. Stiles that the practice lingered longest on Cape Cod, where the English blood was of a purer strain than any to be found in England. (One wonders where, in that case, this pure English blood can possibly have come from. . . .) However, Adams was principally concerned with moral lapses and the efforts of the churches to deal with them, as his title indicates.[31]

I have referred once or twice to Weeden, whose *Economic and Social History of New England* is well known and all too frequently quoted without verification of his statements. His uncritical reliance upon the Rev. Peters led him astray more than once[32] and I have already suggested that he picked up the peculiar use of *tarrying* from an English source. Under the heading of *Amusements*[33] his observations on bundling will be found in the first edition, Volume II, page 864. Those who have taken the trouble to read my long footnote on *tarrying* will be interested to know that he gives precisely two references for the use of this word as a synonym of bundling. They are Burnaby and Anbury. . . . So is history written, and I do not think we need waste any more time on Mr. Weeden.

Of authorities cited by Stiles, one that particularly interests me is the Rev. Alonzo B. Chapin, whose *History of Ancient Glastenbury* is quoted in a long footnote

[31]*Some Phases of Sexual Morality and Church Discipline* (*etc.*). See Proceedings of the Massachusetts Historical Society, Second Series, VI (1891), pp. 477–516.

[32]Particularly with regard to the so-called *Blue Laws*. I dare not allow myself a digression on this subject. . . .

[33]Bundling was described by the Edinburgh *Review* in 1807 as *an amusement in New England* (see Vol. X, p. 109). The occasion was a review of *The Stranger in America,* by C. W. Janson (London, 1807) where there is reference to bundling on p. 88.

(Stiles, p. 52). As I suppose that Glastonbury, Connecticut, owes its name to the town in which I am proud to
have been born (in Somerset) I feel some tenderness for
such records, though I think the term *ancient* somewhat
odd. (My own Glastonbury can boast of a prehistoric
lake village and association with our oldest legends of
Merlin and Arthur, the Round Table, the Holy Graal,
Joseph of Arimathea, the twilight of Celtic and Saxon
history and a host of quite historical saints, plus the ruins
of the finest abbey in the world. . . .) But let that be:
citizens of Glastonbury, Connecticut, have their own history since the Puritan Aeneid, and a fair share of my
Wessex Troy. They will always be welcome if they come
within sight of Glastonbury Tor and the Holy Isle of
Avalon. And it seems they too will have strange tales to
tell, if they have read their own history; for Glastonbury
is one of Dr. Stiles's textbook cases for the decline of
morals in Connecticut, which led to the abuse of the
honest custom of bundling and so to its eventual aboli-
tion. Dr. Stiles, himself proud of Connecticut parentage,
dealt with that decline in public morality in the late
eighteenth century, as it affected another township, in a
work published some years before his book on bundling.[34]

At Dedham, Massachusetts, there was evidently the
same decline. From 1756 the Rev. Jason Haven (ordained in that year) took it upon himself to purge the
morals of Dedham and preached a memorable sermon
against bundling. Stiles, who quotes a local history on
the subject, does not forget to mention the wide effect
of the campaign launched by the formidable Jonathan

[34]*History and Genealogies of Ancient Windsor* (New York,
1859). Relevant portions of this (on, or relating to, bundling) are quoted in the preface to *Bundling: Its Origins*
(*etc.*) and on pp. 51–52.

Edwards on the same subject. We can pass by the pros and cons, the charges and countercharges. The important point historically is that no such campaigns could have been waged against a custom which affected only a negligible minority. The proof of the popularity of bundling is the extent of its anathematisation from the pulpit.

This does not mean that ministers of religion were all equally opposed to bundling—certainly not in its earlier (and no doubt purer) days. A modern author, Edwin Valentine Mitchell,[35] speaks of a candidate for ordination who admitted to bundling *magna cum voluptate*. (Mr. Mitchell also provides—I do not know from what source—an interesting account of safety precautions resembling some we have noticed elsewhere: the swathing of the young lady, tying of legs and even the attachment of sleigh bells to the bed.[36]) But many influences were at work to end the old custom. American opinion was sensitive to the writings of foreigners, as we have seen: Neal had been stirred up, not only by English critics and the views which he erroneously attributed to Chastellux, but by the widely read volumes of the Duc de la Roche-foucauld-Liancourt, whose *Voyages dans les Etats Unis* (Paris, 1799—see Vol. VIII, p. 163, if you are inter-

---

[35]*It's An Old New England Custom* (New York, 1946). See Chapter V, *To Indulge in Bundling.* I salute Mr. Mitchell, a fellow pogonologist, whose book, *Concerning Beards,* I tried in vain to obtain when writing my own treatise on the subject.

[36]Compare Brand's *Popular Antiquities* Vol. II, p. 114. Fletcher's *Night-Walker* is cited for bells hung below bridal beds. Even stranger is the account from the *Contes d'Ouville* of some young men who apparently assembled under the bed themselves *comme on a coutume de faire en pareilles occasions.* And there are various references (e.g., in Herrick) to sewing up the bride in a sheet.

ested) had evidently touched John Neal's pride. It was typical of the situation that, in so vast a work, so short a notice could stand out like an actor in the spotlight.

For all that, bundling died hard. Apart from Abishag the Shunammite,[37] there was biblical warrant for the practice in the peculiar behaviour of Ruth, who unquestionably bundled with Boaz (see Ruth III:4–11). This fact was undoubtedly noticed, as Tom Paine called the book of Ruth *an idle, bundling story*.[38] The Anti-Bundling party, unable to force the issue, on moral and religious grounds, tried ridicule; and *A New Bundling Song,* published about 1785, had a considerable effect, according to Stiles. This I find odd, as—in spite of a supposedly wide circulation in an almanac—Dr. Stiles had great difficulty in finding a copy. And the verse, moreover, is poor stuff.

The song with which the Pro-Bundlers replied was infinitely better. Stiles gives two versions of it. Version A, transcribed from a printed copy in the archives of the American Antiquarian Society, is on the whole happier in its wording; but there is at least one notable exception, to which Stiles does not refer, showing that Version B (from a young schoolmaster's manuscript copy, made

---

[37]Schumann's March of the *Davidsbündler* against the Philistines (Carneval, *op.* 9) was really an anachronism, as David never took up bundling until late in life, whereas his gruesome doings *in re* the Philistines (I Samuel XVIII: 27) were a youthful frolic. But *Davidsbündlerschaft* was an obsession with Schumann. He even wrote *Davidsbündlertänze* and dedicated them to Goethe. This suggests the possibility of a ballet, to be entitled *David and Abishag.*

[38]See *The Age of Reason.* In my own edition (London, 1921), p. 46, the word given is *bungling*. This is clearly a mistake. The whole thing was, on the contrary, very well managed. (I have since noticed that the error dates from the first edition.)

in 1786) recorded memories of an older wording. The MS version of one stanza reads:

> *Whether they must be hugg'd and buss'd*
>> *When sitting up all night*
> *Or whether they in bed may lay*
>> *Which doth reason invite?*

But for one word Version A is better, and probably more authentic. It runs as follows:

> *Whether they must be hugg'd or kiss'd*
>> *When sitting by the fire*
> *Or whether they in bed may lay,*
>> *Which doth the Lord require?*

The word *kiss'd* is clearly an amendment made when *buss* had ceased to be in common use. It also destroys the neat internal rhyming which characterises all the first and third lines. On the other hand, a number of verses which appear in B and not in A, regarded by Stiles as omissions from the printed version, look to me more like a gloss by some scholiast which was later incorporated into the text, after the manner of scholia. These lines concern the unedifying example of a lady who disdained to bundle and came to grief in the snow.[39] The whole story is an obvious interpolation between the two verses following, which I take to be naturally consecutive:

> *Let coats and gowns be laid aside*[40]
>> *And breeches take their flight,*
> *An honest man and woman can*
>> *Lay quiet all the night.*

[39] See Stiles, pp. 61–68. The supposed gloss will be found in stanzas 12–19, pp. 66–67. It was certainly a purely local and personal attack.

[40] B reads: *Let coat and shift be turned adrift*. Again I take this to be the original reading, for reasons already stated. I quote from A because it is in other respects better than B.

> *In Genesis no knowledge is*
> *Of this thing to be got*
> *Whether young men did bundle them,*
> *Or whether they did not.*

The original composition, could it be pieced together from the different versions, was obviously the work of a scholar, in spite of some literary lapses. This is peculiarly evident in the first lines of the second stanza:

> *From Adam's side a crooked bride*
> *The Lord was pleas'd to form. . . .*

Nobody, I am sure, could have written that who was not acquainted with the bent-rib theory expounded in the *Malleus Maleficarum* (see p. 7 of this book).

Yet another Anti-Bundling song was to follow—not particularly notable, except for its ferocious conclusion:

> *Should you go on, the day will come*
> *When Christ your Judge will say,*
> *In* BUNDLES *bind each of this kind*
> *And cast them all away*
>
> *Down deep in hell there let them dwell,*
> *And bundle on that bed. . . .*

And so on (Stiles, pp. 69–71). This Anti-Bundler evidently set out to parody his opponent, in some sense, as he adopted the same metre (the *Nut-brown Maid* arrangement) though not with the same success. The author, according to Dr. Stiles, was a learned divine who wrote c. 1800.[41]

Late survivals of bundling were reported by Stiles (p. 75) among the Dutch settlers of Pennsylvania. He

---

[41]I am inclined to think he had been reading the Early Fathers on syneisaktism. His arguments (see Stiles, p. 71) closely resemble those of Cyprian and others on this subject.

had also a story of a Glastonbury schoolmaster who once bundled in what I have called a secondary sense (i.e., merely for convenience, when travelling) in the early nineteenth century. This too was with a Dutch family. Stiles, as already mentioned, believed that the custom survived longest on Cape Cod—as late as 1827. Here it seems that a bundling lass (on one occasion at least) equipped herself with

> a very appropriate and secure night dress, made neither like a bloomer or mantilla, but something like a common dress, excepting the lower part, which is furnished with legs, like drawers, properly attached. The dress is drawn at the neck and waist with strings tied with a very strong knot. . . .[42]

E. V. Mitchell noted the rumour, which I have already heard myself (notably of certain Dutch citizens), that bundling still exists in some parts of America; but he was doubtful whether it was true of any sizable group. What surprises me most about Mitchell's observations[43] is his statement that bundling was very popular among the Germans. This indicates another claimant to the honour of having introduced the custom into the United States.

This question of origin still remains obscure. Charles Francis Adams, in a paper already quoted, said that it could not have come from England because no trace of it had been reported from any part of that country. On

---

[42]Letter quoted in note by Stiles, p. 76. It will be observed that one could make a formidable list of all such special precautions in different parts of the world: sufficient evidence of the honourable intentions of those who sponsored this custom.

[43]Op. cit., p. 188.

the other hand, we have seen that it was at least ru-
moured in the English Lake District at one time. Holland seems a more likely guess, though Wales and
Scotland are both in the running. (I do not know where
or how C. F. Adams found Ireland among the countries
of which there existed *well-authenticated records of its
prevalence*.) And the Red Indian evidence is altogether
too inconclusive. As to the eventual disappearance of
bundling, the last word shall lie with Ollie M. James,
who certainly did his best to help me by asking the
citizens of Cincinnati what they knew:

> It may be that the price of lumber has gone too
> high for people to be able to afford the center
> board. On the other hand, however, back in the
> old New England days, it was a question of keep-
> ing warm during late evenings of courtship, be-
> cause coal was high and the houses grew cold. In
> other words, your friendly coal dealer and/or
> your friendly gas company loused up that pic-
> turesque custom, but good.

Epilogue and Bibliography

IT IS a common practice to append a bibliography to such a book as this, but I have consulted so many books that the thought makes me feel very tired indeed.

A better idea, so it seems to me, is to append a list of some books which I have *not* read, either because I could not obtain copies or because I had not sufficient time; or maybe it was just what the theologians used to call *accidie*. I have had to leave my bed a number of times in order to wash behind my ears and verify my quotations; but there is a limit to that sort of thing and I have tried, so far as possible, to write this book in the appropriate place. That is why it has so much more local colour than *Cleanliness and Godliness*.

This list of books which I ought to have seen has the advantage of being much shorter than a list of those which I have used. It should also be of some value to those who wish to supplement my survey by further researches of their own. You can even add to it from your private store of knowledge, and have all the fun of feeling superior. And now for my list of unread *dormitantes* and *nyctages*,[1] my neglected confrères of the bed:

Adventures of a Bedstead. Apparently anon. and undated. Described in a bookseller's catalogue as a

---

[1] Words used by St. Jerome to describe certain heretics, but no offence intended.

very curious and diverting history, with coloured plates (London, H. Smith, Hollywell St.).

American Weekly, The, March 21, 1943. Article on Bundling, *on dit*. Unobtainable in London, England.

Burke, Thomas, *The Book of the Inn*. An anthology containing valuable information, I am told, *re* beds in such places—a subject I have hardly touched.

Collinder, Bjorn, *The Lapps* (New York, 1949). Recommended for beds in a cold climate, if you like that sort of thing.

Drepperd, Carl William, *Treasures in Truck and Trash*.

Fielding, W. J., *Strange Customs of Courtship and Marriage* (New York, 1942). I am told that Chapter IV is on Bundling.

Forrester, C. S., *The Bedchamber Mystery*. Why not?

George, N. Dorothy, *London Life in the Eighteenth Century*. Recommended for overcrowding of beds, e.g., in schools. But it would take a vast library to cover this subject properly.

Harris, Frank. I cannot even recall the title of his boring autobiography, nor do I wish to look through its monotonous pages again. But somewhere there is an account of a bed specially constructed for Edward VII, on account of his obesity, for use during his Paris revels. Compare the special construction of the *chaise longue* for accommodating other impedimenta, such as a woman's hairdress (c.f. remark attributed to Mrs. Patrick Campbell: *Oh, for the deep, deep peace of the double bed, after the hurly burly of the chaise longue*).

New England J.V.G. (?), 1930, III, 133–35. Article on Bundling by Parker, H. B. (?), according to an indecipherable MS note of my own.

Noyer, Wallard, *The Witchery of Sleep* (New York,

1903). Apparently unobtainable anywhere in England.

Port Folio, The (Philadelphia). H. R. Stiles cites May 1816, p. 397, on *British Abuse of American Manners.* The *American Glossary* also mentions an issue (1801, Vol. I, p. 308). Both on Bundling.

Spirit of the Farmers' Museum and Lay Preachers' Gazette, The, 1801. Quoted by *American Glossary* on Bundling.

To these I could add a vast list of articles given in the various catalogues of periodical literature, mostly from American magazines, of which there appear to be no files available in Britain. These articles appear to cover almost every imaginable aspect of the subject, from bed warmers to Old Customs in Bed, with many sensational articles on bedbugs.

In order to keep this book a reasonable length I have omitted with regret a wealth of information on hospital beds and bedpans, *savoir mourir* and allied topics, including the joys of convalescence. But if any American lecture agency will supply me with a travelling bed as a rostrum, I am quite willing to visit the States and lecture on any or all of these subjects.

INDEX

Mc Carroll